jim burns
general editor

CD-ROM INCLUDED

uncommon
youth parties

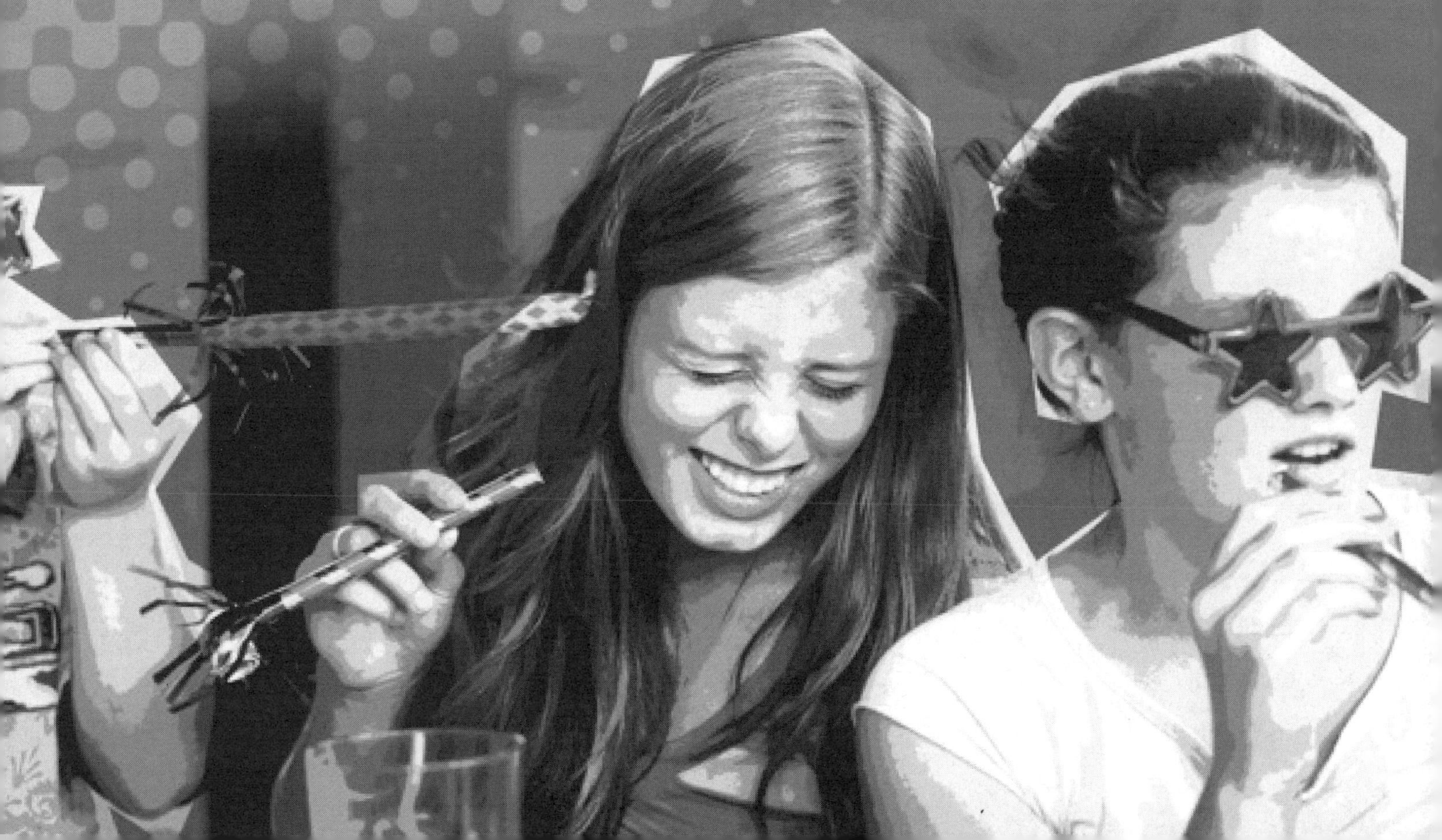

To Pamela Sue Sears Alexander,
our family's favorite person and the best friend any family could possibly have.
A holiday party without you is never the same.
Your laugh, your smile, your servant's heart and your unselfish love and commitment
to our family and your faith are constant inspirations.
Thank you and Craig for your friendship and love. I'm glad you paid for the
houseboat trip, and bring a Diet Coke next time you come over.
You are loved and appreciated.

contents

THEME PARTIES

theme: \\'thēm\\ **1a:** a subject or topic of discourse or of artistic representation **b:** a specific and distinctive quality, characteristic, or concern **2:** a written exercise: composition **3:** a melodic subject of a musical composition or movement

Parties are a great way to reach out to students, help them feel they are part of the group, have some fun together and create a moment that will help them connect with the truth of God's Word. Each party will provide you with an opportunity to impact your group members on a variety of levels: socially, emotionally and spiritually. Having a clear purpose in offering these events is vital to their success.

air band festival

description

This is a fun alternative to a talent show. All the group members can be involved. Most teens love music, so it will be something they will be excited about doing.

key verses

"Love is patient, love is kind. It does not envy, it does not boast, it is not proud. It does not dishonor others, it is not self-seeking, it is not easily angered, it keeps no record of wrongs" (1 Corinthians 13:4-5).

location needed

a room with a stage

materials needed

band sheet (found on page 12)
loud sound system (able to play the music that the students bring)
index cards
pen
hat
several prizes
Bibles

preparation

One week before the party, give the performers the key verses in 1 Corinthians 13:4-5 (write the verse out for them on index cards or have them write it down). Make sure you give the groups the passage at the same time so they have an equal amount of time to work on their performances. You will also need to select a volunteer to emcee the event.

Instruct the performers to pick a song that they think best shows what the verse says. This can be a loose tie-in—but they have to have some rationale for picking the song. Tell the group members that they will be lip-syncing the song in front of the group during the air band festival. In addition, inform the participants that you must approve all songs and costumes *before* the party, and make it clear what costumes, lyrics and gestures are deemed acceptable for the performances. Have the performers give you their music at least two days before the party. Also let the students know that they will be explaining their choice of song after the performances.

Have the group members sign up to bring different types of party food. Before the party begins, you will need to write on an index card one different number for each group that will be performing. Put these cards into a hat. Have a copy of the band sheet and a pen with you.

the event

As the group members arrive, ask them to drop off their food at the party table and sit in the audience area. Let them know they can snack from the party table when they are not on stage. Go over any other rules you want to establish—such as no throwing food on the stage, crowd surfing or moshing.

When everyone is settled, ask each group to draw a number from the hat. Write the number they have selected and their band name on your band sheet. This will determine the order in which the bands will perform. Give the completed band sheet to your volunteer emcee and have him or her begin the show. The emcee will announce each performer or group before they come up on stage.

When all of the performances have finished, have the emcee award prizes by asking the audience to clap for the best performer(s) in the following categories:

- best costumes
- best make-up
- best song
- best moves
- most realistic lip-sync

After this, read 1 Corinthians 13:4-5 aloud. Award a prize to the group that you feel best showed what the Scripture meant.

closing devotion

After the winners have been announced, explain that there are many kinds of love. There is the love that a mother feels for her child—like their moms feel for them (allow time for the collective "ahhhhhh" to subside). There is the love between brothers and sisters (they can admit it—they really do love their siblings). There is the romantic kind of love that some of them may have felt (and others are probably not interested in right now). Then there is the kind of love that God has for each of us.

This type of love is known as *agape* love, and it is a higher form of love than all the others. This is actually the word for "love" that Paul uses in this passage. *Agape* love is a form of love that God has for us and that we are to have for others. It refers to the self-sacrificing love that God had for humanity when He chose to send His only Son to the cross to die for our sins. God extends this love to us even though we don't deserve it and can never hope to earn it. It is a free gift, because "God is love" (1 John 4:8).

Many of the popular songs we hear today talk about "true love" and say it will last "forever." Unfortunately, relationships end and what we thought was love fades away. But God's *agape* love is eternal. It is the only form of love that truly lasts forever—and forever is something we just can't even begin to understand.

band sheet

number	band name

board game party

description

Who is the best board game player in the group? Who is the worst? What is your group's favorite board game of all times? This is your chance to answer these questions. This party is an indoor activity that can be held at any time of the year.

key verse

"So the last will be first, and the first will be last" (Matthew 20:16).

location needed

a large room

materials needed

food and drinks for the party
extra games (in case you don't have enough)
the rules for each game that is going to be played
tables
chairs
several prizes
Bibles

preparation

Ahead of time, have the group members sign up for a board game they would like to bring (this way, you hopefully won't have too many of the same games). You will need to find one adult leader for every different game. Find the rules to these games and give them to your adult leaders ahead of time. Ask them to read through the rules and bring them to the board game party so they will be able to explain them to the students. Set up one table for every game, and then set up the same number of chairs at a table as the maximum number of people who can play that game.

the event

When the group members arrive, have them set up their game on one of the tables. When all of the participants have arrived, welcome them and let them know where the party food table is located. Allow the students to grab some party food and to head to a table. When everyone is seated around the tables, explain how the game time will work. The group members at each game will play for 20 to 30 minutes. At the end of this time, the group that is finishing the game will move one table to the right. Continue this process for as long as you want the party to last. Generally, depending on your time frame, each student will get to play four to five different games.

Introduce the adult leaders and have them go to their respective tables. Let the participants know that their adult leader will be explaining the rules of their game and will be in charge of answering any questions or settling any disagreements that

might arise. The adults will also be keeping a score for each game played. (Note that the adult leaders will be keeping track of the person who loses each game, but they shouldn't share this information with the group members.)

Some of the games will take longer to play than others, so let the groups know that if their game is finished before their time is up, they can play the game again. Some of the groups that are playing short games might end up playing their games several times. However, shorter games will have fewer points awarded.

Here is the scoring system for your adult leaders to use during the party:

- Award 100 points to a person who loses a long game (one that takes the full playing time).

- Award 50 points (per game) to a person who loses a medium-length game (one that can be played twice during the playing time).

- Award 25 points (per game) to the person who loses a short game (one that can be played several times during the playing time).

Give the adult leaders a few minutes to explain the rules of the games their group members are playing, and then start the games. When the game time is finished, collect all the scores from the adults. Award prizes to the players who lost the most games. When you are finished, ask the group members the following questions

- Why is the game that you brought tonight your favorite game?

- What did you like about playing the number of games you did? What did you dislike?

- Did you think it was fair that the person(s) who lost the most games won the prize? Why or why not?

closing devotion

Begin the devotion by explaining that there is an interesting story in the Bible about a group of workers who felt they were being treated unfairly. Read Matthew 20:1-16 aloud. When you are finished, ask the group members the following questions:

- The workers who were hired in the morning agreed to work for how much money? (*One denarius. This was the amount that workers of the time were usually paid for a day of work.*)

- Did the landowner hire any more workers? If so, when did he hire them? (*Yes. He hired workers at 9 AM, 12 PM, 3 PM and 5 PM.*)

- At the end of the day, what group of people did the landowner pay first? (*The ones who were hired at 5 PM.*)

- How much did he pay them? (*One denarius.*)

- How much did he pay those who were hired first in the early morning? (*One denarius.*)

- Did these workers think their payment was fair? Why or why not? (*No. They wanted more because they had worked all day but had been paid the same amount of money as those who had only worked a couple of hours.*)

- What was the landowner's response to this? (*He said in verses 13-15, "I am not being unfair to you, friend. Didn't you agree to work for a denarius? Take your pay and go. I want to give the one who was hired last the same as I gave you. Don't I have the right to do what I want with my own money? Or are you envious because I am generous?"*)

- Do you think the landowner was being fair? (*Allow students to respond.*)

Share with the group that sometimes it is hard for us to see other people getting better grades and better things and, generally, having an easier time in life than us. However, we need to remember that only God truly knows what a person is dealing with in life. He knows what each of us needs and wants. He doesn't give all of us the same things because we need different things from Him. Everything that God does, He does for our good, whether we can see it or not. We need to trust that what He gives us is the right thing for us because He loves us so much.

Explain that in fact, the parable that Jesus told had very little to do with justice in the fields. The parable was actually about receiving the gift of salvation from God. Jesus was saying that some people come into the kingdom of God early and some come in late, but each of us receives the same gift of eternal life. This is because salvation isn't something that is earned—it is a *free* gift from God. In fact, if God were being fair, none of us would receive salvation at all, because "all have sinned and fall short of the glory of God" (Romans 3:23). We need to remember the blessings that God has given us when we compare ourselves to others and grumble that something isn't fair.

Close by singing "Count Your Blessings" (just kidding). But do close in prayer, asking God to help the group members to begin to see how much God has given to them and how much He loves them.

favorite character party

description

This is a great party in which the group members (and you) get to dress up as a favorite person—either a fictional one or a real-life individual. This party works well indoors and will even give your group members the chance to use their acting skills.

key verse

"Woe to you, teachers of the law and Pharisees, you hypocrites! You shut the door of the kingdom of heaven in people's faces. You yourselves do not enter, nor will you let those enter who are trying to" (Matthew 23:13).

location needed

a large room

materials needed

copies of "Who Do You Think I Am?" (see page 19)
pens or pencils
prizes
party food and drinks
Bibles

preparation

Ahead of time, let the group members know that this will be a costume party. They can come dressed as any character from books, television, computer games, movies or even real life. Tell them that they will need to be prepared to share with the rest of the group why they chose that particular character. (*Note*: You will need to set specific guidelines as to what is and is not an acceptable costume according to what you and your church feel should be allowed. You will also need to decide ahead of time what will happen if a student shows up in an unacceptable costume. Be sure to share this information with the group members before the party.) Make enough copies of the handout "Who Do You Think I Am?" for every student.

the event

As the group members arrive, give them the "Who Do You Think I Am?" handout and a pen or a pencil. Ask them not to tell anyone who their character is. To play the game, the participants will need to approach as many characters as they can in an allotted amount of time. Each student will need to guess who the other person's character is by writing his or her guess on that character's handout. Each student will also need to allow the other person to guess who he or she is by doing the same thing on his or her handout. Allow 15 to 20 minutes for the group members to do this.

When the group members are finished with this exercise or the time has expired, ask them to write their names and true identities on the top of their papers. Collect all of the handouts, and then score the sheets. Announce a winner based on the following criteria:

- the character who received the lowest number of correct guesses on his or her handout
- the character who received the highest number of correct guesses on his or her handout

Have the winners come forward and receive their prizes. Announce that the party food table is now open, and allow the group members to have some time to eat and hang out. After a few minutes, begin the following games (modify and adapt these based on your group dynamics and the amount of time you have available).

honey walk

Choose five students at a time to come forward. Have them form a line so that the side of their bodies are facing the audience. Ask the five to walk in place. Next, have the rest of the group come up with something the five have to pretend to walk on or through (such as honey, ice, gelatin). As an option, have the five also do these things in a way the character they are portraying would do it. (For instance, if someone came as Spider-Man, they could pretend to shoot webs from their wrists as they walked.) Play for a few minutes, and then call five more group members up to play the game.[1]

character freeze

Choose three volunteers to come forward and then assign one of the following actions to each player:

- one player is crying because he or she just dropped an ice cream cone on the ground
- one player just stubbed his or her toe
- one player is trying to help the other two

Have the participants act out their assigned tasks. As an option, you can also have each person act the way his or her character would act in this situation. Let the group members know that when they want to step in and replace one of the players, they must call out "freeze." The players have to freeze in position, and then the person who called "freeze" must tap the player on the shoulder to replace him or her. The person who has been tapped must sit down, and the new person must start a whole new scenario by doing something or saying something. This process is then repeated until your allotted time for this game is up.

three things

Choose two group members to be actors and have them come forward. Ask the rest of the group to call out ideas for each of the following categories:

- a place (the top of the Empire State Building, at the bottom of a pool)
- an object (chewed gum, a hot potato)
- an action (dancing, bobsledding)

17

As the group members are calling out ideas, pick one for each category. The two actors must then act as if they are in the selected location, with the chosen object, doing the chosen action. For a challenge, have them also act the way their characters would act with each. Allow several different players to play.

closing devotion

When you are finished playing the games, ask the group members to discuss the following questions:

- Who is your favorite character that came tonight? Why?
- Was it easy to guess who the different characters were when you first came in?
- Why did you choose to be the character that you are dressed up as?

After the group members have had some time to respond, ask one person to read Matthew 23:13. Explain that in this verse, Jesus was addressing a group known as the Pharisees. The Pharisees were the religious leaders in Jesus' time, and they prided themselves on following the rules of the Old Testament. However, as is evident from this verse, when Jesus spoke about the Pharisees, He had little positive to say about them. He accused them of being hypocrites—of putting on the appearance of being righteous but not really being righteous in their hearts, where it mattered the most.

This is not to say that Jesus *hated* the Pharisees. In fact, it is evident that quite the opposite is true. Jesus *loved* the Pharisees—otherwise, He wouldn't have bothered to try to show them the error of their ways. In fact, in John 3:1-21, Jesus had a lengthy conversation with a Pharisee named Nicodemus, who was curious about how a person could enter the kingdom of God. Jesus told him, "I tell you the truth, no one can see the kingdom of God unless he is born again" (verse 3). Nicodemus came to Jesus as a man seeking truth (albeit under the cover of night), and Jesus responded to him in love—in spite of the fact that he was a member of the Pharisees.

Explain that there are many types of different characters in both fiction and in real life, as is evident from the costumes that the group members wore for this party. Oftentimes, these characters are not evil or "bad" people, but they have made wrong choices along the way. This was true of the Pharisees as a whole. They assumed an attitude of superiority and viewed others as being inferior because they followed the letter of the law. They prayed about themselves and how good they were, saying things like, "God, I thank you that I am not like other men—robbers, evildoers, adulterers—or even like this tax collector" (Luke 18:11). As Jesus showed, being religious is obviously not enough to become part of God's kingdom.

Conclude by stating that the way we can keep from becoming like these Pharisees is by keeping a humble heart. Every day we are characters in our own story, and we can choose to do the things that will bring us closer to God. This includes putting others before ourselves and not thinking we are better than them. We must remember that Jesus is the one who is perfect, and only He can remove our sin and "create in [us] a pure heart" (Psalm 51:10).

Note

1. This game is based on an idea found in "Improv Games" at Freedrama.net. http://free drama.net/improv.html.

who do you think I am?

1. _______________________________
2. _______________________________
3. _______________________________
4. _______________________________
5. _______________________________
6. _______________________________
7. _______________________________
8. _______________________________
9. _______________________________
10. _______________________________
11. _______________________________
12. _______________________________
13. _______________________________
14. _______________________________
15. _______________________________
16. _______________________________
17. _______________________________
18. _______________________________
19. _______________________________
20. _______________________________

harvest festival

description

As the name implies, this is a perfect event for the autumn season. It can be used in place of a Halloween party or even be held at a different time during the fall.

key verse

"There is a time for everything, and a season for every activity under heaven" (Ecclesiastes 3:1).

location needed

It is preferable that you hold this festival at a farm with a barn, but you can also decorate a suitable space (such as at your church) and hold the event there. You will need enough space for your group members to compete in the events.

materials needed

kettle corn, fruit pies, hot apple cider and any other harvest-type food items
items for the harvest festival games
prizes for the games
items for harvest festival events
Bibles

preparation

You will need to prepare a few items before the party for the harvest festival games and events. In addition, you will need to prepare the harvest festival food items you select (see following pages).

the event

When the group members have arrived, welcome them and let them know the schedule of games and events you have selected. Open your party food table. Note that you can mix and match the schedule—you can hold your events first or intersperse them in between the games.

harvest festival game ideas

The following are a list of possible game ideas for you and the group to try at the harvest festival.

ain't no flies on me
This is a great game to play when the guests first arrive at the party. The materials you will need are as follows:

- a picture of a fly
- mailing labels

Print the picture of the fly onto the mailing labels to make fly stickers. Make enough stickers so that each person at your party gets three. Come up with five words that your group members would say easily and without thinking. These need to be very common words, such as "hay," "scarecrow," "barn," "pumpkin," or the name of one person who is playing the game. These will be "taboo" words that the players are not allowed to use during the game.

To begin the game, give each person three fly stickers and have him or her put the stickers on his or her clothes. Then explain these rules to the group:

- The object of the game is for the players to get rid of the three fly stickers that they have.
- Players do this by giving a sticker to anyone they hear say one of the "taboo" words (list them).
- Players must keep talking to the other players throughout the game.

End the game after an allotted amount of time (10 minutes or so). Any player who can say "ain't no flies on me" (who doesn't have any fly stickers) wins a prize.[1]

crazy scarecrow dress and dash
For this game, you will need oversized clothing (plaid shirts, goofy pants, floppy hats and other silly items that a scarecrow might wear), and prizes. Create one pile of clothes for each team. Each pile must have one item from each of these categories (again, all clothes need to be large and baggy):

- long-sleeve plaid shirt
- colorful goofy pants
- thick wool socks
- silly shoes
- a bandana
- a floppy hat
- ugly garden gloves

Divide the group into the same number of teams as you have piles of clothes, and then have each team stand in a line. Make sure there is a pile of clothes for each team at the other end of the room. Each player must run to his or her team's pile of clothes, put on the entire outfit, and then run back to the next person in line. Once there, the dressed player must take the clothes off and give them to the next person. The next person must put the entire outfit on, run to the other end of the room, take all of the clothes off, put them in a pile and then run back to the next person in line. This process is repeated until every player on the team has had a turn. The first team to get through all of its players first is the winner. Give prizes to the winning team.[2]

pumpkin seed spittin' contest
For this game, you will need the following:

- pumpkin seeds (five per player)
- a prize
- rope or tape

Use the rope or tape to make a line for the players to stand behind (they will stand side by side). Begin by giving each player five pumpkin seeds. The players must try to spit their seeds, one at a time, as far as they can. They are not allowed to step over the line—if they do, they are out of the game. When all the players are finished, award a prize to the person who spit his or her seed the farthest. You can play this game once with the whole group, or you can play several rounds and allow the winners of each round to play a final game to see who is the ultimate pumpkin seed spitter.

hanging apples

To play this game, you will need one apple for each player, string, scissors, tape and a prize. Cut the string into lengths, making sure that each length is long enough to hang from the ceiling down to the students' mouth level. Tie the string to a secure place in the ceiling. Tie the apple to the bottom end of the hanging string. The object of the game is for the players to try to eat the hanging apples while keeping their hands behind their backs. The first player who eats his or her apple wins a prize.

harvest festival event ideas

Depending on your location and the time frame you have allotted, you may want to incorporate some or all of these additional events into the harvest festival.

hayrides

If you choose to hold your activity at a farm, a hayride can be a fun activity that the group members will remember. There are a few different ways to do this event, depending on what is available at the farm where the party is held. The traditional hayride is a large horse-drawn cart filled with hay, but many hayrides today are made up of a flatbed filled with hay or hay bales and pulled by a tractor. Another idea would be to fill the flatbed of a large truck with hay and allow a few of the group members at a time to ride in it.

hay bale maze

If you have access to many bales of hay, you can create a fun maze. The bales need to be stacked high enough so that your tallest student cannot see over the top. Make one path that leads from the beginning of the maze to the end, and then add several dead ends throughout the maze to confuse the group members. Another option is to set up a corn maze, either by (1) stacking up cut cornstalks to form the walls of the maze, or (2) cutting down corn stalks and setting up the maze in the actual cornfield. (This second option can only be done if you know a farmer who wouldn't mind having some of his corn stalks destroyed!) The nice thing about the hay bale maze is that nothing is destroyed—the bales can still be used after you are finished.

scarecrow making contest

For this event, you will need the following materials:

- many pieces of strange-looking clothing
- hay (or another type of stuffing material)
- permanent markers in several colors for every team
- one pair of nylons per team
- a large container
- prizes

- paper
- tape

Make sure that you have several pieces of each item of clothing—shirts, pants, stockings, socks, gloves, shoes, skirts and accessories (ties, hair bands, scarves, aprons, purses, sports equipment, and so on). Put each category of clothing in a large container (such as a clean garbage can). Make a pile out of the hay or stuffing materials, and then write the name of each clothing category on a separate piece of paper. Tape the label to the large container that houses these items.

Next, divide the students into teams of five people each. Let them know that they will be making a scarecrow—but not just any old scarecrow. Point out the containers with the different clothing items and the pile of hay. The teams must send one person to collect at least one item from every container (note that a pair of something, such as shoes, counts as one item). The teams will then send another person to get the hay, which they will use to stuff their scarecrows.

Pass out one pair of pantyhose and the permanent markers to each team. The teams will need to stuff the top of the pantyhose with their hay and secure it so that the hay doesn't fall out. This will be their scarecrow's head. They will need to use their markers to draw the parts of the face. They will also need to stuff the clothing and put the whole scarecrow together. If they need clothing items during the game, they can go back to the containers for more. They will have 20 minutes to make their scarecrow.

When the event is over, award prizes based on the following categories (or make up your own):

- most original idea
- fanciest outfit
- most likely to scare someone (birds or people)
- best use of accessories
- most lifelike (actually looks like a person)
- weirdest looking

Allow the group members to vote on who the winner should be in each category by their applause as you stand behind each scarecrow. Award prizes to the winners.

closing devotion

When all the games and events are finished, gather the group members together and discuss the following questions:

- What was your favorite game or event? Why?
- What was your least favorite game or event? Why?
- What do you like best about the fall season?
- What do you like least about the fall season?

Explain that in Genesis 8:22, the Lord says, "As long as the earth endures, seedtime and harvest, cold and heat, summer and winter, day and night will never cease." God has given us each of the seasons, and each one is unique. Here are some interesting facts about the fall season:

- In the northern hemisphere, autumn begins in September. In the southern hemisphere, it begins in March.
- The word "autumn" comes from the Latin word *autumnus,* meaning "drying-up season."
- The word "fall" comes from the Old English *feallan* and refers to the leaves that fall from the trees during this season.
- Prior to the sixteenth century, "autumn" was known as "harvest" in most of Europe. The term "harvest" lost meaning as people began moving from the farms to the cities.
- In poetry, autumn is associated with sadness.
- Television stations and networks typically begin their regular season in autumn (football season also begins at this time).
- Most schools open in early fall.
- Since 1997, "Autumn" has been one of the top 100 names for girls in the United States.

Continue by reading Ecclesiastes 3:1-8. Explain that in this passage, the author (whom most believe was King Solomon) talks about how God has set up a time for everything that occurs on this earth. In Deuteronomy 10:14, we read that all things belong to God—the heavens, the earth and everything in it—and that He is in perfect control of events. Everything that happens takes place according to God's will. We may not always like when God chooses to do things—and we may try to rush it—but His timing is always perfect.

Just as the seasons in the natural world come and go, the seasons in our life will come and go. We will have seasons of happiness and seasons of sorrow. We will have seasons where we are really growing in our faith and seasons when it seems like we are standing still. We will have seasons when we are getting along well with others and seasons when it seems like no one wants to be our friend. Yet in all of these times, we can be confident that God is always with us. As He has promised in His Word, "Never will I leave you; never will I forsake you" (Hebrews 13:5).

Conclude with prayer, thanking the Lord for making all of the seasons and for the changes that He brings to our lives. Ask Him to be with the group members and guide them in whatever season of life they find themselves.

Notes

1. Adapted from Denise Witmer, "Fun Party Games for Birthdays and Other Teen Parties: *Ain't No Flies on Me*." http://parentingteens.about.com/od/birthdays/qt/partygames33.htm.
2. Adapted from Maggie Stewart, "15 Fun Fall and Harvest Outdoor Party Games for Children," Yahoo! August 7, 2007. http://voices.yahoo.com/15-fun-fall-harvest-out-door-party-games-children-476244.html.

hawaiian luau

description

This is a wonderful outdoor party that you can plan for an evening in the summer months. It can be as big or as small as you want it to be.

key verse

"How, then, can they call on the one they have not believed in? And how can they believe in the one of whom they have not heard? And how can they hear without someone preaching to them?" (Romans 10:14).

location needed

an outdoor space (you will need enough room for the group members to compete in the events)

materials needed

tiki torches (you can make fake ones from flashlights, yellow cellophane and tape)
leis (a Hawaiian garland or wreath)
tables and chairs
hawaiian table decorations
ingredients for the Hawaiian luau food
items for the Hawaiian luau games
items for the Hawaiian luau entertainment
Bibles

preparation

Ahead of time, you will need to recruit adult volunteers to serve as greeters and cooking staff. Ask your greeters to help you set up the Hawaiian decorations on the tables. Ask your cooking staff to have the food ready before the luau begins. The luau should begin as the sun is going down so the group members will be able to see the tiki torches (be sure to put these up in places where they will not be a fire hazard). Light the torches just as the group members begin arriving.

If you opted to have fake torches, you will need to create the torches. Cut the cellophane into a strip. Make the top edge of the cellophane jagged like a flame and tape the cellophane to the light end of the flashlight. The jagged edge of the cellophane needs to be slightly above the light on the flashlight. Secure the flashlights so they are up off the ground and the light is pointing up to the sky. Turn your torches on just as the guests begin arriving. Meet with your adult volunteer greeters and ask them to greet the group members as they arrive.

the event

As each group member arrives, he or she will be met by one of your Hawaiian greeters. The greeter will welcome the student with the Hawaiian word for hello,

which is "aloha." The greeter will then place a lei around that student's neck and direct the student to the buffet table. After the group members get their food, they can choose a place to sit.

When all the guests have arrived, introduce the entertainment for the night. Halfway through your entertainment line-up, have your servers bring out the dessert. As students eat their dessert, allow the second half of the entertainment to take place. When students are finished eating or the entertainment is over, explain the games that the group members will be playing and have the students go to the games area.

hawaiian luau food

The following are some ideas for food to prepare for the party. If you follow this menu, you will need the following:

- teriyaki pineapple burgers (cook the burgers and add a canned pineapple slice)
- fruit salad (your choice of fruit)
- seasoned jo jo potatoes (see recipe below)
- hawaiian punch (see recipe below)
- haupia (see recipe below)

seasoned jo jo potatoes

This recipe makes 24 Jo Jo's. You will need the following ingredients:

- 6 medium baking potatoes
- 2 tbsp. seasoning salt
- 2 cups vegetable oil

Wash and scrub the potatoes and cut into quarters. Put oil and seasoned salt in a large zip-lock bag. Add the potatoes and shake well. Put the potatoes on a sheet pan. Cook at 400° F oven until the potatoes are tender when tested with a fork.[1]

hawaiian punch

This recipe serves 10 to 20 people. You will need the following ingredients:

- 4 cups orange juice
- 4 cups guava juice
- 4 cups pineapple juice
- ½ cup red grenadine
- 4½ cups ginger ale

Use frozen juice concentrate for each of the above juices. Make sure the juices are well chilled by the time you make it for the party. To make the punch, pour the juices into a large bowl and add the grenadine and ginger ale. Add additional ice cubes as desired.[2]

haupia (hawaiian coconut pudding)

This recipe serves 8 people. You will need the following ingredients:

- 2 cups coconut milk
- 1 cup whole milk

- 6 tbsp. sugar
- 5 tbsp. cornstarch
- ¼ tsp. vanilla (if desired)

Pour one cup of coconut milk into a saucepan. Combine the sugar and cornstarch in a separate bowl, and then stir this into the coconut milk. Add vanilla if desired, and then heat the mixture over low heat, stirring constantly until it is thick. Add the remainder of the coconut milk and whole milk, and continue to heat the mixture until thickened. Pour the pudding into an 8-inch square pan and chill until it is firm.[3]

hawaiian luau game ideas

What's a luau without a few games? The following are some great Hawaiian theme-related games that your group can play during the event.

hawaiian limbo

♫ Limbo . . . everybody limbo! ♫ How low can you and your luau guests go? For this game, you will need the following:

- a broom or long stick
- hawaiian music
- a way to play the music for your group
- a prize

Give the broom or long stick to two participants. Have them stand across from each other and hold up the stick. Have them hold the broom up high to begin with, and then as the rounds progress, have them lower the height to add to the difficulty. Play your favorite Hawaiian music while the participants try their luck. Give a prize to the person who can limbo the lowest.

poi eating contest

As with all timed eating events, if you choose to do this game, you need to make sure that your participants do this safely so they don't choke. Here is what you will need:

- poi (a Hawaiian staple made from the taro root)
- a bowl for each contestant
- a way to time the contestants
- a prize

Place a small bowl of poi in front of each participant. The object of the game is for all participants to eat as much poi as they can without using their hands or utensils. Set your timer for two minutes and let them go at it. The person who eats the most poi before the two minutes is up wins a prize.[4]

lei-stringing contest

When the group members arrived they were given a lei to wear, but this game will allow them to create their own. For this option you will need the following:

- one bag of fake flowers (that have holes in their centers) for each team
- one long piece of yarn with a large knot at the end for each team

- large plastic needle for each team
- prizes

Divide the group into teams of 10 people each, and have the teams line up. Give each team a bag of fake flowers, a piece of yarn and a plastic needle. Explain that the first person in line must thread the yarn through the needle—that person is allowed to get help from the rest of the team—and then use the needle to string one flower onto the yarn. The first person will then hand the lei to the next person in line. Each person must only string *one* flower.

When the lei reaches the last person in line, that person must run to the front, string the flower and pass it to the next person. Make sure that the teams know that they must push the flowers to the knot at the end of the string. When a team has filled the string with flowers, they must tie the two ends of the string together. The first person in line must put the lei around his or her neck and yell out, "I love Hawaii!" The first person to yell this wins the game for his or her team. Give prizes to the winners.

hula-hoop contest

This is an easy game to set up and play at any time during the event. To do this game, you will just need several hula-hoops, a prize, and your Hawaiian music soundtrack. Give a hula-hoop to each contestant and start the Hawaiian music. Whoever keeps the hoop going the longest wins the prize.

hawaiian luau entertainment ideas

What's a luau without a little entertainment? In between the games, you might want to consider doing some of these ideas for your group.

hawaiian entertainers

If there is anyone in your church who can play a ukulele or Hawaiian guitar, ask him or her to come and perform for your luau.

hawaiian translator

This is a fun activity in which either you or one of your adult volunteers translates the group members' names into Hawaiian names.[5] To do this, you will be using the 12 letters in the Hawaiian alphabet: A, E, H, I, K, L, M, N, O, P, U and W (there is a thirteenth letter called *okina* that is written with an apostrophe, but you won't be using it). Use the following table in translating names:

English Letter	Hawaiian Letter	English Letter	Hawaiian Letter
A	A	U	U
E	E	B, F, P	P
H	H	C, D, G, K, Q, S, T, X, Z	K
I	I		
M	M	J, Y	I
N	N	L, R	L
O	O	V, W	W

Using this table, the name "Amber" would be "Ampel." However, there are two more steps to take to translate the name:

1. If a person's name ends in a consonant, add a vowel.
2. Place a vowel between consonants.

Using these two rules, the name "Amber" would be "Amapele." Regarding pronunciation, the consonants H, K, L, M, N, P and W are pronounced exactly as in English. Vowels are pronounced as follows:

A: *ah*
E: *ay*
I: *ee*
O: *oh*
U: *oo*

Thus, "Amber" ("Amapele") would be pronounced *ah-m-ah-p-ay-l-ay*. Here are a few other name translation examples:

Brad:	Palaka	Jen:	Leni
Ralph:	Lalepa	Noreen:	Nolina
Stuart:	Kuaka	Emily:	Emele
Shane:	Kane	Kim:	Kimi

If all of this is too complicated and you have a laptop that you can take to the luau, just search online for a site that translates English names into Hawaiian.[6]

hawaiian storyteller
For this option, have one of the adult volunteers in your group share an ancient Hawaiian legend. You can find a few samples on the CD-ROM included with this book, or your storyteller can look them up online. Find out what story the person is going to tell ahead of time to make sure it is appropriate for your group.

closing devotion

After the games are finished, have everyone regroup in the dinner area. Ask the following questions:

- Has anyone ever taken a trip to Hawaii? Tell us about it.
- What did you like the best about tonight—the food, the entertainment or the games?
- Was any of the food you tried new to you?
- Have you ever played any of these games before?

After you have allowed some time for the group members to respond, state that you have a few interesting facts about Hawaii to share with them:

- The state of Hawaii was formed by an underwater magma source known as a "hotspot."

- Hawaii is made up of eight major islands, though there are as many as 137 all together. It is the only state entirely made up of islands.
- Hawaii was the fiftieth state—the last star added to the flag.
- Hawaii has the fourth longest coastline in the United States after Alaska, Florida and California.
- Hawaii's tallest mountain is Mauna Kea, which stands at 13,796 feet. If you were to follow this mountain all the way to the bottom of the Pacific Ocean (where it begins), it would be higher than Mount Everest.
- Hawaii used to be called the Sandwich Islands, so named by a British explorer named James Cook who sailed there in 1778.
- The state fish is the humuhumunukunukuapua'a.
- Most of the vegetation grows on the northeast sides of the islands, which tend to face the wind.

State that in the book of Acts, we read of how the apostle Paul was called by Christ to take the gospel to a group of people known as the "Gentiles." In the early years following Jesus' death, resurrection and ascension into heaven, the Church was comprised of mainly Jewish believers. This only makes sense, as Jesus was Jewish, His disciples were Jewish, and the people to whom they ministered were Jewish. But with Paul, we begin to see the church planted in other nations surrounding the Mediterranean—such as in modern-day Turkey, Syria, Greece and Italy.

Paul started a long tradition that continues to this day. In 1820, the first missionaries arrived in Hawaii on a ship called Thaddeus. Onboard the ship were seven married couples from Boston, Massachusetts, under the leadership of Reverend Hiram Bingham. At the time, a king ruled the nation of Hawaii, and he allowed the missionaries to preach the gospel to the people. A large number of the population became Christians, and by 1830 Protestantism was designated as the official religion of Hawaii. (Today, about 29 percent of the population is Christian.) The missionaries were the first to give the Hawaiians a written alphabet.

Unfortunately, many of the missionaries who came to Hawaii were not familiar with the customs of the Polynesian people, and many became involved in internal politics and economic investment on the island. They influenced the passage of new laws and started to invest heavily in industries such as sugar cane production. A phrase eventually was coined to describe these missionaries: "They came to do good and ended up doing well." In spite of all this, the people on the islands were exposed to the truth of the gospel and found God.

There are several things that we can learn from these missionaries. First, we must be open to God's call to bring the gospel to others. We need to be willing to respond and reach out to others in faith. Second, we need to be sensitive to where people are in life. Sometimes God is calling us to just plant the seed in a person's life. We must remember that He brings transformation in people, not us. Third, when we are sharing our faith, we need to make sure that we are doing it in love. People will see through us if we have other ulterior motives. In all things, we need to remember that "God so *loved* the world [loved us] that he gave us his one and only Son" (John 3:16, emphasis added).

Notes

1. Recipe adapted from "Seasoned Jo Jo Potatoes" at Yahoo! Answers. http://answers.yahoo.com/question/index?qid=20080823103757AAb6mEG.

2. Recipe adapted from "The Best-ever Hawaiian Punch Recipe," Squidoo.com. http://www.squidoo.com/hawaiian-punch.

3. Recipe adapted from John Fischer, "Haupia—Hawaiian Coconut Pudding," About.com Hawaii Travel. http://gohawaii.about.com/od/luaurecipes/r/haupia.htm.

4. Game adapted from "All the Poi You Can Eat," Polynesian Culture Center of Hawaii. http://www.polynesia.com/luau-games.html.

5. This activity is adapted from "Hawaiian Luau Party Supply: Games and Activities." http://www.hawaiianluauparty.com/luauparty/luau-activities.cfm.

6. One site is http://www.hawaiianring.com/translate.php.

middle ages feast

description

This feast is similar to what a person would find at a restaurant like Medieval Times, only it goes much deeper. Through this event, your students will learn about discrimination and its effects on people.

key verse

"My brothers, as believers in our glorious Lord Jesus Christ, don't show favoritism" (James 2:1).

location needed

a large room or outdoor area (you will need enough space for the group members to compete in the events)

materials needed

tables (see ratio below for the number you will need)
nobleperson's table settings (with nice table decorations)
peasant's table settings
crowns (one for each nobleperson)
pre-written name badges
ingredients for Middle Ages menus
items for the Middle Ages sporting events
Bibles

preparation

You will need to enlist the help of several adult volunteers to serve the group members at the party. To set up the area, you will need a ratio of four "peasants" tables for every one "noblepersons" table. Place the noblepersons' tables together at the front of the room and decorate them with beautiful and elaborate table settings. Give them matching tablecloths, dishes, glasses and eating utensils.

Place the peasant tables together at the back of the room. Leave the tables bare or throw a simple sheet over the tables. Make sure everyone has mismatched cups and dishes, and either one spoon or no eating utensils. Refer to the sections below for items you will need for the menus and the entertainment and sporting events.

Throughout the event, the "noblepersons" will be treated with honor while the "peasants" will not. Instruct your adult volunteers to serve an individually prepared plate of food for each person sitting at the nobleperson's table. They should respond to requests from the nobleperson and be near tables to refill glasses or bring the next course of food. When serving the peasants, they should bring one large dish out and one large pitcher of water. The peasants will then have to serve themselves from the one large dish. The volunteers may respond to requests from the peasants, but most of the time they should ignore them.

The crowns for the noblepersons can either be made from thick paper, or you can purchase cheap ones from a party supply store. If you have people who can do some medieval-type entertainment (see the following section for ideas), have them perform at the front of the room to the noblepersons only. They can take special requests from the noblemen's tables, but they should ignore the peasants' requests.

Buy nametags that say, "Hello, my name is." You will need one nobleman nametag for every three peasant nametags. You will need to write a name and an occupation on each one. An example of a peasant nametag would be, "Grimald/Swineherder." An example of a nobleman nametag would be, "Colin/Knight." The following are some additional medieval-type names you could use.[1]

men's names

Ailwin	Chararic	Giles	Hildebald	Norman	Sigismund
Alard	Colin	Gladwin	Huneric	Odo	Silvester
Aldred	Edwin	Godwin	Imnachar	Osbert	Terric
Amalaric	Engeram	Grimald	Ingomer	Otker	Theobald
Anselm	Ernald	Gunderic	Jocelin	Pepin	Thierry
Aubrey	Eustace	Gunthar	Leofwin	Ranulf	Thurstan
Audovald	Fabian	Hamo	Leudast	Rathar	Umfrey
Badegisel	Fordwin	Harding	Lothar	Reccared	Vulfoliac
Baldric	Fulk	Hartmut	Magneric	Samer	Waleran
Berthar	Gamel	Helyas	Masci	Savaric	Warin
Bertram	Gervase	Herlewin	Meginhard	Sigeric	Wimarc
Blacwin	Gilbert	Hervey	Munderic	Sigibert	Ymbert

women's names

Acilia	Avoca	Faileuba	Helewise	Linota	Premeveire
Adelina	Basilea	Felicia	Hilda	Lora	Radegund
Agnes	Bela	Fina	Ida	Malota	Richenda
Albreda	Berta	Galswinth	Idonea	Margery	Richolda
Aldith	Bertrada	Goda	Ingunde	Marsilia	Rigunth
Aldusa	Brunhild	Golda	Isabel	Matilda	Roesia
Alina	Cecilia	Grecia	Isolda	Mazelina	Rotrude
Amabilia	Celestria	Gundrea	Joanna	Millicent	Sabelina
Amicia	Clarice	Gundred	Lettice	Nesta	Sabina
Amiria	Clotild	Gunnora	Leubast	Nicola	Sybilla
Annora	Dionisia	Haunild	Leubovera	Parnel	Theoderada
Avelina	Estrilda	Hawisa	Liecia	Philippa	Wymarc

Here are some medieval-type occupations to also place on the nametags. Note that these titles can be repeated for more than one individual.

noblemen's jobs

Prince	Archduke	Marquess	Viscount	Knight	Squire
Viceroy	Duke	Earl	Baron	Lord	

noblewomen's jobs

Princess	Arch-dutchess	Marchioness	Viscountess	Dame
Vicereine	Duchess	Countess	Baroness	Lady

peasants' jobs

Apothe-cary	Book-binder	Clerk	Farmer	Miner	Scullion
Armorer	Bottler	Clothier	Fletcher	Minstrel	Serf
Atilliator	Bower	Cook	Furrier	Peddler	Shoe-maker
Bailiff	Bricklayer	Cord-wainer	Grave-digger	Porter	Spinster
Baker	Butler	Cottar	Innkeeper	Potter	Steward
Barber	Candle-maker	Ditcher	Janitor	Reeve	Swine-herder
Black-smith	Castellan	Ewerer	Messenger	Scribe	Watchman

the event

When the party begins, you will need to have several of your adult volunteers at the door holding a box full of pre-written nametags that have been mixed together well. When a guest arrives, the volunteer will have that person draw a nametag from the box and put it on. The volunteer will then seat that student at a noblemen's or peasant's table according to what his or her nametag says.

The servants will also need to place a crown on the head of a nobleperson. If the nametag says any of the occupations listed above for a nobleperson (prince, princess, duke, dutchess, and so forth), that person will be seated at a nobleperson's table. If the nametag lists an occupation for a peasant (bricklayer, janitor, swineherder, and so forth), that person will be seated at the peasant's table. From that moment on, the students will be treated differently. Everyone sitting at a nobleperson's table will receive special treatment.

When all the guests have arrived, have the volunteer adult servers bring food out to the noblemen's tables first. When those tables have been served, they can then serve food to the peasant tables. If you have scheduled any performers, have them begin the entertainment at this point.

Just before you serve dessert, begin the sporting events. At first, only the noblepersons will be allowed to participate. When the events are finished, have the servers bring out the desserts. Once again, they will need to serve all the noblepersons' tables first. Then they can serve the peasants.

middle ages menu

The following are some ideas for food to prepare for the party. If you follow this menu, serve the following to the two different types of tables at the event.

noblepersons' menu:
roast turkey or chicken
loaves of French bread
cooked vegetables
punch or juice
dessert: apple spice cake

peasants' menu:
soup
bread
water
dessert: one small piece of fruit with a slice of cheese

middle ages entertainment ideas

If you have some talented individuals in your church or community, ask them to perform at the event. Ideas for entertainment include a troubadour and minstrel (a singer and someone to accompany him or her on an instrument), a jester (a comedian or someone who tells jokes—make sure you know the routine and that it is appropriate), musicians (a band) or jugglers.

middle ages sporting events

During the Middle Ages, the nobility entertained themselves by holding feasts, banquets, jousts, tournaments and fairs. The following events are a take-off on some of these sporting events. Remember that initially, only the noblepersons will be allowed to participate in these events while the rest of the group watches from their tables.

ye olde hoop shoot
For this game, you will need a basketball, a basketball hoop or a garbage can, and masking tape. Ahead of time, place three sets of tapelines with the masking tape on the floor, going from the closest hoop to the farthest one. Have players try to get a basketball through a hoop or into a garbage can from each tapeline. Give them three tries to make a basket, scoring three points for the farthest hoop, two points for the next closest, and one point for the closest hoop. Tally up the score and give the winner a prize.

foot race
This is an easy game that requires little preparation. Have the players take off their shoes and run barefoot a certain number of times around the room. The winner gets a prize.

archery event

This is actually more of a bowling event (after all, you don't want arrows flying around during your party). Ahead of time, get a soft football (such as a Nerf) and three to five bowling pins (or other object that can be knocked down with the football). Set up a start line using the masking tape, and stack the pins some distance away. Have the players stand behind the start line and try to knock down as many pins. Award a prize to the winner at the end of the round.

jousting tournament

This requires the most setup and the most supervision during the contest. Ahead of time, set up some floor mats in an area, and then place a small raised platform in the middle of the mats. The platform should be a few inches off the group and be just wide enough for two people to stand two to three feet away from each other. Have the participants wear football helmets or headgear, and give each player a long sofa cushion or other large, spongy pillow. The idea is for one player to knock the other person off the platform using only the cushion. State that any player who strikes the other person in the head with the cushion will be disqualified. The game is over when one player successfully pushes the other off the platform. Award a prize to the winner after a few rounds.

closing devotion

When the games are over, serve the desserts. As the group members are eating, discuss the following questions:

- Did you notice a difference in the way some people were treated at this feast? If so, how?
- If you were from the noblepersons' table, did you like the way you were treated? Why or why not?
- If you were from the peasants' table, did you like the way you were treated? Why or why not?
- Do you think that everyone at the feast was treated fairly? Why or why not?

Explain that this event was structured to give the group members not only an idea of the inequalities that existed in medieval times but also the inequalities that exist in the world today. When you look at the inequalities between the richest and poorest countries on earth, the statistics are staggering:

- The average income of a person living in the United States is $39,945, which works out to roughly $109 per day.[2] Almost half the population of the world—3 billion people—live on less than $2.50 per day.[3]
- More than 80 percent of the world's population lives in countries where the gap between rich and poor is widening.[4]
- The richest 20 percent of the world's population account for 75 percent of the world's income, while the poorest 40 percent account for only 5 percent of the world's income.[5]
- An estimated 93 million dogs and cats in the United States are overweight or obese (54 percent of all dogs and cats).[6] Each day, 22,000 children in the world die of poverty.[7]

- Nearly a billion people entered the twenty-first century unable to read or write.[8] In the United States, 99 percent of the population over age 15 is literate.[9]

In 1 Corinthians 11, Paul wrote that this type of inequality was happening in one of the churches he had planted in the city of Corinth. During the days of the Early Church, the believers would all gather together to share what was known as an *agape* feast, or "love feast." Those who could afford to bring food brought it to the feast and shared it with the other believers. In Corinth, however, the rich were gathering early and indulging in the food, leaving the poor to go hungry. As Paul wrote, "When you come together, it is not the Lord's Supper you eat, for as you eat, each of you goes ahead without waiting for anybody else. One remains hungry, another gets drunk. . . . What shall I say to you? Shall I praise you for this? Certainly not!" (1 Corinthians 11:20-22).

In the book of James, the author saw this going on in churches as well, and he wanted to strongly point out the problem to believers. He asks his readers to suppose that they see a person coming into their church with nice clothes and a gold ring, and also a person coming in with shabby clothes. If the believers give preferential treatment to the guy with nice clothes, but make the poor guy stand in the back, then they are acting as "judges with evil thoughts" (James 2:4). As James puts it clearly, "My brothers, as believers in our glorious Lord Jesus Christ, don't show favoritism. . . . If you show favoritism, you sin and are convicted by the law as lawbreakers" (James 2:1,9).

In Deuteronomy 15:7, God told His people, "If there is a poor man among your brothers in any of the towns of the land that the LORD your God is giving you, do not be hardhearted or tightfisted toward your poor brother." God does not want us to discriminate against poor people. He wants us to love others in the same way that we love ourselves (see Mark 12:31). When God looks at us, He doesn't see rich people or poor people—He sees what is in our hearts (see 1 Samuel 16:7). One of the things that He wants us to have in our hearts is compassion for others, regardless of how much money they have or how they happen to be dressed. As Christians, we need to set an example for the world as to how we should treat one another, and this begins by treating others as God would want us to treat them.

Close the devotion time in prayer, asking God to help the group members not to judge others and to look for ways that they can reach the poor and needy in their communities. When the devotion time is concluded, allow all of the group members to participate in the games (and eat any of the desserts, if there are any left!).

Notes

1. Names taken from "Gothic Names," The Middle Ages.Net. http://www.themiddle ages.net/people/names.html.
2. "Per Capita Personal Income by State: 1990 to 2010," U.S. Department of Commerce, Released September 2011. http://bber.unm.edu/econ/us-pci.htm.
3. Shaohua Chen and Martin Ravallion, "The Developing World Is Poorer than We Thought, but no Less Successful in the Fight Against Poverty," World Bank, August 2008. http://www.globalissues.org/article/26/poverty-facts-and-stats#src1.
4. "The 2007 Human Development Report," United Nations Development Program, November 27, 2007, p. 25.
5. Ibid. http://www.globalissues.org/article/26/poverty-facts-and-stats#fact3.
6. "Obesity Facts and Risks," Association for Pet Obesity Prevention, 2010. http://www.pet obesityprevention.com/pet-obesity-fact-risks/.

7. Anup Shah, "Today, Around 21,000 Children Died Around the World," Global Issues, September 24, 2011. http://www.globalissues.org/article/715/today-21000-children-died-around-the-world.

8. "The State of the World's Children," UNICEF, 1999. http://www.unicef.org/sowc99/index.html.

9. "Literacy," The World Factbook, Central Intelligence Agency, 2003 estimate. https://www.cia.gov/library/publications/the-world-factbook/fields/2103.html.

middle ages feast

7

olympic games event

description

This event requires more setup time and materials, but it makes for an exciting day packed with physical activity. Everyone gets a chance to be an athlete in this event.

key verse

"Do you not know that in a race all the runners run, but only one gets the prize? Run in such a way as to get the prize" (1 Corinthians 9:24).

location needed

a large outdoor space (you will need enough room for the group members to participate in the events)

materials needed

large open field with a paved area
several different colors of ribbon
a flashlight
yellow cellophane
olympic anthem music (and a way to play it for your group)
one tricycle for every team
suction cup archery bows, arrows and targets
several large buckets of water
several long ropes
several pairs of wooly mittens (enough for two teams)
equipment for badminton
equipment for volleyball
equipment for croquet
one stick horse (or broom) for every team
items needed to make the obstacle course for the equestrian event (see below)
a copy of "Summer Olympics Quiz" (found on page 44)
one bell for each team
one clipboard with paper for each team and yourself
pens or pencils
ingredients for the Olympic games party food
several "gold" medals (buy these at a party supply store or make them out of cardboard and foil—you will need enough so that each person on a team can have one)
several "silver" medals (enough so that each person on a team can have one)
several "bronze" medals (enough so that each person on a team can have one)
energy snacks and drinks for group members to munch on throughout the games
Bibles

preparation

Ahead of time, you will need to recruit a student volunteer to be your torchbearer and one adult volunteer for each team. Cut the different colors of ribbon into strips that are long enough to tie around each student's arm. Cut a strip of the yellow cellophane and make the top of the strip jagged so that it will look like a flame. Wrap the cellophane strip around the light end of the flashlight so that the "flames" stick up above the top. Make sure your group knows what they should wear for this event (shorts, T-shirts and apparel in which they can play sports). Set up the different event areas, using and reusing the long ropes for the finish lines. Also, create a special tricycle course and an obstacle course with jumps for your equestrian event. Give each adult volunteer a clipboard with blank paper and a pen or pencil to keep score for their teams.

the event

Divide the students into four teams (or more if you have a large group). Allow each team to come up with a team name and to pick a color. Write the name each team has chosen next to the color they picked on your clipboard. Let the teams know that there will be food and drinks available throughout the day and point out where those tables are located.

olympic games food ideas

The following are some ideas for food to prepare for the party. Here are the food items that you will need:

- hamburgers/chiliburgers
- chips
- power veggies—a tray filled with vegetables such as carrot sticks, celery, radishes, and so on
- whole fruit
- ice cream sundaes
- sports drinks (make available during the events)

olympic games events

After the teams have been decided and the team colors and names have been assigned, begin the games!

opening ceremony

Have everyone stand in a large circle and play your Olympic anthem music. As you announce the opening of the "first-ever [your church name] Olympic games," have your torchbearer arrive. When you announce each team name, ask that team to go to the center of the circle and wave their color ribbons. When all the teams have been announced, ask the group members to tie their ribbons around their arms or in a place where the color will be visible to everyone. Let the participants know in what events they will be competing. Use and adapt the ideas given below, or create your own unique events.

ten-lap tricycle pedal

In this event, one person from each team will ride a tricycle around a circular area 10 times. The fastest rider gets 100 points.

suction cup archery

Everyone on each team gets to make one shot. Every time a player hits the target, the team receives 25 points.

trikeathalon

Each team needs to pick five people to compete in this event. Each athlete must do the following in succession:

1. Hop on one leg 10 times. If the athlete has to use his or her other leg, or if he or she, falls down, that person must begin again.
2. Ride 10 laps around the designed course you set up above with the tricycle.
3. Pour a large bucket of water over his or her head.
4. Run to the finish line.

The first person who crosses the finish line wins 150 points for his or her team; the person who crosses second wins 100 points; the person who crosses third wins 50 points; and everyone else who finishes wins 25 points.

badmitton

Two teams at a time will compete against each other in this event. Have the players put on the wooly mittens and play a standard game of badminton. The first team that reaches 15 points wins the game. Award a score of 100 points to the winning team.

volleyball

Two teams at a time will compete against each other in this event. Have two teams play a game of volleyball to 15 points. For an added challenge, have the teams put on the wooly mittens from the last event. Award a score of 100 points to the winning team.

croquet

Two teams at a time will compete against each other in this event. Have two teams play a standard game of croquet. Once again, have the teams wear the mittens for an added challenge. The first team to hit all of the balls through the hoops and hit the final stake wins the game. Award 100 points to the winning team.[1]

equestrian

Each team will pick one player to participate in this event. Each player must ride his or her stick horse through the course that you have set up, including jumps. The first person to cross the finish line wins 100 points for his or her team.

tug-of-war

You can have several tug-of-wars going on at once to determine the top teams for this event. After each round, have winning teams play against each other until you have an overall winner. Award the overall winning team 100 points.

summer olympics quiz

One player from each team will participate in this event. Read the questions from the "Summer Olympics Quiz" handout (see page 44). After reading the question, if a player thinks he or she knows the answer, then that person needs to grab his or her

olympic games event

bell and ring it. The first person to ring his or her bell will be allowed to answer the question. If that person is correct, he or she is awarded the number of points indicated on the handout. If that person is incorrect, allow the other players a chance to answer the question. If no one can answer the question, all players get 10 points.

closing ceremony

As you can see, a lot of points will be awarded during these games, which is why it is important to have one adult leader assigned to each team to keep track of that team's points. After the group members have finished all the events, have them assemble near the party food table. While your group members are eating, play your Olympic anthem music again and announce the winners. The team with the most points wins gold medals; the team in second place wins silver medals; and the team in third place wins bronze medals. Have each winning team come forward to receive their medals.

closing devotion

After the presentation, discuss the following questions as a group:

- What was the hardest event? Why?
- What was the easiest event? Why?
- Did you want to quit any event that you were in today? Why?
- Did you actually quit or did you keep going? Why or why not?

Explain that the games the group members played today were modeled after the events in the Olympic Games, which in turn were modeled after a series of competitions held in ancient Greece. Historians believe that the first games occurred around 776 BC, and the apostle Paul made references to some of these events in many of his letters in the New Testament. One such passage is found in 1 Corinthians 9:24, where Paul states, "Do you not know that in a race all the runners run, but only one gets the prize? Run in such a way as to get the prize."

In ancient times, there was nothing easy about running these races. It is believed that there were four different types of running events in the ancient Olympics. In the first three, the athletes ran different distances: (1) 630 feet, (2) 1,260 feet, and (3) a distance between 4,410 feet to around 3 miles. The most grueling race was the fourth one, where a runner ran a distance of 1,260 feet to 2,520 feet *in armor*. This race was especially useful to the Greeks in building up the speed and stamina of their soldiers.

When a runner won his race, he received a crown of leaves as part of his reward. Paul refers to this crown in 2 Timothy 2:5, where he writes, "If anyone competes as an athlete, he does not receive the victor's crown unless he competes by the rules." Although back then—as today—running was grueling, winning that crown made it all worthwhile. Today, modern athletes receive bronze, silver and gold medals for winning, but the principle is the same. They train for years to be the best in their event so they can win the prize.

Paul states that the same is true in our lives. As Christians, we go into strict training so we can hear God's commands and follow what He wants us to do. We train so we won't give up when things get tough and the end doesn't seem to be in sight. We train and participate in the race so that we can receive the ultimate prize: eternal life with Jesus in heaven—a "crown that will last forever" (1 Corinthians 9:25).

This is why we must always keep our focus on Christ in this life and never stop running the race. As the writer of Hebrews states, we "fix our eyes on Jesus, the author and perfecter of our faith" (12:2), and run a good race for God.

Note

1. Check online for specific rules on how to play badminton, volleyball and croquet. See http://www.livestrong.com/article/112967-badminton-rules-groupmembers/; http://www.kidzworld.com/article/4963-playing-volleyball; and http://www.backyardsteward.com/croquet.php.

43

summer olympics quiz

1. In what city was the first modern Summer Olympic Games held?

   Answer: Athens (25 points)

2. In what year were the first modern Summer Olympic Games held?

   Answer: 1896 (25 points)

3. True or False: Women were not allowed to participate in these early games.

   Answer: True. In 1896, a woman from Greece named Stamata Revithi ran the marathon anyway. She ran the race one day after the men had completed the official event and turned in a time of 5 hours and 30 minutes (25 points).

4. What African-American sprinter and long jumper won four gold medals during the 1936 Summer Olympic Games in Berlin?

   Answer: Jesse Owens. Hitler and his Nazi party hosted the Olympic Games that year. They only allowed Aryan (white skinned, fair-haired, blue-eyed) men and women to compete on the German team, because they thought it would show the world they were the better race of people. Jesse Owens blew this theory out of the water (50 points).

5. What did the Olympic sport *jeu de paume* eventually become?

   Answer: Tennis (50 points)

6. True or False: Since 1896, only Australia, Great Britain and Switzerland have sent athletes to every Olympic Games.

   Answer: True (50 points)

7. In what year did the United States refuse to send athletes to participate in the Summer Olympics being held in Moscow?

   Answer: 1980 (75 points)

8. What significant event occurred during the 1972 Summer Olympics held in Munich, Germany?

   Answer: A terrorist group known as Black September held 11 members of the Israeli Olympic team hostage. During a failed rescue attempt, all 11 Israeli athletes, the 5 members of the terrorist group, and a German police officer were killed (75 points).

9. What significant event occurred during the 1996 Summer Olympics held in Atlanta, Georgia?

   Answer: A bomb was detonated in a main park in the city, killing 2 people and injuring 111 others (75 points).

10. True or False: Basque Pelota is a drink that is served to players in the Olympics.

    Answer: False. It is the name for a variety of court sports that originated in the Basque area of Spain and France (100 points).

8

outdoor
cinema party

description

This party is based on outdoor cinema events that take place throughout the United States during the summer months. Moviegoers are treated to one of their favorite old movies, which are usually projected on the wall of a building. This can be a memorable event for your group and should be held on a warm and dry evening.

key verses

"The father said to his servants, 'Quick! Bring the best robe and put it on him. Put a ring on his finger and sandals on his feet. Bring the fattened calf and kill it. Let's have a feast and celebrate'" (Luke 15:22-23).

location needed

parking lot or yard with a light-colored wall (or you can put a white sheet over a wall)

materials needed

extra chairs
popcorn machine (if available—otherwise, you need a way to make popcorn)
hotdogs, nachos, candy, popcorn and soda (for the snack table)
a copy of "Disney® Movie Trivia Questions" (found on page 48)
several small prizes
three special prizes
an appropriate movie for your group
a way to project the movie onto a wall (the projection must be visible)
Bibles

preparation

Ahead of time, recruit adult volunteers or responsible teens to man the popcorn machine and party snack table. Also recruit adult volunteers to act as movie ushers. Tell the group members that they will need to bring their favorite chairs to this event (lawn chairs, bean bag chairs, and so on). Let your movie usher volunteers know that they are there to help group members with any problems they may have during the movie and for the group members' safety.

the event

As the group members arrive, have them visit the party snack table to load up on popcorn, movie goodies and drinks. When the guests come back to their seats, ask the "Disney® Movie Trivia Questions" before you begin the movie (see page 48). Give out small prizes for correct answers. Give out special prizes for the three challenge questions at the end. Following this, introduce the movie and any rules of conduct

you want the group to know ahead of time. Also let the students know that they can get popcorn, drinks or snacks anytime during the movie. Introduce your ushers for the evening and let the group members know that they are there to help.

closing devotion

When the movie is over, discuss the following questions as a group:

- Who was your favorite character in the movie? Why?
- Was there a character in the movie that you didn't like? Why?
- What is one lesson you learned from this movie?

Explain that all stories have characters and a plot—a problem the main character must solve. When we watch a movie, we find out before the end how the character solves his or her big problem. Many times, the stories we see in movies can teach us lessons about the consequences of our actions. As we watch the lead character make mistakes and attempt to solve his or her big problem, we discover how we should make decisions in our lives to avoid having to go through the same consequences.

Jesus told many stories with real-life characters and wonderful plots. He called these stories "parables," which can roughly be defined as a simple story that illustrates an important life principle. One of Jesus' longer parables is called the Parable of the Prodigal Son. Read Luke 15:11-32, and then discuss the following questions:

- Who was the main character in this story? (*The younger son.*)
- Who were the secondary characters? (*The father and older son.*)
- What was the main character's big problem? (*He squandered his money and found himself starving.*)
- What caused the main character's problem? (*His own decision to spend his inheritance and leave home.*)
- What ultimately caused the main character to do something about his problem? (*He realized the pigs were being fed better than him.*)
- How did the father react when he saw his younger son? (*He rejoiced and ordered a celebration to be held.*)
- How did the older son react? (*He became angry with his father and refused to join the party.*)

Conclude by stating the main message of this story: It is never too late to make a good decision and turn back to God. If we go to God, He will be there. He will forgive us and love us and celebrate the fact that we have come back to Him. As the father in the story said, "This son of mine was dead and is alive again; he was lost and is found" (Luke 15:24). God rejoices in the same way when we come back to Him.

However, there is yet another message in this story: Those who do not wander away from God get to experience His blessings every day of their lives. The older son in the parable was angry that his father was paying so much attention to the younger son who had turned his back on the family, but, as the father reminded him, "You are always with me, and everything I have is yours" (verse 31). As Paul states in Galatians 4:7, we are sons and daughters of God, and because of this, God has also made us His heirs. Unlike those who wander from God, we maintain our fellowship with God and get to witness His blessings in our lives every day.

outdoor cinema party

46

Close in prayer, asking God to help any group members who have fallen away from God to make the choice to come back home. Remind them that they can always ask forgiveness of their sins, and God will forgive them. Also say a praise of thanks for those who have chosen to follow God's calling wherever He has led them.

47

disney® movie trivia questions

1. In the movie *The Jungle Book*, what kind of animal was Bagheera?

    Answer: A black panther

2. In the movie *Aladdin*, what kind of pet does Aladdin have?

    Answer: A monkey named Abu

3. In the movie *Bambi*, what was the skunk's name?

    Answer: Flower

4. What was the prince's name in the movie *The Little Mermaid*?

    Answer: Prince Eric

5. What was the name of the villain who tried to kill the beast in the movie *Beauty and the Beast*?

    Answer: Gaston

6. What was the name of the evil lion who killed the king in *The Lion King*?

    Answer: Scar

7. In the movie *Cinderella,* what sort of creatures made the dress that Cinderella was to wear to the ball?

    Answer: Mice and birds

8. In *Robin Hood,* what sort of animal was the lead character?

    Answer: A fox

9. What would happen to Pinocchio when he lied?

    Answer: His nose would grow

10. Does anyone know all the words to a song from a Disney movie?

    (Have the person sing it!)

challenge questions

1. What were the names of the seven dwarves from the movie Snow White?

    Answer: Dopey, Sneezy, Happy, Sleepy, Grumpy, Bashful and Doc

2. What were the names of Ariel's six sisters in the movie *The Little Mermaid*?

    Answer: Aquata, Andrina, Attina, Adella, Arista and Alana

3. What were the names of the four crows in the movie *The Jungle Book*?

    Answer: Ziggy, Dizzy, Buzzie and Flaps

pirate's quest

description
This is a scavenger hunt-type event with a piratey twist. Arr!

key verse
"Get yourselves a bank that can't go bankrupt, a bank in heaven far from bank robbers, safe from embezzlers, a bank you can bank on" (Luke 12:33, *THE MESSAGE*).

location needed
a mall or other shopping area with a lot of stores in one location (you will also need an area where you can share the group's photos and they can eat after the event is over)

materials needed
one digital camera for each group
a copy of "Pirate's Quest List" for each person (see page 51)
stickers
pen
paper on a clipboard
party food
treasure chest
many small prizes
Bibles

preparation
You will need one adult volunteer for each group. This person will be taking the pictures, keeping track of the time, and making sure the group members are being safe. Make sure that each adult volunteer has a watch or other time-keeping device. Ahead of time, write a different number on each sticker (you will be putting one sticker on each camera). Also, fill the treasure chest with prizes and pick out a location where the group members can meet after the event.

the event
When the group members arrive at the mall, divide them into groups of seven people each (if your group is small, decrease the number of people per group). Assign one adult volunteer per group. Introduce that adult leader to the group and let the group members know that the adult is there to take the pictures, keep track of the time, and basically keep the group safe.

Begin by having the groups come up with a "piratey" name for their team. Give one camera to each team and, on your clipboard, write down the name of each group and the number that is on the camera you give to them. Explain to the teams that each camera represents an empty treasure chest. All the teams will have one hour to fill their treasure chests.

Pass out a copy of "Pirate's Quest List" to each person. (Note: Feel free to change any of the quest pictures if you have a better idea of what would fit your mall's situation.). The teams will need to take pictures of as many things as they can find on the list. This will require bravery on their part—they will need to talk to people at the mall to be able to capture some of these pictures. Pick a store or other location where everyone will meet up, and make sure the teams know that they must meet you there in one hour. If any team is late, 10 points will be deducted for every minute.

Begin the game. When one hour has passed, make sure you are at the agreed-upon rendezvous point. Collect the cameras as the teams arrive and take the group members to the area where you will be having the party (this could be in the food court or other open area). Allow the participants to get their food and find a seat.

Announce a pirate ship name from your list and show that group's pictures. Mark off on your list the things the team was able to capture on the camera. Do this for each team, and then tally the points. Announce the winning team with the most points, and present that team with the treasure chest that holds the prizes.

closing devotion

After the winner has been announced, discuss the following as a group:

- Which was the hardest picture to take on the list? Why?
- Which was the easiest to take? Why?
- Which was the craziest picture you took?
- Which picture do you like the best? Why?

Explain that for as long as there have been ships on the ocean, there have been pirates nearby to relieve those sailors of their possessions. While pirates still exist today, the ones that come to mind when we think of the term were generally active from the 1560s to the 1720s. The most famous among these were Edward Teach (Blackbeard), Calico Jack Rackham, Henry Morgan and the most successful pirate ever, Bartholomew Roberts (Black Bart), who captured more than 400 ships during his career. And, of course, there is Captain Jack Sparrow from the *Pirates of the Caribbean* movies.

When you put aside these men's colorful names and even more colorful personalities, they were basically just common thieves who took other peoples' money. That is the real problem with earthly possessions—they can always be lost or stolen. Jesus recognized this fact when He said, "Get yourselves a bank that can't go bankrupt, a bank in heaven far from bank robbers, safe from embezzlers, a bank you can bank on. It's obvious, isn't it? The place where your treasure is, is the place you will most want to be, and end up being" (Luke 12:33-34, *THE MESSAGE*).

Jesus told us to invest in a bank that couldn't fail—a bank that is heaven. How do we do that? By investing our time in other people and doing the work that God wants us to do on this earth. When we do God's will and follow His commands, we build up reserves in our heavenly bank account—a place where "thieves do not break in and steal" (Matthew 6:20).

pirate's quest

pirate's quest list

Here be a list of treasures ye must try ta take for yer treasure chest. The number next to the treasure is how much that treasure be worth. Now git goin', fore ye only have one hour to get yer treasures!

1. A picture of everyone in your group wearing a wig: 90 gold doubloons. (If you opt for everyone in a hat: 75 gold doubloons.)

2. A picture of everyone on his or her knees proposing to a store mannequin: 50 gold doubloons.

3. A picture of everyone holding up a basketball: 75 gold doubloons.

4. A picture of everyone with a yellow tennis shoe on his or her left foot only: 80 gold doubloons.

5. A picture of everyone sleeping on beds in a mattress or furniture store: 50 gold doubloons.

6. A picture of at least one person in the group taking an order at one of the mall's restaurants: 100 gold doubloons.

7. A picture of everyone in the projection room of a movie theater: 100 gold doubloons.

8. A picture of one member of the group washing another member's hair in one of the mall's hair salons: 100 gold doubloons.

9. A picture of everyone lying on the floor of a store reading a Curious George book: 50 gold doubloons.

10. A picture of one person in your group wearing earrings, a necklace, a bracelet, a ring, an ankle bracelet and a hair accessory in a store: 75 gold doubloons.

11. A picture of everyone inside a family bathroom: 50 gold doubloons.

12. A picture of everyone on the mall's stage area or another elevated place singing the sea shanty, "Aweigh, Santy Ano," on the following page (you can sing it to any tune you would like, but you must sing it as a true pirate): 100 gold doubloons.

aweigh, santy ano

From Boston Town we're bound away,
Heave aweigh (Heave aweigh!) Santy Ano.
Around Cape Horn to Frisco Bay,
We're bound for Californi-o.
So heave her up and away we'll go,
Heave aweigh (Heave aweigh!) Santy Ano.
Heave her up and away we'll go,
We're bound for Californi-o.

She's a fast clipper ship and a bully crew,
Heave aweigh (Heave aweigh!) Santy Ano.
A down-east Yankee for her captain, too.
We're bound for Californi-o.
So heave her up and away we'll go,
Heave aweigh (Heave aweigh!) Santy Ano.
Heave her up and away we'll go,
We're bound for Californi-o.

Back in the days of Forty-nine,
Heave aweigh (Heave aweigh!) Santy Ano.
Those were the days of the good old times,
Way out in Californi-o.
So heave her up and away we'll go,
Heave aweigh (Heave aweigh!) Santy Ano.
Heave her up and away we'll go,
We're bound for Californi-o.
When I leave ship I'll settle down
Heave aweigh (Heave aweigh!) Santy Ano

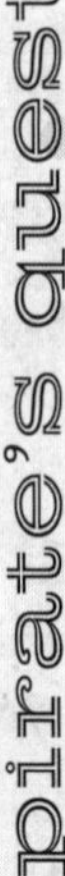

progressive dinner party

description
This is a party where your group members will eat each course of their meal at different houses. At each house, they will have the opportunity to taste that family's secret recipes and hear interesting stories told by the hosts.

key verse
"For many are invited, but few are chosen" (Matthew 22:14).

location needed
a number of different houses

materials needed
items for the meal (check with your hosts to see what they need)
Bibles

preparation
For this party, the group members will be moving from place to place for the different courses of the meal. Get the group members' parents involved by asking them to host one of the courses in their homes. The courses should be:

- hors d'oeuvres
- soup
- main course
- dessert

Ask the hosts to try to incorporate a family recipe in the course that they are sponsoring. Let them know that this will be a time for them to share family stories with the group members. Check with the hosts to see if there is anything the youth group can do to help.

If the houses that are hosting the courses are close to each other, the students can walk from house to house. Otherwise, you will need a way to transport the group members to each location.

the event
When the group members arrive at a house, they will be served one course of their meal. During this time, the hosts should share some family stories—possibly about the food that the group members are eating and why it is their family's specialty. Have the group members go from house to house until they get to the last location, where dessert will be served.

closing devotion

After the group members have had the final course at the last house, have a brief devotional time. Begin by asking the students the following questions:

- What did you find interesting about this experience?
- What was the most interesting story you heard?
- What was one thing you learned from this experience?
- Why is it important to preserve stories of your family's heritage?

Explain that in the Bible, we find Jesus often telling stories (called parables) to people when He wanted to teach them important truths. One of the stories He told was about a king who prepared a wedding feast for his son. The king invited many people to the banquet, but they wouldn't come. One person said he had to work in his field, and one said that he had some business to which he had to attend. Some of the invitees actually seized the king's servants!

The king became enraged at the response he received. He told his servants, "The wedding banquet is ready, but those I invited did not deserve to come. Go to the street corners and invite to the banquet anyone you find" (Matthew 22:8-9). So the king's servants went out into the streets and gathered all the people they could find.

At the end of the story, Jesus said, "For many are invited, but few are chosen." Ask the group members what they think Jesus meant by this statement. The answer is that Jesus invites all of us to be in a relationship with Him—He wants all of us to have salvation, which is what this parable is all about. However, we have been given the freedom to choose. We can choose to be like the guests who turned down the king's invitation and not receive Christ as our Savior and Lord. Or we can choose to be like the people on the streets who dropped what they were doing when the king summoned them and joined the party. The choice is given to each of us, and we must choose what we will do for ourselves.

Close in prayer, thanking God for all the wonderful hosts and their food and stories they provided. Ask God to help the group members make the right choice—to accept Jesus' invitation and choose to follow Him.

54

stargazer event

description

As the name implies, this is an event in which your group members will be able to appreciate the wonders of God's creation by viewing the stars at night. This is a great event for a summer evening or other time of year when the sky is clear. For an added twist, you can also give your group members the opportunity to send model rockets soaring into the sky.

key verse

"The heavens declare the glory of God; the skies proclaim the work of his hands" (Psalm 19:1).

location needed

a location away from city lights that has an open area and campfire sites available

materials needed

kindling and firewood
matches
telescopes
hot dogs
graham crackers
chocolate bars
marshmallows
hot cocoa
metal skewers or sticks
items needed for the model rocket launches (optional—see below)
Bibles

preparation

Ahead of time, recruit adult volunteers who like astronomy to help with the stargazing event, an adult volunteer to supervise the rocket launches (if you choose to do this activity), and adult volunteers to man the campfire. Also ask a worship leader from your church to come to this event to lead the group members in some worship songs around the campfire.

You will need to find a place that has an open area so the group members can easily view the sky. The location needs to be away from city lights and have campfire sites available. You will need to plan this for a clear night—no clouds.

If you choose to launch model rockets, do so when you first arrive at the site, before nightfall. (The group members will need to bring their own rockets to the event.) Ask your adult volunteer who is helping with the launches to help set up the rockets and be in charge of safety. Note that all states, with the exception of Rhode Island and California, currently adhere to a common Federal code of regulations

55

known as the National Fire Protection Association Code 112. This code defines the power, weight and other limits to which a rocket must comply to be considered a "model" rocket. Check this regulation online if you choose to do this option.[1] If you live in California and Rhode Island, you will need to obtain a permit or special permission from the local fire department before setting off any rockets.

Before sunset, ask your adult astronomers to set up their telescopes. You will want to get the campfire started as soon as the group members begin looking through the telescopes. Make sure that the fire is a little ways from where they are trying to view the stars so that smoke won't be a problem. Have all of the party snacks available, and make sure that the group members have the metal skewers or sticks you brought so they can heat their food over the fire. Ask the adult volunteer(s) who is helping with the campfire to keep the fire going, be in charge of fire safety, and help with snacks.

the event

Arrive at the site before sunset and have the group members go to the rocket launch area (if you choose to do this activity). Have your adult volunteer supervise the rocket launches. When it grows dark, take the group to the area where they will be stargazing. Introduce your adult volunteer astronomers and let the group members know they can visit the different telescopes and speak with any of the astronomers if they have questions or want more information. Also let them know where the campfire will be if they want to warm up or have snacks.

At the campfire, the group members can make s'mores, hot cocoa, hot dogs, or anything else you want them to cook on the fire.[2] Toward the end of the evening, have all of the group members come and sit around the campfire. Have your adult volunteer lead the teens in a few worship songs and then conclude with the devotion time.

closing devotion

After the group members have sung a few worship songs, discuss the following questions together:

- What types of things did you see through the telescopes tonight?
- Did you see anything that surprised you? If so, what?
- What is one thing you learned tonight that you didn't know before?
- What was your favorite constellation? Why?
- What do you think about God when you see these stars and planets?

Begin by stating that it was the ancient Babylonians who, from 1800 BC to 600 BC, first recorded many of the constellations that the group has viewed tonight. The Greeks and Romans adopted this system beginning around 400 BC, giving the constellations the names by which we identify them today—Ursa Major, Orion, Draco, Cassiopeia, Gemini, and so forth. The book of Job in the Bible mentions several of these ancient constellations, such as Job 9:9, where God is said to be "the Maker of the Bear and Orion, the Pleiades and the constellations of the south."

In Psalm 19:1, David wrote, "The heavens declare the glory of God; the skies proclaim the work of his hands." David, a shepherd, would have spent many nights out in the open as he watched his flock, observing the stars and reflecting on the awesome power of the God who created it all. To David, the universe itself was evidence of just how mighty God truly was. Perhaps even more amazing is that, unknown to

stargazer event

56

David, many of the "stars" he was seeing were actually *galaxies*—complete solar systems with their own sun and planets. We think our galaxy is huge, but it is only *one* of the many, many galaxies that exist. God created them all, and He keeps everything in perfect order—down to the smallest particles in atoms.

If you doubt this, consider the following: All atoms are made up of "particles" called protons, neutrons and electrons. As you may remember from science class, protons have a positive charge, electrons have a negative charge, and neutrons have no charge. Science tells us that the strength of the positive charge in a proton is *exactly equal and opposite* to the negative charge in an electron. If this were off by even the tiniest of fraction, nothing in our world would stick together. In other words, if this über-precise balance were not in place, we wouldn't *have* a world.

God designed it to work this way, and He keeps it all functioning perfectly. But there's more: this incredible, all-powerful God—who made everything that exists—*cares about each and every one of us*. We know this is true from such verses as 1 John 4:7-8, which states, "Dear friends, let us love one another, for love comes from God. Everyone who loves has been born of God and knows God. Whoever does not love does not know God, because God is love." God loves us, because *God Himself is love*. We may feel insignificant and small when we consider the complexity and size of God's creation, but the truth is that we *matter* to Him. How awesome is that!

Notes

1. See the National Fire Protection Association Code for Model Rocketry (NFPA 1122) at http://www.nfpa.org/aboutthecodes/AboutTheCodes.asp?DocNum=1122&cookie_test=1.
2. If you are unfamiliar with s'mores, roast a marshmallow over the fire, holding it on a long stick or wire coat hanger. When it is golden brown, squeeze it between two squares of graham crackers along with a piece of milk chocolate. After eating one, you'll want s'more!

travel the world party

description
This event will give the group members a chance to experience a bit of the world without ever leaving your church. If your church has a missions convention, this would be a great event to put on during this time.

key verse
"He said to them, 'Go into all the world and preach the good news to all creation'" (Mark 16:15).

location needed
a church or other venue with five separate rooms and a meeting area

materials needed
food from each of the five countries chosen
pictures and objects from each of the five countries chosen
costumes from each of the five countries chosen
five rooms that will be used as countries
refreshments
index cards
pens or pencils
Bibles

preparation
If your church is having a missions convention, invite the visiting missionaries to speak at your party. Also ask them to bring any interesting items/costumes from that country that they can show to the group. You will need five different speakers. For a high-tech option, you could also have a missionary speak from wherever he or she is located via a webcam. You would just need to set up a laptop in the room and make sure you have a good Internet connection so you don't lose the link in the middle of the presentation.

If you do not have access to visiting missionaries (or do not have five missionary speakers), choose several adult volunteers to represent five foreign countries. Ahead of time, the volunteers will need to do the following:

- choose a country that they will represent
- know some of the history of that country and be ready to share it[1]
- obtain pictures and/or interesting objects from that country
- prepare a food that is unique to that country

- bring or wear clothes or costumes from that country
- be prepared to answer questions

The representatives do not have to do all of the work—ask what they need help with and recruit teens (and parents) to be involved in areas where help is needed. Also, ask a few of the group members and their parents to bring refreshments.

the event

When everyone has arrived, divide the students into groups of 5 to 10 people each. Send each group to a different country (room). Allow each group to have about 20 minutes in each room, and then have them move to the next room. When all the groups have visited all the rooms, instruct them to come back to the main meeting area where refreshments will be available.

closing devotion

When everyone is back in the main room, discuss the following questions as a group:

- What was your favorite country? Why?
- What was the weirdest thing you ate?
- What was the tastiest?
- What was the most interesting fact that you learned?

Begin the closing devotion by reading Mark 16:15, in which Jesus told His disciples to "go into all the world and preach the good news to all creation." Explain that in making this statement, Jesus provided us with some concrete instructions to follow: We are to go everywhere, telling others the good news that Jesus came to save them from their sins and give them eternal life. Although most of us probably won't get to go to a foreign country for a while, we can start telling our friends *right now* about Jesus. It is the *best news* they will ever hear, so we shouldn't be shy about telling them.

Will everyone receive the good news about Christ? No. In fact, Jesus told the following parable about the types of people we will encounter when we share the gospel with them:

> A farmer went out to sow his seed. As he was scattering the seed, some fell along the path, and the birds came and ate it up. Some fell on rocky places, where it did not have much soil. It sprang up quickly, because the soil was shallow. But when the sun came up, the plants were scorched, and they withered because they had no root. Other seed fell among thorns, which grew up and choked the plants. Still other seed fell on good soil, where it produced a crop—a hundred, sixty or thirty times what was sown (Matthew 13:3-8).

Ask the group members who they believe each of the four types of different soil represent (soil along the path, rocky soil, thorny soil, good soil). When they have had time to answer, read the following explanation of the parable from Jesus:

> When anyone hears the message about the kingdom and does not understand it, the evil one comes and snatches away what was sown in his heart. This is the *seed sown along the path*. The one who received

travel the world party

the seed that *fell on rocky places* is the man who hears the word and at once receives it with joy. But since he has no root, he lasts only a short time. When trouble or persecution comes because of the word, he quickly falls away. The one who received the seed that *fell among the thorns* is the man who hears the word, but the worries of this life and the deceitfulness of wealth choke it, making it unfruitful. But the one who received the seed that *fell on good soil* is the man who hears the word and understands it. He produces a crop, yielding a hundred, sixty or thirty times what was sown (Matthew 13:19-23, emphasis added).

After the devotion time, ask the group members to think about one country for which they will commit to pray this week. Pass out the index cards and pens or pencils and ask the group members to write the name of this country on the card. Have them keep the card in a place where they will see it every day to remind them to pray for that country. Close in prayer, asking God to help the group truly care about the people in the nations for whom they are praying and to have confidence in sharing the good news of Jesus with their friends.

Note

1. The best way to find out information about a specific country is to Google it. For information on a specific country, use the Web search. For pictures of the country, the way the people dress and what they eat, use the images search. A great site for finding food recipes and histories from other countries is located at http://www.foodbycountry.com/.

unbirthday party

description

This is a party that your group members put on for a group of children in need. The event includes food, gifts, games and entertainment from your students to the children.

key verse

"I tell you the truth, anyone who doesn't receive the Kingdom of God like a child will never enter it" (Mark 10:15, *NLT*).

location needed

an indoor or outdoor space with enough room for playing games

materials needed

items for the unbirthday craft
items for the unbirthday games
party food
items for unbirthday cookie making
items for the unbirthday gifts to the children
children's tables and chairs
party decorations
extra presents
a DVD of *Alice in Wonderland* or a way to play a short clip of the movie from the
    Internet (optional)
Bibles

preparation

For this party, every child invited will have a happy *un*birthday—he or she will get a gift just because it isn't his or her birthday! Ahead of time, you and your group will need to select some children that you want to invite. Ideally, you want to select children in your church or community who are in need and who might not always receive presents on their birthday or on Christmas. Speak with your pastor or other leaders in your church to find out which specific families to invite.

A month before the party, ask your pastor if the church members could donate small empty boxes and bright-colored wrapping paper. Explain to the parents or guardians of the children you want to invite that your group is having a "happy unbirthday" party. This is taken from the book *Alice in Wonderland* by Lewis Carroll, in which the characters have a party and celebrate when it *isn't* a person's birthday. In other words, you want to celebrate and give gifts to the children just because. Ask the parents or guardians what small items the children want and need. Create a list of these items and make enough copies for your group members.

Give each person in your group the name and age of one of the children who will be attending the party. Also give each student one copy of the wants and needs list

for the children. Give each group member a box, and ask him or her to fill it with items from the list for their child. Instruct them to bring the full boxes to the church one week before the party is to be held. You may want to have each group member pick one area that he or she needs help in preparing, and be sure to contact parents as well and ask them to help out or bring needed items.

One week before the party, have the group members wrap their boxes with the wrapping paper. They can also make cards for the children at this time if they choose. A day before the event, have a team of students set up children's tables and chairs and decorate the room. Also, recruit a team of teens who will help with the cleanup when the party is over. For the actual party, if you choose to do a craft, play games or make cookies, see the individual instructions below for what you will need.

the event

When the children arrive, have your group members introduce themselves and show the children to the party area. The teens can help the children go through the line at the food table and find a seat. The group members should sit at the tables with the children that you have assigned to them. Give them and the children a chance to eat and get to know each other a bit. Introduce yourself during this time and let the children know that the "Happy Unbirthday" party has begun. Following this, start the cookie making, crafts and games (or all three).

unbirthday party food

Keep the food simple: have a cracker and cheese plate, a fruit plate, a vegetable plate, a make-your-own-sandwich plate, and small bottles of water. If you choose to decorate cookies with the children (see below), they can eat the cookies for dessert. If not, you might want to bring in some cookies or cupcakes. Use disposable plates and plastic ware with bright colors and patterns.

unbirthday cookie making

If you choose to have the children make cookies with the group members, you will need the following:

- sugar cookie dough (pre-made)
- animal cookie cutters
- baking sheets
- several kinds of sugar sprinkles
- an oven

Use a simple sugar cookie recipe or buy already made dough. The dough needs to be ready and rolled out before the party begins. Let the children use cookie cutters to cut shapes into the dough, and have different kinds of candy sprinkles for them to put on the cookies before you bake them. (This way, the children won't have to frost them after they are baked.) Recruit a volunteer baker to be in charge of collecting the cookies on the sheets, baking the cookies, and putting the finished cookies on plates.

unbirthday colorful cats craft

The following is a craft idea that will be a lot of fun for the children and the group members. To do this craft, you will need the following materials:

- wooden craft spoons
- acrylic paint
- white card stock
- glue
- pipe cleaners
- tiny beads (about the size of a seed)
- fine-point permanent marker
- silver or gold tissue paper
- red beads or glitter

The children and group members will be making colorful cats out of wooden spoons for this project. Begin by completely painting a wooden craft spoon. Paint a patch of the same shade of paint onto a piece of white card stock and allow both to dry. Next, cut a ½-inch square from your white card stock. Cut the square in half diagonally and glue the two triangles to the top of the spoon. (These will be the cat's ears.) For a tail, curl a six-inch piece of pipe cleaner around and glue it to the back of the spoon.

Use the tiny beads for the cat's eyes (black works best) and draw a cat's face on the spoon with the fine-point permanent marker. Create the cat's collar by twisting several one-inch squares of gold or silver tissue paper around the tip of a pencil. Glue these in place on the spoon, adding a few tiny red beads or glitter. Glue on more beads for buttons. Let the glue dry completely before you send the cat crafts home with the kids.[1]

unbirthday games

The following is a list of possible game ideas for you and the group to try at the unbirthday party:

doggy dash

This is a great warm-up game for the kids to play. The materials you will need are as follows:

- vaseline
- black construction paper

Cut the construction paper into circles to create black "doggy noses." Divide the children into two teams. Have half of the kids stand at one end of the room and the other half at the other end. Each child will need to put Vaseline on his or her nose. When the game begins, the first child in each line must put a black circle on his or her nose and then race to the other end of the room, where he or she will stick the black nose on the next child in line. If the black nose falls off, put a little more Vaseline on the child's nose and stick a new black circle on it. Allow the child to go again. Make sure that every player gets at least one chance to run with the black nose.[2]

freeze it

For this game you will need the following:

- music
- a way to play it for the group

Begin playing the music. Everyone must move and dance around until the music stops. When this occurs, they must "freeze" in whatever position they happen to be in. Have a spotter watching to see if anyone moves after the music stops or if they are too slow in getting into the freeze position. These players will be out of the game. Play until you have only one person left.

frog and the flies

For this game you will need some index cards and a pen or pencil. Count out the same number of index cards as you have players in the game. Write the letter "D" (for detective) or draw a magnifying glass on one of the cards. Write the letter "F" (for frog) or draw a frog on another card. Write the letter "X" or draw a picture of a fly on the rest of the cards.

Have all of the players sit in a circle. Put the cards into a hat or other container and have each person draw out one slip of paper. The players can look at the cards, but they shouldn't show them to anyone else. The player with the "D" or magnifying glass on his or her card is the "detective." Have that person sit in the center of the circle. The player with the "F" or frog is, of course, the frog. The rest of the players are flies.

On your signal, the frog is to "eat" the flies by sticking out his or her tongue quickly when the detective isn't looking. Any fly who sees the frog do this must fall over "dead." The detective's job is to try to figure out who is the frog by watching the players carefully and catch the frog with his or her tongue out. If the detective does this, he or she wins the game. However, if the frog eats all of the flies but one, that player wins the game.[3]

mummy race

For this game, you will need several rolls of toilet paper. Divide the players into two separate teams. Have the teams choose one person to be the "mummy." The object of the game is for each team to wrap up the mummy using all of the toilet paper. Make sure that the teams leave the nose and eye areas open so the mummy can see and breathe. Once a team has finished wrapping its mummy, that person has to hop (without breaking any of the wrapping) down to a finish line. If the wrapping breaks, the person must go back to the starting line and begin the hop again. The mummy who does this first without breaking any wrappings during his or her hop wins the game.[4]

unbirthday gifts

When you have finished your activities, tell the children that it is time for them to open their unbirthday gifts. Have each group member hand out the gift that he or she put together. The teen will need to call out the child's name if he or she has not met that child yet and then take the present (and card) to the child. In the event that some of the children do not end up with presents, have extra presents on hand that you can give out. After all the presents have been opened, begin the brief devotional.

closing devotion

Because you have children with short attention spans at this party, you will want to keep the closing devotion short and make it entertaining. One idea is to explain the "Unbirthday Party" theme by showing a short clip from the Disney version of *Alice in Wonderland*. Either bring in the DVD and find the scene where Alice meets the Mad Hatter and the March Hare at the tea party, or look online for a YouTube clip.

After showing the clip (if you choose to do so), explain that you and your group members are celebrating the fact that each of the children in attendance is important to them and to God. Explain that in the Bible, we read that people would bring children to Jesus. Some of the disciples told the people not to do this—after all, Jesus was a very busy guy. When Jesus saw them do this, He wasn't happy about it. Here is what He said to the disciples:

> Let the children come to me. Don't stop them! For the Kingdom of God belongs to those who are like these children. I tell you the truth, anyone who doesn't receive the Kingdom of God like a child will never enter it (Mark 10:14-15, *NLT*).

Talk to the children about how important they are to God and how He wants to be their friend. Close in prayer, asking God to help the children know that He loves them and that He is always with them.

Notes

1. Idea adapted from "Colorful Christmas Cats," from Disney *FamilyFun* magazine. http://familyfun.go.com/christmas/christmas-decorations/christmas-ornaments/colorful-christmas-cats-812044/.
2. Idea adapted from Sharon Mehl and Alecia Dixon, "Rudolph Dash," Kaboose. http://holidays.kaboose.com/xmas-party.html.
3. Idea adapted from "Frog Detective," MomsWhoThink.com. http://www.momswhothink.com/birthday-party-games/frog-detective.html.
4. For additional craft, food and activity ideas, see www.kaboose.com and www.familyfun.go.com.

waterworld event

description

This is a warm-weather event that should be held on a long, hot summer day. All food and activities have to do with water. **Warning**: You and your teens *will* get wet!

key verse

"Jesus answered her, 'If you knew the gift of God and who it is that asks you for a drink, you would have asked him and he would have given you living water'" (John 4:10).

location needed

a large field (where it won't matter if you saturate the grass)

materials needed

sprinklers and hoses
wading pools
water slides
super soakers
plastic decorations in bright colors
setup for the group water games (see below)
items for the group water games (see below)
food for the waterworld party (see below)
Bibles

preparation

Ahead of time, you and your team of party planners will need to set up the "waterworld." This can be as complex or as simple as you want to make it. The idea is to have different areas with sprinklers, hoses, pools, water slides, super soakers, and so on—kind of like a funhouse with water. Use plastic decorations with bright colors and set up your food table in an area where the snacks won't get wet. Ask some of the group members to help you design the layout. Have fun with it.

the event

When the group members arrive, have them enter the waterworld. They can hang around this area and eat party food until the group games begin. You can put your group events together or intersperse them with break times.

waterworld party food

The following are some ideas for types of food to serve at the party. If you follow this menu, you will need the following:

- "waterfreeze"—shaved ice with flavorings or frozen juice pops
- "waterlegs"—barbequed chicken drumsticks

- "waterpunch"—a citrus water punch (see recipe below)
- "watermelon"—well, that's just a typical watermelon

For the "waterfreeze," you will need a machine for making shaved ice and the flavorings. Another option is to bring frozen juice pops or some other frozen treat for the participants to enjoy. To make the "waterpunch," you will need the following ingredients:[1]

- 2 tablespoons citric acid (you can find this at most pharmacies or natural food stores)
- 5 quarts water
- 2 cups sugar
- 2 tablespoons pure lemon extract
- 3 sliced lemons
- 3 sliced limes
- crushed ice

Stir together the water, sugar, citric acid and lemon extract in a large bowl. Keep stirring until all the sugar dissolves. Add the sliced lemons and limes and serve! This recipe makes enough for 12 to 14 people.

waterworld group games

The highlight of your waterlogged—sorry, that's water*world*—event will be the group games. Here are a few options for games you and your group can play.

water relay

For this fun exercise in frustration, you will need the following items:

- 5 spoons
- 5 pop bottles
- 5 buckets of water
- prizes

Divide the group members into five teams and have each team form a relay line. Give each team one spoon and one bucket of water. Place one pop bottle for each team at the other end of the area. Explain that when you signal for the game to begin, the first person in line must dip the spoon into his or her team's bucket and then carefully walk to where the bottle is. When the player reaches the bottle, he or she must pour the water into the pop bottle. After this, the player must run back to his or her team and give the spoon to the next person in line. The teams must repeat this process until the game ends, at which point the team that has the most water in their pop bottle will be declared the winner. Allow the group members to run the relay for 10 minutes, and then signal the end of the game. Award prizes to the winning team.

mud bowl

This is basically "king of the mountain" played in mud. As the name suggests, this is a messy game, and it will require some advance preparation. Ahead of time, you will need the following:

- a large circular area of dirt
- a way to fill this area with water

waterworld event

67

- shovels
- a way to wash the group members off

Begin by filling a dirt area with water so that you have a mud pit. Shovel some mud into a large mound in the middle of the pit to make the "mountain" on which the players will stand. Have the hoses ready for the cleanup after the game.

Divide the group into two teams. Explain that when the game begins, each team will try to get its players on the mound and the players from the other team off the mound. Set some ground rules ahead of time to ensure that this is a fun game where no one gets injured. Players must keep their arms crossed when blocking or trying to move someone off the mound. There is no hitting, tackling, slapping, holding anyone under muddy water, grabbing, kicking . . . you know your group, so enforce any rules you believe are necessary. Explain to the group that if anyone breaks the rules, he or she must leave the mud bowl area at once.

It will be difficult for a team to get all of its players on the mound, but that is why it is so much fun. In fact, the fun in this game is less about winning than in just playing it. By the end of the game, the players will be so covered with mud that they won't be able to recognize their teammates.

Give the group a specified amount of time to play. If no team is able to get all of its members on the mound by the specified amount of time, signal the end of the game. Use the hoses to spray the mud off the players.

water balloon toss
The classic game of skill. For this game, you will need the following:

- water balloons
- a large open area
- prizes

Fill the balloons with water and have the group members get into pairs. Give each pair one water balloon and have them stand face to face. Explain that when you call, "toss," the person with the water balloon must toss it to the other person without breaking it. This will be extremely easy at first, but after each toss, the players must take two steps back. The distance between the pairs will grow, and the game will become much harder. If a pair breaks its balloon, they are out of the game. The last pair left with an unbroken balloon wins the game. Award prizes to the winners.

water war
This is another great game that allows your group to wage war against each other using super soakers and water balloons. You will need the following:

- several super soakers
- water balloons
- buckets of water
- a long piece of rope
- adult volunteers to referee
- prizes

Begin the game by laying the long piece of rope across the field to use as the dividing line between the two teams. Make sure both sides have buckets of water so they can refill their super soakers. Also make sure that both sides have an equal number of water balloons.

Divide the group members into two teams and have each team go to a different side of the rope. Allow the teams to fill their super soakers. Explain that the object of the game is to hit players from the other team with either a water balloon or with their super soakers without themselves getting hit. They can come up to the rope line, but they cannot cross over it to the other team's side. Players cannot hit anyone in the face—period—or they must leave the field.

When a player is hit, he or she must leave the game. Have several adult volunteers on hand to referee the game and make sure everyone is following the rules. The team with the last player that has not been hit wins the game. Award prizes to that team.

closing devotion

At the end of the party, gather together as a group and discuss the following:

- What was your favorite food at the party today?
- What was your favorite game or event?
- What was your least favorite game or event?
- Are you tired of water yet?

Begin the devotion time by asking the group members how much of the human body is made up of water. The answer is around *60 percent.* In addition, our brains are made up of 70 percent water, and our lungs are made up of nearly 90 percent water.[2] We must have water to survive, and if we don't get enough of it, we will die.

Given this fact, it's no wonder that people have gone to war over water. Unlike the "water wars" we fought today, these wars were often between groups of people for the rights to a well or other water source. We read about one of these ancient wars in the book of Exodus. After Moses led the Israelites out of Egypt, the people went into an arid region known as the Desert of Sin. There, God gave the people food in the form of quail and manna, a white bread-like substance that appeared on the ground each morning (see Exodus 16). However, the people still needed water.

God solved this problem by having Moses strike a rock. Water flowed out, and the people were saved. However, this new water source attracted the attention of a band known as the Amalekites, and they attacked the Israelites to get it. After a lengthy battle, they were defeated (see Exodus 17).

In the New Testament, towns had a well that provided water to the community, and the women and children would go there to get water for their homes. One of these wells, named "Jacob's well," was located near the town of Sychar in Samaria. Jesus and His disciples were passing through the area one day when He saw a woman there getting water. Jesus approached her and asked for a drink—which surprised her for two reasons. First, Jesus was a man, but He was addressing her as an equal. This was unheard of in the culture at the time. Second, Jesus was a Jew, while she was a Samaritan. The two groups didn't get along with each other.

Jesus told the woman that He had "living water." The woman didn't understand—after all, Jesus didn't have anything to use to draw water, and the well they were sitting by was deep. In truth, Jesus wasn't talking about well water at all, but about life that comes from God (see John 4). This is the type of "water" that He offers to us as well, and when we drink of it by giving our lives to Christ, He satisfies our cravings for things that aren't good for us. He gives us eternal life.

water world event

Notes

1. http://www.melskitchencafe.com/2010/04/citrus-water-punch.html.
2. "The Water in You," U.S. Geological Survey (USGS). http://ga.water.usgs.gov/edu/propertyyou.html.

whodunit mystery party

description
This is a mystery dinner theater. The group members will not only enjoy a great dinner at this event but will also be able to experience the play "The Case of the Cat's Meow" taking place all around them.

key verses
"In reading this, then, you will be able to understand my insight into the mystery of Christ, which was not made known to men in other generations as it has now been revealed by the Spirit to God's holy apostles and prophets" (Ephesians 3:4-5).

location needed
a large banquet room with a stage

materials needed
enough copies of "Lord and Lady Wellington's Dinner Invitation" (found on page 73) to mail to each student
a copy of "The Case of the Cat's Meow" (found on page 74) for every actor
costumes for each actor (refer to the play for details)
props for each actor
the Cat's Meow Statue
the Diamond
food items for the dinner menu
enough tables with tablecloths and settings for all the invited guests
Bibles

preparation
Several weeks before the party, enlist the help of teens in your group or adult volunteers to serve as cooking staff and cleanup crew. Also, choose actors for the play "The Case of the Cat's Meow," which will be performed at the event. Give each actor a copy of the play and assign costumes and props for each actor to bring (or have a special team of people working on this). Make sure that your actors have memorized the play and have had a chance to practice where you will be holding the dinner. Be sure to announce the event at your youth meetings. Two weeks before the party, mail out (or email) the invitations to the group members. Meet with your cooking staff and go over the menu and what will be happening during the evening.

the event
Before the event the guests will receive a copy of "Lord and Lady Wellington's Dinner Invitation," which will provide them with all the information that they need

to attend the party. As the guests arrive on the evening of the dinner, seat them according to the directions given in "The Case of the Cat's Meow." Follow the directions for serving the dinner and beginning the drama. During the event, serve the following courses:

- Appetizer: drinks (soda, water, juice, punch) and rolls with butter
- Main course: Beef Wellington (this can consist of steak, or you can use chicken); cooked vegetables (corn, peas, carrots) and a baked potato
- Dessert: Chocolate Diamond Surprise (a slice of chocolate cake with a scoop of chocolate ice cream, sprinkled with silver sugar sprinkles)

closing devotion

When the play is over, ask anyone who guessed who stole the diamond before it was revealed to raise his or her hand. Call on a few people to tell how they figured it out. Was it based on the evidence given, or just a gut feeling?

Explain that in the Bible, we often find the word "mystery" being used. For example, in Matthew 13:11, Jesus says, "To you it has been granted to know the *mysteries* of the kingdom of heaven" (*NASB*, emphasis added). Likewise, in Ephesians 3:4-5, Paul writes, "In reading this, then, you will be able to understand my insight into the *mystery* of Christ, which was not made known to men in other generations as it has now been revealed by the Spirit to God's holy apostles and prophets" (emphasis added).

What was this "mystery" that Jesus and Paul were talking about? Was it some secret that could never be known? Was it some puzzle that people had to figure out? In fact, the word for "mystery" used in these verses refers to God's plan for salvation through Christ. When Jesus came to earth, He unlocked many of the mysteries of the kingdom of God and revealed how God wanted to work in the earth. Likewise, Paul revealed that the "mystery of Christ" was God's plan for bringing people back into relationship with Him—a plan that had been kept "hidden" in ages past but now, because of Christ, was available to everyone.

Because of the Bible, God's Word, we don't have to wonder about God. We don't have to guess what will make Him happy or what He wants us to do. And we don't have to try to decipher how we can be saved from our sins and have eternal life. The Bible unlocks all of these mysteries and shows us how to find God—if we believe and have faith in His Son, Jesus Christ.

The Cat's Meow

Here's what you need to know:

The Cat's Meow is a famous Egyptian statue of a Sphinx-like cat that is meowing. The statue has two sapphires for eyes, a ruby nose and one of the largest diamonds on the planet inside of its meowing mouth. Lord and Lady Wellington have been financing an Egyptian dig in which the famous archaeologist Jerold Tarter has been uncovering some amazing tombs and artifacts.

Five months ago, Mr. Tarter discovered the Cat's Meow in a deep tomb. He returned one week ago to the Wellingtons' palatial estate in the English countryside, where he turned the statue over to its new rightful owners, Lord and Lady Wellington.

Tonight, the Wellingtons are throwing an extravagant party. They have invited many important guests, including their niece Hortence Hathaway and their son, Tommy. They will unveil the statue for the first time during the dinner.

In attendance will be the famous archaeologist Jerold Tarter, a young reporter named Etta Williams, Prince Hubert of Liechtenstein and many dukes, duchesses, barons and baronesses. As an important and high-class person in society, you have also been invited to the party.

You will need to dress appropriately for the 1920s time period. Remember that you are royalty—or at least very, very rich. You will also need to present this invitation at the door to be admitted to the dinner.

Please arrive by [time] at the following address:

[Add the address of your dinner here]

the case of the cat's meow

time and setting
The grand dining room of Lord and Lady Wellington's estate, around the 1920s

characters
Lady Wellington
Lord Wellington
Jerold Tarter (an archaeologist)
Etta Williams (female reporter)
Jiles (the Butler)
Other servants
Hortence Hathaway (Lord and Lady Ellington's niece)
Tommy Wellington (Lord and Lady Ellington's son)
Prince Hubert of Liechtenstein (rich and eligible—also interested in archaeology)
Detective Miles Long
Many dukes, duchesses, barons, baronesses and other important people (played by the guests in the audience)

props
For the Cat's Meow statue, use a wooden or stone figurine of a cat, or wrap a toy cat in aluminum foil. Use two green plastic or stone "gems" for the eyes and a red plastic or stone "ruby" for the nose. For the diamond, use a shiny piece of crystal or anything else that resembles a precious stone. The diamond should be larger than the other "gems" and placed inside the cat's mouth. For the costumes, have the actors dress in clothing that represents the styles of the 1920s as much as possible (long coats, bowler hats, suits and ties, and so on). Check online for ideas, be creative, and have fun with it.

Place the diamond into the pocket of a coat. You will also need a disguise of some sort for Jiles to wear—a fake mustache, glasses, wig, or other items. Place these with the coat. Put the coat on a coat rack located at the back of the room.

background information
The Cat's Meow is a famous Egyptian statue of a Sphinx-like cat in the process of meowing. The statue has two sapphires for eyes, a ruby nose and one of the largest diamonds on the planet inside its meowing mouth. Lord and Lady Wellington have been financing an Egyptian dig in which the famous archaeologist Jerold Tarter has been uncovering some amazing tombs and artifacts.

Five months ago, Mr. Tarter discovered the Cat's Meow in one of the deepest tombs. He returned one week ago to the Wellingtons' palatial estate in the English countryside, where he turned the statue over to its new rightful owners, Lord and Lady Wellington.

Tonight, the Wellingtons are throwing an extravagant party. They have invited many guests, including their niece Hortence Hathaway (in hopes of helping her find an eligible and rich young man to marry) and their son, Tommy. Also in attendance will be Jerold Tarter, a young reporter named Etta Williams, Prince Hubert of Liechtenstein, and many dukes, duchesses, barons and baronesses. During the party, the Wellingtons plan to unveil the Cat's Meow for the first time.

directions

Lord and Lady Wellington, Jerold Tarter and Detective Miles Long will be offstage until they make their entrances. The Cat's Meow statue should be onstage and draped with a cover so no one can see it until it is presented.

Jiles, the butler, and his staff will be at the entrance of the dining room when the guests arrive. They will seat both the actor guests and the student guests at their tables. They will also be serving the various courses of the dinner. As soon as the guests are seated, the servants will bring out the appetizer.

Etta Williams will be seated at one of the student tables. She will spend the dinner trying to get information on the Wellingtons, Mr. Tarter and the Cat's Meow. She will also be taking notes on her reporter notepad during the dinner.

Hortence Hathaway and Prince Hubert will be seated together at the same table. Hortence will spend much of the dinner trying to engage the prince and any other male at the table in conversation—very boring conversation. The Prince will spend his time trying not to talk to Hortence.

Tommy Wellington will be seated at one of the student tables. He will spend the dinner talking about himself—how wonderful, good looking and talented he is. He will be quite aggravating to the other guests at the table.

the play

As soon as the main course is served, Lord and Lady Wellington should go to the stage and stand on either side of the Cat's Meow statue. Have them keep the statue draped with a cover until the moment comes in the play when they reveal the statue.

Lord Wellington: Ladies and gentlemen, I wanted to thank you on behalf of my wife and myself for coming this evening. Many of you are family, dear friends and esteemed colleagues. I would now like to introduce you to the archaeologist who, aided by our support, discovered the treasure you will see today. Jerold Tarter, please come and join us.

(Jerold enters the stage and stands next to Lord Wellington.)

Lord Wellington: Mr. Tarter, will you briefly share what it was like to uncover the Cat's Meow?

(Etta Williams begins writing furiously on her notepad to get every word that Mr. Tarter says. Prince Hubert watches the stage with interest. Hortence stares at Prince Hubert with interest. Tommy rolls his eyes and prepares for the boring speech that he has already heard several times.)

Jerold Tarter (in a whiney voice)**:** Thank you, Lord Wellington. My team and I had been in Egypt for more than three years making discoveries in several Egyptian tomb sites.

75

(Tommy mouths the next sentence with Mr. Tarter.)

Jerold Tarter: It was exactly five months ago today that we found something we had never seen before—a plant that usually cannot be found in that part of the world. This was my first clue. As I began to dig up the plant, my shovel hit something hard. My team assisted me in clearing the area, revealing what looked like a door. It was sealed. We stood on one side, and a thousand years of Egyptian secrets stood on the other.

(Tommy begins to fall asleep.)

Jerold Tarter: Still, the sealed door was no match for me. I had a special tool I had invented on a previous dig that was helpful in such situations as this. I put the "Tarter Pry Bar," as I have named it, into position, and we were able to open the sealed door. As soon as it was open, I was the first to enter, of course.

(Tommy begins to snore loudly. Hortence sees him, comes to his table and smacks him on the head. He wakes up grumbling.)

Jerold Tarter: We found many artifacts, but the prize was the statue that you will be viewing this evening. I named it "The Cat's Meow." It is a beautifully carved cat statue with emerald eyes, a ruby nose and one of the largest diamonds the world has ever seen in its mouth. Right away—
Lord Wellington (interrupting): Very good. Fascinating, just fascinating. Thank you for your enthralling account, Mr. Tarter. And now it is time for the unveiling. (To Lady Wellington) My dear, will you do the honors?

(Lady Wellington, giggling with glee, yanks the cover off the statue. The statue sits there with jeweled eyes and nose, but the mewing mouth is empty. Lady Wellington shrieks in horror. Lord Wellington gasps. Mr. Tarter states the obvious.)

Mr. Tarter: The diamond is gone! Someone has stolen the diamond!!!

(Detective Miles Long enters the dining room. He makes his way past each table, inspecting the people and the food. Mr. Tarter paces back and forth, and Lord Wellington tries to console Lady Wellington. Jiles stops the detective, and they say some words that the rest of the audience cannot hear. Jiles nods his head and leads Detective Long up on stage.)

Detective Miles Long: My dear Lord and Lady Wellington, it has come to my attention that you are in need of my services. I am Detective Miles Long, and I am here to investigate the alleged theft of one said diamond from the mouth of this statue. I will need to examine the scene of the crime and interview possible suspects. (To Jiles) Please lock the door. No one is to leave this room until I say so.

(Detective Long goes over to inspect the statue. Jiles signals to one of his staff to secure the doors. The rest of the staff begins to serve the dessert. After a few minutes,

Detective Long calls Jiles over and talks to him. Jiles goes into the room and escorts the following people to the stage: Etta Williams, Hortence Hathaway, Tommy Wellington, Prince Hubert of Liechtenstein, and one of the student guests. They are seated in chairs facing the audience. While the interrogation is in progress, Jiles sneaks to the back of the room and takes the coat that has been placed there on the coat rack. He should put on the disguise and sit down at one of the tables.

> **Detective Long** (to Lord Wellington): When is the last time you saw the diamond in the statue's mouth?
> **Lord Wellington:** Why, just before the dinner. Lady Wellington and I made sure that it was there. You see, we have been quite nervous about putting the statue—especially the diamond—on display.
> **Detective Long:** Has something happened recently to make you nervous?
> **Lord Wellington:** As a matter of fact, yes. Yesterday when we returned home from a trip to the city, we found the diamond lying on the floor in front of the statue. We didn't think that anyone had tried to take it, but we didn't know what it was doing on the floor.
> **Detective Long:** Interesting.

(Detective Long spins around and looks at Tommy.)

> **Detective Long:** You are Lord and Lady Wellington's son?
> **Tommy:** Yes.
> **Detective Long:** The same son who has been having money problems as of late?
> **Tommy:** Now, I don't believe that is any of your business.
> **Detective Long:** On the contrary, it is my business. Where were you just before the dinner tonight?
> **Tommy:** I was in my room getting ready.
> **Detective Long:** Was anyone with you there to corroborate your story?
> **Tommy:** Yes.
> **Detective Long:** Who?
> **Tommy:** Well . . . if you must know . . . my mother. I haven't gotten the whole tie thing down yet, and she had to tie it for me.

(Lady Wellington nods as everyone else snickers. Detective Long spins around again and points at Hortence.)

> **Detective Long:** And you, Miss . . .
> **Hortence** (whispers): Hortence.
> **Detective Long:** Miss Hortence, why did you come tonight?
> **Hortence** (stumbling over her words): Well, I . . . I . . . wanted to support my aunt and uncle.
> **Detective Long:** Wrong!

(Hortence starts to cry.)

> **Detective Long:** In fact, weren't you here because you want a diamond about as much as you want a rich husband—say, a prince, perhaps?

77

(Prince Hubert looks sick. Hortence is now wailing. Detective Long spins yet again and stares at Prince Hubert.)

> **Detective Long:** So, you're a prince, eh? What are you a prince of?
> **Prince Hubert:** Well, I'll have you know that I am the prince of Li—
> **Detective Long:** Lincoln, Nebraska, isn't it? In fact, you are the "prince" of the Royal Foods chain. You are only pretending to be royalty so you could get near one of the greatest archaeological finds of the century.
> **Prince Hubert:** Yes! It's true! But I didn't take it. I just wanted to be near it.

(Detective Long walks over to Etta Williams, who is still furiously writing down every word and doesn't notice him.)

> **Detective Long:** So, Miss Williams, what might you be writing on that notepad of yours?

(Etta jumps in surprise.)

> **Etta:** The news. I'm a reporter from the *Gazette*. I'm here to report the facts of this—
> **Detective Long:** Wrong! Isn't it true in fact that you are not a *Gazette* news reporter but a gossip columnist from the *Tattle Tale Times*?
> **Etta** (flustered): I . . . I . . . may not be from the *Gazette,* but I *am* a reporter just the same.

> **Detective Long:** Sure you are. Weren't you sent here by the paper to dig up any dirt you could find on these poor unsuspecting folks?

(Etta looks down. Detective Long approaches the student.)

> **Detective Long:** And what are you doing here?

(Whatever the student says will cause Detective Long to shake his head.)

> **Detective Long** (to everyone): Well, the case is solved. I know who has the diamond.
> **Lord Wellington:** How could you possibly know? You haven't even questioned the other people in this room yet.
> **Detective Long:** I don't need to do so. You see, as I began the questioning, my trained eye noticed something taking place in another part of the room. How much do you know about your butler, Jiles?
> **Lord Wellington:** He has been with us for years.
> **Lady Wellington:** He had the highest letters of recommendation from his last employer.
> **Detective Long:** Would that employer have happened to be Diamond Pockets—the sneakiest diamond thief in town?

(Lord and Lady Wellington gasp in disbelief. All the actors on stage begin to talk excitedly. Detective Long leaves the stage and heads to the table where the now-disguised

Jiles is sitting and looking very nervous. Detective Long pulls Jiles to his feet and rips off his disguise. He finds the diamond in one of the pockets in the coat Jiles is wearing and holds it up. Everyone onstage rushes down to the table. Lord and Lady Wellington lovingly take possession of the diamond.)

Detective Long: Jiles is one of Diamond Pockets's best thieves. I'll be taking him down to the station. We might be able to use him to bring down Diamond Pockets's entire ring.

(Detective Long leaves, dragging Jiles behind him. Everyone thanks him for his amazing detective work. Lord and Lady Wellington return to the stage, followed by the cast. Lady Wellington hands the diamond to Mr. Tarter, who places it in the mouth of the statue.)

—The End—

winter carnival

description

This party is based on the winter carnivals held during cold months in many areas of the world. You will need lots of snow and some chilly weather for this event.

key verse

"Though your sins are like scarlet, they shall be as white as snow" (Isaiah 1:18).

location needed

a large field or other outdoor location where you can set up carnival tents (make sure you also have an indoor area where the group members can go to warm up)

materials needed

booths or tents for the snow arcade
maps of the carnival area
handout with times of each event
ingredients for the winter carnival food
items for the winter carnival events
items for the winter carnival snow arcade games
Bibles

preparation

Ahead of time, make sure that your group members wear warm clothes to the event. Set up the booths and tents in the carnival area for the winter snow arcade games you want to play. (Note: Seven options are listed below, but you can adapt and modify these to fit your group and location.) These should be simple structures similar to what you would find at a carnival or fair—nothing complex is needed. Have treats and hot drinks available in the indoor area before the carnival begins so that your group members will have a place to warm up. Also set up any winter carnival events that you want to have available at the party (see section following). You will also want to create a map showing the location of the different winter snow arcade games and winter carnival events and schedule listing times when these will be held (these could be put on the same handout). Your map should have the following areas listed:

- indoor area (indicating where food and snacks are available)
- individual tents for the winter snow arcade
- locations of any winter carnival events
- general meeting areas where the group members can hang out
- location where you will gather for the closing devotion

For the schedule, list the starting time, the times when you will be holding the winter carnival events, any times when the winter snow arcade games will close, and the time when the group should gather together for the closing devotion or to conclude the party.

the event

Welcome the group members as they arrive and hand out the maps and schedules. Let the group members know that the indoor area will be open throughout the event if they want to grab a snack or hot drink or just warm up. Allow the students to eat, play games in the winter snow arcade or mill around in the indoor area. Remind the group members to move to the winter carnival event location approximately 10 minutes before the event is scheduled to begin.

winter carnival food

For this event, provide hot chocolate, coffee and/or tea and any other snacks that you would like to serve. For a fun twist, you can provide the following two winter-themed treats.

trapper's delight

This recipe makes about 30 fried dough treats. You will need about an hour and a half to make these, so you will likely want to make these ahead of time and have a way to keep them warm in your indoor area. Here are the ingredients you will need:

- ½ cup warm water
- 5 teaspoons active dry yeast
- 1 pinch white sugar
- 1 cup warm milk
- ⅓ cup white sugar
- 1½ teaspoons salt
- 1 teaspoon vanilla extract
- 2 eggs
- ⅓ cup vegetable oil
- 5 cups whole-wheat flour (or as needed)
- 1 quart oil (for frying)
- 2 cups white sugar (or as needed)
- 1 teaspoon ground cinnamon (optional)

Get a large bowl and combine the yeast, warm water and pinch of sugar. Let the mixture stand for about 5 minutes. When the mixture becomes slightly foamy, add the remaining ⅓ cup white sugar, milk, vanilla, eggs, oil and salt, and stir until smooth. Mix in about 3 cups of the flour and stir with a spoon. Gradually add in more flour. When the dough becomes firm, transfer it to a floured surface. Knead the dough for 5 to 8 minutes and add flour as needed to make it firm and elastic. Place the dough in a greased bowl and cover. Let it rise until it is about double in size (approximately 30 to 40 minutes).

When the dough has risen, gently deflate it and pinch off a golf-ball sized piece. Place the dough ball on a lightly floured surface and use a rolling pin to flatten it into an oval shape. Cover the oval dough with a towel and set aside. Do this with the rest of the dough until you have a number of oval-shaped pieces. Pour the oil into a deep fryer (you can also use a Dutch oven or wok) and heat to about 375° F. (You can test the temperature by tossing in a bit of the dough to see if it sizzles and swells up.)

winter carnival

81

Grab the dough ovals you made and stretch them out into a flat tail shape. Carefully place the dough into the hot oil. Fry the dough, turning once, until they are a deep brown color (about 1 to 2 minutes per side). Remove the dough using tongs and drain on paper towels. Place the remaining 2 cups of sugar in a large bowl and stir in cinnamon (if desired). Toss the fried dough into the sugar bowl while they are still hot and shake off the excess.[1]

maple snow taffy

This is a tasty if odd-looking frozen treat. For this recipe you will need to have access to a stove in your indoor area, as you will need to pour the taffy over snow (or ice cream) and serve immediately. You will need the following ingredients:

- 1 cup maple syrup
- ¼ cup salted butter
- clean snow (or ice cream)

Place a plate into a refrigerator (you will need this to be cold later to test the taffy). Pour the syrup and butter into a pot and heat over medium heat. Stir and heat until the mixture reaches 220° F to 235° F on a candy thermometer (approximately five minutes after it comes to a boil). Test whether the taffy is ready by pouring a small amount of the mixture onto the plate that's been cooling in the refrigerator. When the mixture is ready, it should thicken up into soft taffy on the plate (if this doesn't happen, cook it for a minute or two more). Let the mixture cool for several minutes and then pour it over bowls of clean snow (or ice cream). It should harden into a maple-flavored taffy lump.[2]

winter snow arcade games

To create a true carnival atmosphere—even if it is 20 degrees outside—you will want to set up some fun fair-type games for your group members to play. Most of these games can be broken down into the following categories:

- tossing rings around an object
- throwing a ball to knock down a stack of objects
- tossing an object into a container
- hitting a target with an object

Create your own games using these categories or use the following ideas.[3]

pop bottle ring toss

For this game, you will need several 2-liter pop bottles, several rings (large enough to fit over the top of the pop bottles), and several small prizes. You might want to make the rings out of rope rather than using wood or plastic ones, as rope rings tend not to bounce off the bottles as much. Use the 2-liter bottles for the targets and set them up in a challenging but not overly difficult manner. When a player gets a ring around the top of a bottle (or several bottles), he or she wins a prize.

can knockdown

For this game, you will need several empty metal cans, three tennis balls and small prizes. Stack cans in a pyramid formation. Give each player three balls to throw at the cans. When a player knocks down all the cans, he or she wins a prize.

bucket toss

This game requires five small buckets, three balls and, of course, some small prizes. Set up the five buckets in a straight line. Place the first bucket a short distance away from the player. Set up the next bucket about six inches beyond the first one, but still in front of the player. Continue in this manner until you have set all five buckets. The player must try to toss a ball into the buckets in order, from the closest to the farthest. If the player does this, he or she wins a prize.

break-a-plate

For this game, you will need cheap dinner plates, three baseballs and small prizes. Set up the plates on the far wall of the booth and give three baseballs to the player. The player must throw the baseballs and try to break a plate. If the player does this (or breaks some other set number of plates), he or she wins a prize.

penny pitch

This game requires a bag of pennies, paper targets (you can use funny photos of youth leaders) and small prizes. Place the paper targets at random locations. The player must throw a penny and have it land on the specific target in order to count. Award prizes for the number of targets hit or for specific spots on the target that are hit.

soccer kick

You will need a target, soccer ball and small prizes to set up this game. Make the target out of plywood and paint it with a fun sports design or winter theme (snowmen, icicles, snowflakes). Cut out some holes that are large enough for a soccer ball to go through. Give each player three chances to kick the soccer ball through the holes in the target. If the player does this, award him or her with a prize.

flying disc throw

For this game, you will need a target made out of plywood and some flying discs. Similar to the soccer kick target, you can paint this with a sports design or winter-related theme. Cut out rectangular holes in the target that are wide enough for the discs to go through (make these challenging but not impossible). Give each player three chances to throw the disc through the holes. Award prizes to the winners.

winter carnival events

As previously mentioned, you will want to establish specific times to hold each of these events and list those times on the schedule you give to the group members when they first arrive. The following are some ideas for winter-themed activities that you can do at your carnival

snow rafting

This is a fun take on inner tubing that requires a small hill. Use a rubber raft for a sled—the bigger the raft, the better. Injuries can occur when sledding, so make sure you set some ground rules to keep everyone safe.[4]

castle conquest

Divide the group into teams. Have each team build a snow castle and stock up on a good supply of snowballs. Set up targets on each of the snow castles (something that can be knocked over with a snowball, such as aluminum cans). The players

must stay behind their castle and lob snowballs at the other teams' targets. The last team with targets left standing is the winner. Make sure that the players know to duck behind their snow castle to avoid snowballs to the face. Instruct players not to lob snowballs at the heads of the other players (disqualify anyone who intentionally breaks this rule).[5]

sleigh rides
If you have the funds or know someone in the area who can provide a sleigh ride, this can be a one-of-a-kind event for the group members to enjoy.

snow sculpture contest
This event can be done either in teams or individually. Give the contestants a certain amount of time to build a snow sculpture. Award prizes for the most creative, most realistic, largest, smallest, and so on.

snow obstacle course
Navigating an obstacle course in the snow can be twice as difficult to do as on dry ground. Set up a simple course in an area where the snow is a bit deeper. Award prizes for the fastest time.

closing devotion

Toward the end of the party, gather all of the group members together inside to thaw out. Ask the students the following questions:

- Even though it was cold, did you still have fun?
- What game did you like the best?
- What special event was your favorite? Why?
- What was the strangest game or event you did?

Begin the devotion time by asking the group if they know where the coldest inhabited place is on earth. If they guess "the South Pole" or "Antarctica," they are technically correct. It is true that Antarctica is the coldest place on earth, with average temperatures reaching between -112° F and -130° F in the interior region during the winter. Antarctica is also populated year round, though most of the people there are scientists and only stay part of the year. The coldest permanently inhabited place on earth is Oymyakon in Siberia (Russia), which reaches an average daily temperature of -51° F in January.[6] Kind of puts the current cold weather into perspective, doesn't it?

The word "snow" is mentioned 23 times in the *New International Version* of the Bible. Often this word is used to describe what a person with leprosy looks like. For instance, in Numbers 12:10, Miriam, Moses' sister, appears "leprous, like snow." In other places, the word "snow" is used for exactly what it is—the cold white stuff that falls from the sky. There's a great story in 1 Chronicles 11:22 where a warrior named Benaiah goes down "into a pit on a snowy day" and kills a lion. In other places, however, "snow" is used to describe a person who has a clean and pure heart before God. David writes about this in Psalm 51:7 when he states, "Cleanse me with hyssop, and I will be clean; wash me, and I will be whiter than snow."

In Isaiah 1:18, the Lord says, "Though your sins are like scarlet, they shall be as white as snow." In Hebrew, the word "scarlet" in this verse is actually the name for a worm (*towla*). This worm would attach itself to a tree when it was ready to lay its eggs

84

and die in the process, leaving a red stain on the wood. (Pretty gross.) "Scarlet" came to represent "sin" in the Bible, while "snow" came to represent purity and total cleansing. From this, we see that what God is saying is that even though we have made a mess of our lives, He can turn them into something clean and beautiful. We just need to release ourselves to God, ask for His forgiveness, turn from our sins and embrace His forgiveness.

Close your time in prayer, thanking God that each of us can come to Him just as we are, and He accepts us and forgives us our sins.

Notes
1. Recipe taken from "Canadian Fried Dough from a Real Canadian," available at All Recipes.com. http://allrecipes.com/recipe/canadian-fried-dough-from-a-real-canadian/.
2. http://family.go.com/food/recipe-780690-maple-snow-taffy-t/.
3. These winter snow arcade games are adapted from "Carnival Game Ideas," School Carnivals. http://www.schoolcarnivals.com/Games/alphabetical.htm.
4. Adapted from "KRAFT Snow Rafting," Quebec Winter Carnival 2013. http://www.carnaval.qc.ca/en/carnival-2013/family-activities.
5. Adapted from "METRO Castle Conquest," Quebec Winter Carnival 2013.
6. "Antarctica" and "Extremes on Earth," Wikipedia.org. http://en.wikipedia.org/wiki/Antarctica; http://en.wikipedia.org/wiki/Extremes_on_Earth.

85

HOLIDAY PARTIES & EVENTS

holiday: \ hä-lə-dē\ **1:** a day on which one is exempt from work; specif- ically a day marked by a general suspension of work in commemora- tion of an event **2:** *chiefly British*: vacation—often used in the phrase on holiday—often used in plural **3:** a period of exemption or relief (cor- porations enjoying a tax holiday)

new year's celebration
january 1

description

This a fun event to get the group members thinking about the upcoming year and setting some practical goals for themselves. As an option, hold this event a day early to free up the group members for other New Year's events with their families or at church.

key verse

"He who was seated on the throne said, 'I am making everything new!'" (Revelation 21:5).

location needed

a large room (and a bowling alley for the bowl-a-thon)

the event

Ahead of time, decide which events you want to do with your group. Each of the events requires different materials and setup, so see the specific directions below. If you decide to do the bowl-a-thon, you will need a way to transport a television set (or two) to your venue (if one is not already there) and possibly transportation for the group members to the bowling alley. In addition, invite someone who can lead the group members in a few worship songs, or play some pre-recorded worship music to which the group can sing along.

new year's prophecies

This is a take-off of magazines that have prophecies for the upcoming year. For this option, you will need the following:

- paper
- pens or pencils
- envelopes

Have a time for the group members to suggest spiritual-growth prophecies for the upcoming year about their lives and the lives of their friends. Hand out paper and pens or pencil and ask them to write down these predictions. Give the students an envelope, and instruct them to address the envelope to themselves and place their prophecies in it. Mail the envelopes to them in about six months. (As an option, they could also give their predictions on things such as upcoming football games and events around the world.)

new year's resolutions

Most people like to start the New Year off by making resolutions (weight loss goals, reading the entire Bible during the year, spending more time with family, and so on). For this option, you will need the following:

- a copy of "My New Year's Resolutions" for every group member (see page 92)
- pens or pencils

Give each person a copy of "My New Year's Resolutions" and ask him or her to write at least three personal resolutions for the upcoming year. When everyone has finished, go around the room and ask volunteers to share their resolutions.

new year's verse

For this option, group members will find a passage of Scripture they would like to adopt as their personal verse for the upcoming year. You will need the following:

- a copy of "My New Year's Scripture Verse" for every group member (see page 93)
- pens or pencils
- Bibles

Give everyone a copy of "My New Year's Scripture Verse," and make sure each person has access to a Bible. Have the group members write out their chosen verse and complete the other information on the handout. Then have them commit their verse—or at least the reference—to memory and give their papers to you. Mail the papers to them in six months. As an option, you can also buy a packet of Scripture promises online (or type up several verses yourself—more than enough for the number that will be attending the party!). Place the slips of paper in a basket or other container. Shortly before (or after) midnight, pass the container around the room and invite students to select a verse. When everyone has a verse, ask the group members to share their verses aloud.

new year's magazine search

This is a fun scavenger-type activity that your group members can do without leaving the premises. You will need the following for this option:

- copies of "New Year's Magazine Search" (see page 94)
- magazines and newspapers
- poster board
- scissors
- glue or tape

Have the group form several teams. Give each team a copy of "New Year's Magazine Search" and a pen or pencil. Place the stack of magazines and newspaper on the floor or on a table (the group members will be finding pictures and articles in these magazines and newspapers). Also give each team a piece of poster board and tell them to glue or tape their finds onto these boards. Decide on a time limit and announce the start of the competition. The first team to finish its list or the team with the most items complete when the time is up wins the game.

new year's celebration

new year's bowl-a-thon

Many group members will want to spend time with their families on New Year's Day, but others may need something to do. For those students, this is a great way to have fun together—while you still get to watch the bowl games yourself! You will need the following to do the activities in the bowl-a-thon:

- television set (or two)
- football information sheets
- prizes
- munchies and drinks
- Bibles

Ahead of time, set up a television set. Create some football-fanatic information sheets with national rankings, season records and game scores—there are many fantasy football sites that have this information. Ask group members to help in making this sheet, as this will be a great way to involve students who don't normally participate in meeting and/or special event preparations. (You may also want to come up with some activities for non-football fans who want to come to the party.)

Assign each individual a football team for each game. Every time their team scores a touchdown, they must sing "The Star Spangled Banner" or do push-ups or something to celebrate. As an option, you can even set up *two* televisions sets at opposite sides of the room and have the individuals rooting for each football team at their respective locations. Another option is to set up a football pool and award prizes for correct predictions. Whatever you decide, the idea is to make it fun!

For the second half of your *bowl*-a-thon, take everyone in the group to your local bowling alley. Most bowling alleys are open on New Year's Day, and they are usually not busy.

closing devotion

Regardless of which activities you choose to do, end with a short devotional time. If you chose to have your group members do the New Year's prophecies or New Year's resolutions, ask a few individuals to share what they wrote. Following this, state that New Year's is a great time to make these types of resolutions because it gives you a specific time frame in which to reach these goals—one year from today. It's easy to measure what you've accomplished when you set a goal on January 1, because you know how well you have done when that day rolls around again next year.

People set all kinds of resolutions each year to make a "new start." What's interesting is that this is exactly what Christ does when He comes into our lives. When we accept Jesus as our Savior and Lord, we put aside our past life and embrace the new life that He gives us. As Paul puts it in Galatians 2:20, we are "crucified with Christ," and it is no longer us who lives but Christ who lives in us. This is the best goal we could ever make—to commit to serving Christ and Christ alone each day of our lives.

In Revelation 21:5, Jesus says, "I am making everything new!" It is Christ who gives us new life. In John 3:3, He explained this to a man named Nicodemus, who was a Jewish religious leader of the time, stating that Nicodemus could have eternal life if he were "born again." When Nicodemus understandably questioned how one could physically be born a second time, Jesus stated that the "birth" He was talking about was spiritual in nature. He also told Nicodemus how he could get that new birth: "everyone who believes in [Me] may have eternal life" (John 3:15).

Today, as you look over your resolutions or think about what you want to achieve this year, remember that Christ is the one who can truly help you to make a new start. He is there to help you if you ask Him, and through the power of the Holy Spirit you can lead a life that is pleasing to Him!

Close in a time of worship and prayer, thanking God for always being with the group members and for His help in allowing them to reach their goals.

my new year's resolutions

With God all things are possible.
Matthew 19:26

This is the beginning of a whole new year in my life! To celebrate new beginnings, I want to make the following resolutions:

resolution one

____
____
____
____
____

resolution two

____
____
____
____
____

resolution three

____
____
____
____
____

Everything is possible for him who believes.
Mark 9:23

Thank You, God, that I can count on You to guide me and help me do the things You want me to do. I commit my resolutions to You and ask that You will help me meet these goals. Amen.

Signed _________________________________ Date _________________

my new year's scripture verse

This is the Scripture verse I have chosen for this year . . .

____

____

____

____

____

____

____

This is the reason I chose this Scripture verse . . .

____

____

____

____

____

____

____

This is how I want to apply this Scripture verse to my life this year . . .

____

____

____

____

____

____

____

new year's magazine search

Use the magazines and newspapers provided to find the following photos and/or articles. Check off the box when you find the item, cut it out, and paste it to your team's board.

❑ Find an article about a New Year's Day college football game.

❑ Find a picture of a bowl (any type of bowl will work).

❑ Find a list of the top 10 collegiate football teams. Write down those teams in order of ranking.

1. _______________________	6. _______________________
2. _______________________	7. _______________________
3. _______________________	8. _______________________
4. _______________________	9. _______________________
5. _______________________	10. _______________________

❑ Find an ad for a weight-loss program or product.

❑ Find something that mentions a New Year's resolution.

❑ Find an advertisement that mentions something "new" about its product.

❑ Find a picture of a present a team member received for Christmas.

❑ Find an article describing the beginning of a politician's or other official's new term in office.

❑ Find a photo of a baby who could have been born within the last year.

❑ Find a photo that captures new life and new beginnings.

dr. martin luther king, jr., day
third monday in january

description

Recognizing this national holiday with your group can help promote healing, understanding and racial reconciliation. The ideas below can be incorporated into a general meeting time with the group or built around a general time of fellowship.

key verse

"He has told you, O man, what is good; and what does the LORD require of you but to do justice, to love kindness, and to walk humbly with your God" (Micah 6:8, *NASB*).

location needed

a large room

materials needed

copies of "I Have a Dream" for every group member (see page 97)
copies of "A Call to Action" for every group member (see page 99)
laptop (optional)
pens or pencils
snacks and drinks
Bibles

preparation

Ahead of time, make copies of each of the handouts. For added impact, you might want to bring a laptop computer and play footage of Dr. King's speech from YouTube or another Internet site. You can play the entire speech, or you can search for the part of the message that corresponds with the words on the handout and run the clip from that point. Set up your snack and drinks table before the event begins, and let the group members know that they can visit it throughout the party.

the event

Begin by explaining that Dr. Martin Luther King, Jr., was an American clergyman who was a prominent leader in the Civil Rights Movement during the 1950s and 1960s. He began his career as an activist in 1955 by organizing the Montgomery Bus Boycott, in which the African American community of Montgomery, Alabama, refused to ride the city's public transit to protest its policy of racial segregation. Although Dr. King was assassinated in 1968, he did more for civil rights in a short time period than any other human being in recent history. He helped bring freedom

where once existed ungodly segregation, and he brought hope where once there was only bitterness.

One of Dr. King's most popular and inspiring messages was his "I Have a Dream" speech, which he delivered on the steps of the Lincoln Memorial in Washington, DC, on August 28, 1963. Since this incredible speech was made, changes for the better have been made in the United States, but racial reconciliation is still needed in our lives. The words spoken by Dr. King moved racial reconciliation to higher ground and, more than 40 years later, continues to be an inspiration to all.

Ask a volunteer to read the excerpt from Dr. King's "I Have a Dream" speech, or play the clip that you found online. After the speech has been read (or played), distribute copies of "A Call to Action." Give the group members some time to complete the questions on the handout, and then gather back together as a group or form smaller groups for discussion.

closing devotion

If you had the group members break into smaller groups, begin the devotion time by asking one member from each group to share the main ideas that were discussed. Following this, lead into the devotion time by stating that one of the most well-known quotations of all time is from the Declaration of Independence, which states, "We hold these truths to be self-evident, that all men are created equal." This document was drafted and put into effect in 1776.

Unfortunately, the Declaration of Independence did not halt the practice of slavery in America. In fact, many of the drafters of the document (such as Thomas Jefferson) owned slaves and continued to own them throughout their lives. This attracted comments from abolitionists (those who wanted to do away with slavery) from the time the Declaration of Independence was first published. Thomas Day, one such abolitionist, stated, "If there be an object truly ridiculous in nature, it is an American patriot, signing resolutions of independency with the one hand, and with the other brandishing a whip over his affrighted slaves."[1]

It wasn't until the American Civil War in 1861–1865 that slavery was officially abolished everywhere in the United States. However, by this time racial prejudice was so engrained in places that segregation (a separation between races) continued on well into the 1960s. It was these types of laws that led Dr. King and others to protest and finally bring national attention to this injustice that was taking place.

In Deuteronomy 10:18, Moses told the Israelites, "[God] administers justice for the fatherless and the widow, and loves the stranger [the foreigner], giving him food and clothing." Our God is a God of justice and mercy, and He requires us to treat each other with love. As He said to the prophet Micah, "He has told you, O man, what is good; and what does the LORD require of you but to do justice, to love kindness, and to walk humbly with your God" (Micah 6:8, *NASB*).

Note

1. David Armitage, *The Declaration Of Independence: A Global History* (Cambridge, MA: Harvard University Press, 2007), pp. 76–77.

I have a dream

Speech delivered by Dr. Martin Luther King, Jr.,
at the Lincoln Memorial in Washington, DC, on August 28, 1963

I am not unmindful that some of you have come here out of your trials and tribulations. Some of you have come fresh from narrow jail cells. Some of you have come from areas where your quest for freedom left you battered by storms of persecutions and staggered by the winds of police brutality. You have been the veterans of creative suffering. Continue to work with the faith that unearned suffering is redemptive.

Go back to Mississippi, go back to Alabama, go back to South Carolina, go back to Georgia, go back to Louisiana, go back to the slums and ghettos of our modern cities, knowing that somehow this situation can and will be changed. Let us not wallow in the valley of despair.

I say to you today, my friends, so even though we face the difficulties of today and tomorrow, I still have a dream. It is a dream deeply rooted in the American dream.

I have a dream that one day this nation will rise up and live out the true meaning of its creed: "We hold these truths to be self-evident that all men are created equal."

I have a dream that one day on the red hills of Georgia the sons of former slaves and the sons of former slave owners will be able to sit down together at the table of brotherhood.

I have a dream that one day even the state of Mississippi, a state sweltering with the heat of injustice, sweltering with the heat of oppression, will be transformed into an oasis of freedom and justice.

I have a dream that my four little children will one day live in a nation where they will not be judged by the color of their skin but by the content of their character.

I have a dream today.

I have a dream that one day, down in Alabama, with its vicious racists, with its governor having his lips dripping with the words of interposition and nullification; one day right there in Alabama, little black boys and black girls will be able to join hands with little white boys and white girls as sisters and brothers.

I have a dream today.

I have a dream that one day every valley shall be exalted, every hill and mountain shall be made low, the rough places will be made plain, and the crooked places will be made straight, and the glory of the Lord shall be revealed, and all flesh shall see it together.

This is our hope. This is the faith that I will go back to the South with. With this faith we will be able to hew out of the mountain of despair a stone of hope. With this faith we will be able to transform the jangling discords of our nation into a beautiful symphony of brotherhood. With this faith we will be able to work together, to pray together, to struggle together, to go to jail together, to stand up for freedom together, knowing that we will be free one day.

This will be the day when all of God's children will be able to sing with new meaning, "My country 'tis of thee, sweet land of liberty, of thee I sing. Land where my fathers died, land of the pilgrim's pride, from every mountainside, let freedom ring."

And if America is to be a great nation, this must become true. So let freedom ring from the prodigious hilltops of New Hampshire. Let freedom ring from the mighty

dr. martin luther king, jr., day

mountains of New York. Let freedom ring from the heightening Alleghenies of Pennsylvania!

Let freedom ring from the snowcapped Rockies of Colorado!

Let freedom ring from the curvaceous slopes of California!

But not only that; let freedom ring from Stone Mountain of Georgia!

Let freedom ring from Lookout Mountain of Tennessee!

Let freedom ring from every hill and molehill of Mississippi. From every mountainside, let freedom ring.

And when this happens, when we allow freedom to ring, when we let it ring from every village and every hamlet, from every state and every city, we will be able to speed up that day when all of God's children, black men and white men, Jews and Gentiles, Protestants and Catholics, will be able to join hands and sing in the words of the old Negro spiritual. "Free at last! free at last! thank God Almighty, we are free at last."[1]

Note

1. Reprinted by arrangement with the Estate of Martin Luther King, Jr., c/o Writers House as agent for the proprietor, New York, NY. Copyright 1963 Martin Luther King, Jr., copyright renewed 1991 Coretta Scott King.

a call to action

1. What is the Christ-honoring call to action in Dr. King's "I Have a Dream" speech?

    ____

    ____

    ____

    ____

    ____

2. Why do you think this speech is recognized as one of the greatest and most memorable speeches of all time?

    ____

    ____

    ____

    ____

    ____

3. John 8:32 says, "Then you will know the truth, and the truth will set you free." How does this verse apply to Dr. King's speech?

    ____

    ____

    ____

    ____

Note: To learn more about Dr. Martin Luther King, Jr., visit www.thekingcenter.org.

valentine's day
february 14

description

It was William Shakespeare who said, "Love comforteth like sunshine after rain." This party will allow your group members to share similar sappy sentiments as they celebrate this holiday focused on love.

key verse

"Let us love one another, for love comes from God. Everyone who loves has been born of God and knows God" (1 John 4:7).

location needed

a large room (and a neighborhood or shopping mall for the "Lookin' for Love" activity)

the event

Ahead of time, decide which events you want to do with your group. Each activity requires different materials and setup, so see the specific directions below.

valentine's day panel

Most of us think about that special person in our lives on Valentine's Day. We go out of our way to make the one we love (or like a lot) feel special and let him or her know how much we care. Valentine's Day is also a great opportunity to plant some seeds for what *real* love looks like. This activity will give students a glimpse of what love and marriage looks like over the years, using couples in various stages of their marriage. For this activity, you will need the following:

- tables and chairs for students
- chairs for panelists
- tablecloths and centerpieces for tables
- sound system and several microphones (if necessary)
- desserts and beverages

This activity works best in an informal setting such as a dessert night, where students and panelists can sit at tables and enjoy some time together before the panel begins. For your actual panel, you will need a newlywed couple, a couple who has been married several years, and a couple who has been married for more than 25 years. You will also need to select a moderator for the event. Ahead of time, set the date and time with your panelists (plan for about 60 minutes). Arrange for people to bring in desserts and beverages, and have a team set up some Valentine's decorations on the tables.

Allow some time for the group members to mingle when they arrive. When everyone is seated around the tables, begin the panel. Seat the panelists at the table located at the front of the room. Have the moderator ask the following questions to get things rolling, and encourage the group members to ask questions as well:

- How did you meet?
- Were you initially attracted to each other?
- When was your first kiss?
- How did you know you were in love?
- What is the best thing about being married?
- What is the hardest thing about being married?
- What advice would you give to a couple who is just starting to date?
- Where does God fit into your relationship?
- Does having a relationship with God change how a marriage works?

You can also give the panelists a list of questions ahead of time and let them share from their hearts about their relationships. Tell the panelists that they are also free to share pictures, letters, their special song or whatever else may help the group members get to know them and their stories. Make sure the panelists portray both the good times and the bad times in their responses to the questions or through their stories.

valentine's day caroling

There are many groups who share the joy of Christmas by caroling in their neighborhoods. How about sharing the love Valentine's Day represents by doing some good old love-song caroling? Pick out some old love songs—the mushier, the better (try some oldies). Print out lyrics to the songs ahead of time and make a copy for everyone in the group.[1] If you have someone who can play guitar in your group, get the music as well. (Note: You may need to practice the songs before you go caroling. No sense hurting people's ears!) Here are a few classic favorites:

- "Love Me Tender" (Elvis Presley)
- "Can't Buy Me Love" (The Beatles)
- "Sugar, Sugar" (The Archies)
- "Can't Take My Eyes Off of You" (Frankie Valli)
- "My Girl" (The Temptations)
- "Book of Love" (The Marcels)
- "I Got You, Babe" (Sonny and Cher)
- "Unchained Melody" (The Righteous Brothers)
- "L.O.V.E" (Nat King Cole)

Serenading seniors with the oldies is a great way for students to connect with older members of the church or people at a nursing home. Have the group members bake cookies beforehand to share, or purchase flowers or Valentine cards to give to each person they are visiting. (Note: Nursing-home residents may have special diet needs. Be sure to check with the nursing-home administration to find out what food items can be brought in and shared with participants.)

sappy love poem contest

For this option, you will need paper and pens or pencils. Break the group into teams of three to four people each. Have each group come up with the sappiest love poem

or song they can (make sure they know to use only appropriate content). Here are some ideas for truly sappy sentiments to get them started:

- "Real love stories never have endings." (Richard Bach)
- "Love starts with a smile, grows with a kiss and ends with a tear."
- "I don't want to go to sleep at night, because my life with you is better than a dream."
- "Doubt that the stars are fire, doubt that the sun doth move, doubt truth to be a liar, but never doubt I love." (William Shakespeare)
- "If a star fell each time I thought about you, the moon would truly realize what loneliness is like."
- "You broke my heart, but I still love you with all the little pieces."[2]

lookin' for love

This is a theme-related scavenger hunt. Have the group members form several teams and give each team a copy of "Lookin' for Love" (see page 103) and a pen or pencil. You can either have this scavenger hunt in the neighborhood or at a local shopping area where there are lots of people. If you want to go farther afield, recruit adult drivers to take the group members to different neighborhoods. Assign one adult volunteer to each group to verify the group's findings or take pictures of the items the group locates. Decide on a time limit (one hour or so). The first team to finish its list or the team with the most items complete when the time is up wins the game. Award Valentine's heart candy to the winning team.

closing devotion

Begin the devotion time by asking a group member to read 1 John 4:7. Explain that in this passage, John tells us love comes from God. He is the source of love, and it is actually because He loved us first that we are able to show love to others (see verse 19). Thus, when we show love to others, we are actually reflecting the nature of God.

Some people in our lives are easy to love. If you have recently started dating someone, you know how exciting it is to be around that person. Everything he or she does is funny, interesting—and even inspiring. It is easy to love the other person because you *like* being in his or her presence. But there are others in our lives who are difficult to love. Maybe this is a person who is mean to you at school, or a grumpy neighbor, or even a family member that just bugs you. You would rather run away when you see this person coming near you, much less show love to him or her.

However, this is what God calls us to do. In Romans 12:18, Paul writes, "If it is possible, as far as it depends on you, live at peace with everyone." While we don't have to suffer abuse from that person, we can choose to forgive him or her for any wrong done to us, make amends where necessary, and choose to live at peace. We can choose to show love and, in so doing, reflect God's love to that person. This will not only leave an impression on the person, but it will also help us to grow and develop in our faith. Loving others in the way that God loves will make us more like Him.

Notes

1. Here are some websites you can visit to find the lyrics to your favorite songs: http://www.lyrics.com; http://www.lyricsdomain.com; http://www.absolutelyric.com.
2. Some of these statements were adapted from "Sappy Love Quotes . . . Ugh," http://itsmetaushie03.tripod.com/id18.html.

lookin' for love

- ❑ Find a picture of a heart.

- ❑ Find some Valentine's Day candy.

- ❑ Find a couple (boyfriend and girlfriend or married) and write their answers to the following questions:

    Where did you go on your first date?
    ____
    ____
    ____

    How long have you been married/dating?
    ____
    ____
    ____

    What would be the perfect Valentine's Day gift from the other person?
    ____
    ____
    ____
    ____
    ____

- ❑ Find someone who can tell you the origin of Valentine's Day. Write a brief summary here.
    ____
    ____
    ____
    ____
    ____

- ❑ Find a guy and a girl who are wearing red. Ask them to repeat the following lines from *Romeo and Juliet*:

    Juliet: O Romeo, Romeo, wherefore art thou Romeo?
    Deny thy father and refuse thy name,
    Or, if thou wilt not, be but sworn my love
    And I'll no longer be a Capulet.

    Romeo: I take thee at thy word.
    Call me but love, and I'll be new baptized.
    Henceforth I never will be Romeo.

| **Juliet:** | What man art thou that, thus bescreened in night, |
| | So stumblest on my counsel? |

Romeo:	By a name I know not how to tell thee who I am.
	My name, dear saint, is hateful to myself
	Because it is an enemy to thee.
	Had I it written, I would tear the word.[1]

❑ Find a photo of a couple in love.

❑ Find the definition of the word "love" and write it here.

____

____

____

____

❑ Write out four lines from your favorite love song and sing the lines.

____

____

____

____

❑ Find five names of movies, TV shows or popular songs with the word "love" in the title and list them.

1. ____
2. ____
3. ____
4. ____
5. ____

❑ Find someone who has fallen in love more than five times. Get his or her autograph below.

____

Note

1. "The Tragedy of Romeo and Juliet, Act II, sc. ii," in *Shakespeare: The Complete Works*, G. B. Harrison, ed. (New York: Harcourt, Blake and World, 1968), p. 484.

st. patrick's day
march 17

description
Aye, laddie, there be many ways to celebrate St. Paddy's Day. Even if ye not be Irish, ye can be wearin' the green and enjoy these events!

key verse
"If the Son sets you free, you will be free indeed" (John 8:36).

location needed
a large room

the event
Ahead of time, decide which events you want to do with your group. Each of the events requires different materials and setup, so see the specific directions below.

toss the hat on the leprechaun
This is just a silly aiming-type game with a St. Patrick's Day theme. For this activity, you will need the following:

- something that looks like a leprechaun costume
- a chair
- a bowler hat (a round hat with a brim)
- small prize

For the leprechaun costume, you just need a green sports coat and vest and maybe a green bowtie and a red fake beard (look online for some ideas). Pick up the felt bowler hats at a costume store (ideally in green color). Ahead of time, have a volunteer dress as your leprechaun. Mark off a starting point, and have the volunteer sit in the chair some distance away. The object is for the group members to toss the bowler hat like a Frisbee so that it lands on the leprechaun's head. The leprechaun can move his or her head so that the hat lands on it, but he or she cannot stand up or move the chair. Give the players three chances to toss the hat and award one point for each successful landing. In the event of a tie, have a tiebreaker round and award a prize to the winner.

heave it over
While this is technically a traditional *Scottish* game, it's still fun to play on St. Patrick's Day (hey, Scotland and Ireland are close by, right?). This game is a take-off on the hay sack toss, in which players use a pitchfork to toss a bundle of hay over a crossbar. For this activity, you will need the following:

- several spatulas
- several paper lunch bags
- newspaper
- duct tape
- clothesline (or other makeshift crossbar)
- small prizes

Ahead of time, crumple up the newspaper and stuff it into several of the paper lunch bags (you will need as many bags as you have teams). Tape the lunch bags closed with the duct tape to make a "hay bundle." Set up the clothesline in the room and mark off a starting point on the floor with the tape. Divide the group into teams and give the first person in line the spatula and paper bag bundle. On your go, the first person on each team will attempt to pitch the bundle over the clothesline using the spatula. If the person is successful, he or she hands the spatula to the next person, who must also use it to pitch the bundle over the clothesline. If a person crosses the line, he or she must go to the end of the line and do it again. Award a prize to the first team to have everyone complete the challenge.[1]

quasi-caber toss

This is another traditional Scottish highlands game in which players hoist an 18-foot log (called a caber) onto their shoulders and try to flip it so that it lands in a vertical position with the other end pointing toward 12 o'clock. Players are scored not by the distance the caber is thrown but by the position in which it lands, with the 12 o'clock position being considered perfect. For your version of this game, you will need the following:

- small cat-litter sized pan
- sand (or clean cat litter)
- unsharpened pencils
- small prizes

Pour the sand or cat litter into the pan. Give a pencil to each player and have him or her stand behind a start line some distance away from the sand. The object is for the players to flip the pencil in such a way that it lands in the sand with the eraser end pointing up in the 12 o'clock position. Give each person three tries, and award points as follows:

- pencil eraser in the 12:00 position: 100 points
- pencil eraser in the 9:00 to 11:00 position: 50 points
- pencil eraser in the 1:00 to 3:00 position: 50 points
- pencil eraser in the 6:00 to 8:00 position: 0 points
- pencil eraser in the 4:00 to 5:00 position: 0 points

Tally up the points after everyone has had three chances to toss the quasi-caber and award a prize to the winner.[2]

st. patrick's day quiz

For this option, you will make your group members use their noggins by giving them a fun St. Patrick's Day quiz. Ahead of time, print out enough copies of "It Ain't

Easy Being Green" (see page 109) for each person and have pens and pencils available. Also have some small prizes available (such as a small box of Lucky Charms® cereal). Give the group members about 10 minutes or so to complete the quiz on their own. If you prefer, allow them to work in groups of two. When they are finished, go over the quiz as a group and award prizes to the person or team with the most correct answers. Here are the answers to the quiz:

1. On what date is St. Patrick's Day celebrated each year?
   C.   March 17.

2. In addition to being a successful and famous Christian missionary, what else is Saint Patrick known for?
   B.   He drove the snakes out of Ireland.

3. What did Saint Patrick do while he was enslaved in Ireland before becoming a missionary?
   C.   He herded and tended sheep and swine.

4. There are differing views about the place of Saint Patrick's birth, but he is generally thought to be from either of which two countries?
   B.   Scotland or England.

5. Saint Patrick is known as the patron saint of what?
   A.   Ireland

6. What is a leprechaun?
   C.   An Irish fairy with a hidden pot of gold.

7. Why is the shamrock associated with St. Patrick's Day?
   B.   Saint Patrick used it to tell about the Father, the Son and the Holy Spirit.

8. Where was the first St. Patrick's Day celebration in America?
   C.   Boston, Massachusetts.

9. What does *Erin go bragh* mean?
   B.   Ireland forever.

10. Why is the color green associated with St. Patrick's Day?
   D.   It is the color of spring.

closing devotion

Begin the devotion time by stating that all of us are familiar with the fun that goes along with St. Patrick's Day—it's the day to wear green and eat corned beef. However, few of us are aware of the person for whom the day is named: Saint Patrick. He was, in fact, a remarkable person who was responsible for bringing the gospel to Ireland.

Patrick was born around AD 387 in Wales, located on the western side of the island of Britain. When he was about 16, he was captured by Irish raiders and taken as a slave to Ireland. There he worked herding sheep for six years, and during this time his faith in God grew. One day, Patrick stated that he heard a voice telling him that

he would be freed and that his ship was ready. So he escaped to a port and eventually made his way back home to his family.

After returning home, Patrick entered the Roman Catholic Church and went to Gaul (western Europe) to study for 12 years. At one point, he saw a vision in which the people of Ireland called for him to come back to them and preach the gospel of Christ. When Patrick was appointed the second bishop to Ireland, he returned to the land where he had once been enslaved. There he won many people to Christ, established monasteries and set up schools and churches. He also made many enemies—primarily the Celtic Druids, whose religion Christianity was replacing. Patrick was imprisoned several times, but each time, miraculously, he escaped.

St. Patrick remained in Ireland for 30 years. Throughout his ministry, he lived by Jesus' words in John 8:36: "If the Son sets you free, you will be free indeed." Although the Irish had made him a slave, because of his faith in Christ, he was able to see that it was the Irish themselves who were enslaved to their pagan gods. He had experienced freedom in Christ, and he wanted others to experience this same freedom. By the time of his death on March 17 in AD 461, most of Ireland had come to know Christ.

Close in prayer, asking God to help the group members experience the type of freedom that St. Patrick knew and to help them see the need in this world for those who do not yet know Christ.

Notes

1. Adapted from "Gaelic Games" on Disney Family Fun. http://familyfun.go.com/st-patricks-day/st-patricks-day-games/gaelic-games-704878/.
2. Ibid.

it ain't easy being green

How much do you know about St. Patrick's Day? Take this quiz to find out. Circle only one answer for each question.

1. On what date is St. Patrick's Day celebrated each year?
    A.   The third Sunday in March
    B.   The second Wednesday in March
    C.   March 17
    D.   March 21

2. In addition to being a successful and famous Christian missionary, what else is Saint Patrick known for?
    A.   He found the first four-leaf clover.
    B.   He drove the snakes out of Ireland.
    C.   He declared the shamrock a symbol of Ireland.
    D.   He was a rich landowner.

3. What did Saint Patrick do while he was enslaved in Ireland before becoming a missionary?
    A.   He robbed the rich to feed the poor.
    B.   He converted the Irish to Christianity.
    C.   He herded and tended sheep and swine.
    D.   He tamed wild beasts.

4. There are differing views about the place of Saint Patrick's birth, but he is generally thought to be from either of which two countries?
    A.   Ireland or England
    B.   Scotland or England
    C.   England or France
    D.   Ireland or Scotland

5. Saint Patrick is known as the patron saint of what?
    A.   Ireland
    B.   Snakes
    C.   Britain
    D.   Four-leaf clovers

6. What is a leprechaun?
    A.   The lead Irish dancer
    B.   The national symbol of Ireland
    C.   An Irish fairy with a hidden pot of gold
    D.   A tiny man found at the end of rainbows

7. Why is the shamrock associated with St. Patrick's Day?

    A. It's green and represents the coming of spring.
    B. Saint Patrick used it to tell about the Father, the Son and the Holy Spirit.
    C. It brings good luck.
    D. Four-leaf clovers are hard to find.

8. Where was the first St. Patrick's Day celebration in America?

    A. New York City
    B. Plymouth, Massachusetts
    C. Boston, Massachusetts
    D. Philadelphia, Pennsylvania

9. What does *Erin go bragh* mean?

    A. Happy St. Patrick's Day!
    B. Ireland forever.
    C. Irish luck be with you.
    D. Erin, go out back and feed the pigs.

10. Why is the color green associated with St. Patrick's Day?

    A. Saint Patrick wore a green hat.
    B. Shamrocks and four-leaf clovers are green.
    C. It represents spiritual renewal.
    D. It's the color of spring.

5

passover
late march or early april

description

Passover commemorates God's deliverance of the Hebrews from slavery in Egypt and is the oldest and most important religious festival in Judaism. The focal point of Passover is a meal called the Seder, and in this youth celebration you will be enacting a version of this meal and service with your group members.

key verse

"Get rid of the old yeast, so that you may be a new unleavened batch—as you really are. For Christ, our Passover lamb, has been sacrificed" (2 Corinthians 5:7).

location needed

a room where you can set up tables and conduct a meal

the event

In recent years, there has been increasing interest among Christians to take part in this ancient Jewish festival. This has primarily come about as Christians have realized that the Early Church came out of a predominately Jewish heritage. A Christian Seder is one way of allowing believers to connect with these Jewish roots.

Preparation is needed ahead of time to perform the Seder (both in terms of the food that needs to be brought in and the elements of the service that need to be presented). For this reason, it is a good idea to delegate tasks to adult and student volunteers and ask their assistance in preparing the food items. As a general rule, allow around two weeks of preparation before holding the event. In addition, you may want to circulate a sign-up sheet for this event so you know exactly how many group members will be attending.

In Jewish homes, the Seder is celebrated as a full meal and includes games and songs. For this adapted Seder, the food items will be limited to those actually used in the service. This has the advantage of allowing you to present the main items used in celebrating Passover and allowing your group to participate in the meal as well.[1]

setting up the room

Ideally, you will want to set up the participant tables to accommodate six people. You will need to set up a head table at the front or middle of the room where everyone can see it. If possible, arrange the tables in a *U* shape so that everyone will be facing the head table when seated. The head table should be large enough to seat three to four people. Use a six-foot to eight-foot table and cover it with a simple white tablecloth.

setting up the head table

The head table is where you or another leader will conduct the service, so you will need to have all of the elements on the table required for the Seder. Here is what you need:

1. a copy of "Simple Seder Service for Leaders" (found on the CD-ROM)
2. a linen napkin
3. a linen bag (to hold the *matzot*)
4. a cup of drinking water
5. a clear bowl for the ceremonial hand washing
6. a clear bowl of salt water
7. carafe or pitcher of red grape juice
8. a Seder plate—traditionally, this is a decorated plate with places for the symbolic elements used by the leader (you can purchase these at certain stores, or you can use a wide plate with room so that the elements don't mix together)
9. a piece of horseradish root (for the Seder plate)
10. a hard-boiled brown-shelled egg (for the Seder plate)
11. a lamb shank bone (for the Seder plate—available at grocery stores)
12. a clear bowl holding *charoset* (see instructions on page 114)
13. four clear long-stemmed glasses (a different style for each glass if possible)
14. 2 candlesticks with white candles
15. a bowl of grated horseradish (make sure that you do not use the "creamed" variety that is processed into a white sauce—this should be made from the grated root)
16. several slices of regular bread (these will be hidden around the room)
17. small prizes
18. a pitcher of water
19. an empty basin
20. a plate and place setting
21. a hand towel

Use the following chart to place each of these elements on the head table.

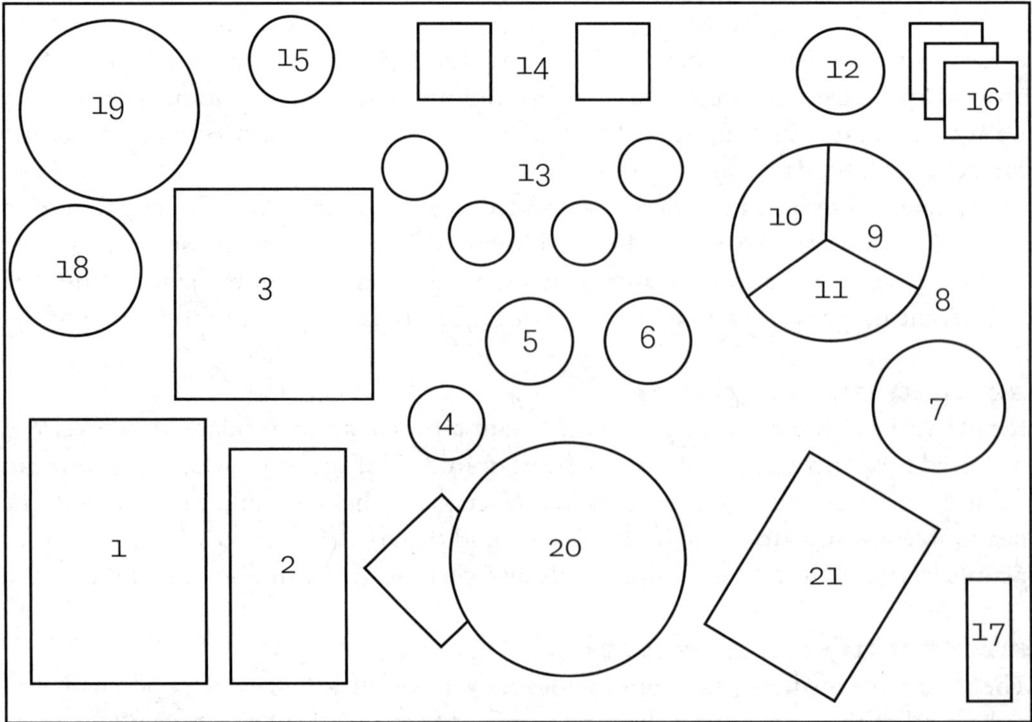

passover

For each group table of six people, you will need the following Seder elements:

1. 2 white candles in candlesticks
2. 1 small bowl of *charoset* (see instructions on page 114—you need enough for each person to have 2 tablespoons)
3. a small bowl of grated horseradish (each person needs 1 tablespoon)
4. a carafe or pitcher of red grape juice
5. a pitcher of water
6. any table decorations you want to include

To cut down on costs and complexity, have two people share the Seder elements. Using this approach, here is what you will need for each two-person setting:

7. 2 copies of "Simple Seder Service for Participants" (found on the CD-ROM)
8. 2 dinner plates (one for each person; fancy paper plates are okay to use)
9. napkins
10. 2 long-stemmed glasses (1 for each person) or 8 small communion cups (4 for each person—these should be pre-filled)
11. 2 water glasses (1 for each person)
12. 2 forks and 2 spoons (1 for each person)
13. a special Seder plate (something different from the dinner plates)
14. a sprig of fresh parsley
15. 3 six-inch squares of *matzot*
16. a bowl of salt water
17. an empty basin
18. a hand towel

Use the following chart to place each of these elements on the participant tables:

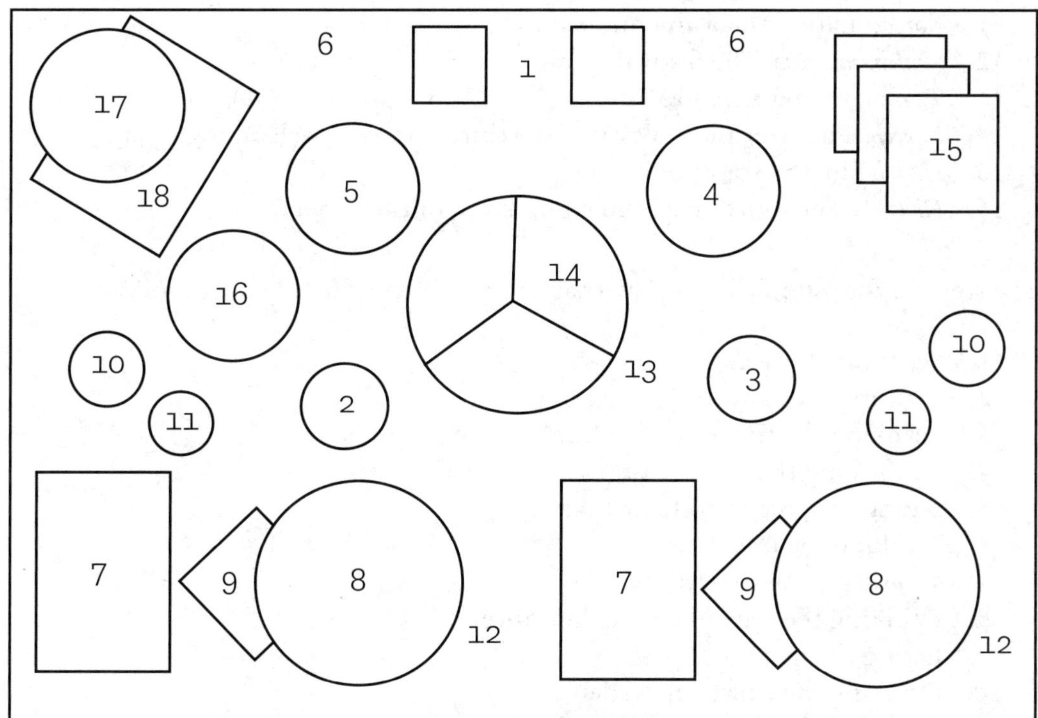

The following is a simple recipe to create the *charoset*:

- 1 cup chopped apples (2 to 3 apples)
- 1 cup chopped walnuts or almonds
- 1 tsp. ground cinnamon
- ¼ tsp. ginger or ¼ tsp. ground cloves
- 1 tsp. honey
- grape juice, wine vinegar or lemon juice

Core and peel the apples and chop them up. Add the walnuts or almonds, the spices and the honey. Add enough grape juice to moisten the mixture to the consistency of mortar. Place in a refrigerator until you are ready to use it (serves 8 to 10 people).

steps of the seder

The Hebrew word *seder* actually means "order," and traditionally it is presented in the following separate steps:

1. *Bedikat Chametz:* Search for leaven
2. *Hadlakat Ha-Nerot:* Lighting the Passover candles
3. *Kaddesh:* Sanctifying blessing and first cup of wine
4. *Urchatz:* First hand washing
5. *Karpas:* Dipping the green vegetable in salt water and blessing
6. *Yachatz:* breaking the middle *matzot* and hiding the *afikomen* (half of the middle *matzot*)
7. *Maggid:* The telling of the story of Passover, and the second cup of wine
8. *Rachtzah:* Second hand washing and blessing
9. *Motzi/Matsah:* Blessing for the bread and eating of *matzot*
10. *Maror:* Eating the bitter herbs
11. *Korech:* Eating the *maror* and *matzot*
12. *Shulchan Orech:* The festival meal
13. *Tzafun:* Eating the *afikomen*
14. *Barech:* The after-meal blessing, the third cup, and welcoming Elijah
15. *Hallel:* Singing songs of praise
16. *Nirtzah:* The fourth cup and completion of the Seder

The steps in the "simplified Seder" that you will be conducting are as follows:

1. Searching for leaven
2. Lighting the candles
3. Drinking the first cup (freedom)
4. Performing the hand washing
5. Eating the green vegetable (parsley)
6. Breaking the bread
7. Telling the Passover story
8. Drinking the second cup (deliverance)
9. Eating the meal
10. Drinking the third cup (redemption)
11. Drinking the fourth cup (thanksgiving)

Refer to the "Simple Seder Service for Leaders" (found on the CD-ROM) for additional instructions on conducting the service. Traditionally, the mother and father lead the Passover Seder, so you will need to designate someone to read the parts of the "leader" and "female leader." The participants also have speaking parts, so they will need a copy of the "Simple Seder Service for Participants" so they can follow along. Before the participants arrive, hide several pieces of regular bread in fairly visible places around the room.

Note

1. The following Seder is adapted from Dennis Bratcher, "Introduction to a Christian Seder" and "The Passover Seder for Christians," from The Voice: Biblical and Theological Resources for Growing Christians. For additional background information and notes on the Seder, visit http://www.crivoice.org/seder.html.

ash wednesday
46 days before easter

description
Unlike the Catholic and Orthodox Church, the Protestant Church typically does not place much emphasis on Ash Wednesday and the Lenten season leading to Easter. This season can be used as a tremendous time of reflection as you prepare to celebrate the resurrection of Christ.

key verse
"I have come that they may have life, and have it to the full" (John 10:10).

location needed
a meeting room with access to an outdoor area that is dimly lit (or not lit at all)

materials needed
several Bibles
copies of "Litany of Penitence" (optional—see page 120)
copies of "All Have Sinned" (found on the CD-ROM), cut into strips
copies of "Crucified with Christ" (found on the CD-ROM) on card stock and cut in business-card size
pens or pencils
comfortable floor cushions
candles
juice
a large stemmed glass or chalice
a loaf of unsliced bread
some low-key, reflective worship music and a way to play it (try to choose some that focus on personal reflection and repentance)
a cross made from rough-hewn wood (large enough for students to nail notes on it)
one nail for each person (adults included)
several hammers
ashes (made of last year's palm branches or any other type of ash), dampened with a small amount of water to create a paste

preparation
Ahead of time, construct a cross made from the rough-hewn wood and set it up in an outside location that is dimly lit. Recruit at least two adult volunteers for the service, one of whom will make the sign of the cross on the group members' heads with the ashes (which you will need to prepare before the service begins). Also consider inviting the senior pastor or elders to serve Communion. Remove most of the furniture from the room where you will be meeting and light the room with candles set in key places so that the room has a warm glow but isn't bright. Arrange cushions on the floor. If the group is small, you can place the cushions around a low table

(either place a large piece of plywood on cinderblocks to make a low-profile table, or keep the legs folded on a folding table and place it on the cinderblocks). Prepare the communion elements.

the event

In John 10:10, Jesus said, "I have come that [you] may have life, and have it to the full." That is the emphasis of this service—to remind the group members of the need to die to one's sinful self and choose to embrace life in Christ. Begin by playing the worship music softly to create a reflective atmosphere as the group members arrive.

greeting and introduction

As the group members arrive, invite them to quietly find a seat and to take the time to think about their lives (where they are with God, how far they've come, and where they want to be). After everyone has arrived, share that Lent is the 40 days before Easter (not including Sundays). While most of them are likely familiar with Mardi Gras (or Fat Tuesday), they probably don't know that it is the last hurrah before Lent, during which many people give up (fast) from certain foods or activities for the 40 days. Ash Wednesday is the start of this fast, and thus marks the first day of Lent.

Why 40 days? The reason is because the number 40 is important in Scripture. God sent rain to flood the earth and all its inhabitants for 40 days and 40 nights (see Genesis 7:12). The Israelites ate manna for 40 years while wandering in the desert (see Exodus 16:35). Jesus fasted for 40 days in preparation for His ministry (see Matthew 4:2; Luke 4:2). The stories surrounding the number 40 point to God's protection, provision and preparation of His people. During Ash Wednesday, many people place ash on their foreheads in the shape of a cross. Ashes are used because throughout Scripture, they signify mourning and fasting. They literally serve as a mark of dying to one's self.

call to worship

Begin the service by reading the following passages (or use your own selections):

> For God did not send his Son into the world to condemn the world,
> but to save the world through him (John 3:17).

> God is our refuge and strength,
>   an ever-present help in trouble.
> Therefore we will not fear, though the earth give way
>   and the mountains fall into the heart of the sea,
>   though its waters roar and foam
>   and the mountains quake with their surging (Psalm 46:1-3).

prayer and worship

Following the Scripture reading, pray for the evening and for the Holy Spirit to move in the hearts of the students. Next, sing a few worship songs that focus on reflection and repentance.

litany of penitence

For this portion, you can either hand out copies of "Litany of Penitence" from the Book of Common Prayer (see page 120) and have the group members read where indicated, or read Psalm 51 as a group, or make up your own corporate confession.

worship and private confession

Without talking, distribute the strips of paper from "All Have Sinned"—each adult leader should get one as well—and pens or pencils. Invite everyone to write down his or her sins on the strips of paper and fold them. Remind the group members that each confession is between God and the person confessing and that *no one* will read the strips of paper, even after the service. When everyone has finished writing, invite the group to the outside location where you have set up the cross. Distribute hammers and nails and instruct the group members to *lightly* hammer their sins to the cross, making sure the paper is secure. (Note: Watch as students nail their sins to the cross. Often the way in which they pound the nail into the cross can give you a clue as to the emotions behind their hammering.)

As the group members are nailing their sin confessions to the cross, remind them that Jesus died for those sins. Pray the following prayer from 2 Peter 3:18:

> *But grow in the grace and knowledge of our Lord and Savior Jesus Christ.*
> *To him be glory both now and forever! Amen.*

Once the group members have nailed their sin confession to the cross, they should go to the door leading back into the room, where a leader will meet them and give them a "Crucified with Christ" card. The leader will then repeat the first part of Galatians 2:20—"I have been crucified with Christ and I no longer live, but Christ lives in me"—dip a finger into the ashes, and make the sign of a cross on the students' foreheads. Before each group member goes through the door to the room, the leader should repeat the last part of Galatians 2:20: "The life I live in the body, I live by faith in the Son of God, who loved me and gave himself for me."

When the students reenter the room, have your second group leader encourage them to sit quietly and reflect as others finish the process outside.

assurance of pardon

After all of the group members have nailed their sin confessions to the cross, invite them to reflect on how they went out into the cold darkness with their sins but came back into the warm and comforting room after giving those sins to Christ. Explain that this activity is symbolic of how our sins put us into darkness, but Jesus leads us to the light. Read 1 John 1:8-9 aloud: "If we claim to be without sin, we deceive ourselves and the truth is not in us. If we confess our sins, he is faithful and just and will forgive us our sins and purify us from all unrighteousness." Announce to the group, "By your confession and God's promise, know that you are forgiven."

communion

Have the group members form a single line and come forward one at a time to take a piece of the bread and dip it in the cup. As you invite them to partake in Communion, let them know that the invitation to participate comes from Christ. Read Revelation 3:20: "Behold, I stand at the door and knock." As the group members receive the bread, the pastor (or other leader giving Communion) will say, "Christ's body, broken for [student's name]." As students take the bread and dip it in the cup, the pastor or leader will say, "Christ's blood, shed for [student's name]." This intimate addition personalizes Communion in a special way.

Invite the group members to stay after Communion as long as they would like to contemplate what has taken place. Help set the tone for further reflection by playing soft instrumental music in the background.

On a Personal Note: We have conducted this service for the past several years, and it is always a highlight to our year. During Lent, we leave the cross displayed with all of our sins nailed to it. On Good Friday, we remove the sins and burn them, so no one ever sees the confessions; and the cross is prominently displayed on Easter with the nails still in it, representing the scars of sin after the sin is removed. Finally, we remove all the nails on Pentecost Sunday.

We use the same cross year after year, so the cross has continued to gain character each year as it has borne the scars of our sins. It continues to represent the resurrected Christ by remaining in its place, empty the remainder of the year. As you challenge students to give something up and then to take something else on, it is good to provide resources on spiritual disciplines from your church or denomination. Have the students sign up for the Ash Wednesday service so that you can follow up during the season of Lent and beyond.

Pete Aubin
Director of Youth and College Ministries,
Roswell United Methodist Church, Roswell, Georgia

litany of penitence
from the book of common prayer

Leader: *Most holy and merciful Father:*

*We confess to you and to one another, and to the whole communion of saints
in heaven and on earth,that we have sinned by our own fault
in thought, word, and deed; by what we have done, and by what we have left undone.*

*We have not loved you with our whole heart, and mind, and strength. We have not loved our
neighbors as ourselves. We have not forgiven others, as we have been forgiven.*

All: Have mercy on us, Lord.

Leader: *We have been deaf to your call to serve, as Christ served us. We have not been true to
the mind of Christ. We have grieved your Holy Spirit.*

All: Have mercy on us, Lord.

Leader: *We confess to you, Lord, all our past unfaithfulness: the pride, hypocrisy, and impatience of our lives,*

All: We confess to you, Lord.

Leader: *Our self-indulgent appetites and ways, and our exploitation of other people,*

All: We confess to you, Lord.

Leader: *Our anger at our own frustration, and our envy of those more fortunate than ourselves,*

All: We confess to you, Lord.

Leader: *Our intemperate love of worldly goods and comforts, and our dishonesty in daily life
and work,*

All: We confess to you, Lord.

Leader: *Our negligence in prayer and worship, and our failure to commend the faith that is in us,*

All: We confess to you, Lord.

Leader: *Accept our repentance, Lord, for the wrongs we have done: for our blindness to human
need and suffering, and our indifference to injustice and cruelty,*

All: Accept our repentance, Lord.

Leader: *For all false judgments, for uncharitable thoughts toward our neighbors, and for our prejudice and contempt toward those who differ from us,*

All: Accept our repentance, Lord.

Leader: *For our waste and pollution of your creation, and our lack of concern for those who come after us,*

All: Accept our repentance, Lord.

Leader: *Restore us, good Lord, and let your anger depart from us;*

All: Favorably hear us, for your mercy is great.

Leader: *Accomplish in us the work of your salvation,*

All: That we may show forth your glory in the world.

Leader: *By the cross and passion of your Son our Lord,*

All: Bring us with all your saints to the joy of his resurrection.

Leader: *Almighty God, the Father of our Lord Jesus Christ, who desires not the death of sinners, but rather that they may turn from their wickedness and live, has given power and commandment to his ministers to declare and pronounce to his people, being penitent, the absolution and remission of their sins. He pardons and absolves all those who truly repent, and with sincere hearts believe his holy Gospel.*

Therefore we beseech him to grant us true repentance and his Holy Spirit, that those things may please him which we do on this day, and that the rest of our life hereafter may be pure and holy, so that at the last we may come to his eternal joy; through Jesus Christ our Lord. Amen.

ash wednesday

121

good friday
friday before easter

description

Good Friday commemorates the crucifixion of Jesus on the cross and is a time for your group members to reflect on the sacrifice that Jesus made to forgive them for their sins. Because it always falls on Friday, it is best to schedule this event in the evening.

key verse

"Greater love has no one than this, that he lay down his life for his friends" (John 15:13).

location needed

a large meeting room

the event

Below are two activities that you can do with your group to get them thinking about Jesus' death on the cross for their sins. After you do these activities, have a time of fellowship and encourage your group members to discuss their thoughts and feelings when they consider Christ's sacrifice on the cross.

a gift of grace

For this activity, you will need Bibles, a tub of bubble gum (or a large amount of candy), and enough copies of "No Greater Love" for every person in the group (see page 125). Begin by showing the group the tub of gum or candy and ask for a show of hands of all those who would like to have some gum. As each hand goes up, explain that you simply don't have enough for everyone in the group, so you are going to have to set up some criteria for deciding who will get a piece.

Ask if anyone in the group believes he or she deserves a piece of gum, and then pick one person from those who raise their hands. Ask why the student believes he or she deserves the gum. After he or she answers, ask the following questions and allow the student to answer each one:

1. Have you ever murdered anyone?
2. Have you ever stolen anything?
3. Have you ever had a desire to steal your neighbor's wife (or husband)?
4. Have you ever lied?
5. Have you ever been sarcastic or disrespectful to your parents?
6. Have you ever called someone a name or said bad things about another person, even if they were true?

The group member will likely say yes to everything except items 1 and 3. However, for these questions the person is not off the hook, because 1 John 3:15 states that "anyone who hates his brother is a murderer," and Matthew 5:28 states that "anyone who looks at [another person] lustfully has already committed adultery." In fact, no one can honestly answer no to every single one of these questions, so let the person know he or she doesn't deserve a piece of gum—and, for that matter, no one in the room does!

After all the moaning dies down, ask someone to read the following passage from Luke 18:10-14:

> Two men went up to the temple to pray, one a Pharisee and the other a tax collector. The Pharisee stood up and prayed about himself: "God, I thank you that I am not like other men—robbers, evildoers, adulterers—or even like this tax collector. I fast twice a week and give a tenth of all I get." But the tax collector stood at a distance. He would not even look up to heaven, but beat his breast and said, "God, have mercy on me, a sinner." I tell you that this man, rather than the other, went home justified before God. For everyone who exalts himself will be humbled, and he who humbles himself will be exalted.

Explain that in this story, the Pharisee thought he was right with God because his actions were better than others. He believed he was special to God because he was good and that God loved him because he *deserved* God's love. The tax collector, on the other hand, knew that if his relationship with God was based on how good he was, he was in trouble. So he asked for mercy.

Continue by stating that *none* of us deserves God's love and mercy, but He gives it to us anyway because of His grace. Hand out copies of "No Greater Love" and explain that the story the group members are about to read will better illustrate this idea. Read the story aloud to the group, or ask a volunteer to read it. After the reading, explain that the drunken man—who really deserved nothing but death for his killing the little boy—received life from the little boy's mother. The mother had so much love for her son that she chose to honor him by giving the man the lifesaving blood he didn't deserve. In this way, she operated much in the way that God operates with us. We are like the drunken man in the story. We deserve only death because of our sins, but God chooses to give us life instead.

Conclude by asking several volunteers to read the following verses: Romans 3:23, 5:6-8, 6:23 and Ephesians 2:8-9. Tell the group members that if our faith is based on what we think we can do for God or what we have already done for Him, it is certain to crumble. However, if our faith is based on the realization that God has freely given us His salvation, then it is certain to grow. God's relationship with us is not based on how good we are but on how good He is. We serve a living, loving God because He loved us enough to die for us, even though we did not—nor will we ever—deserve it.

good friday drama

For this activity, you will need several volunteers to hold up some props as you read the "Good Friday Drama" from Matthew 27:1-66. Here are the items you will need:

- copies of the "Good Friday Drama" for each member in the group (see page 126)
- some coins
- a pitcher of water and a bowl to pour the water into
- a whip (this can be made out of rope or string)

- a robe
- a crown of thorns (you can make this out of paper or just print out a picture from the Internet)
- a wooden cross (this can be any size)
- a hammer or mallet
- large nails
- a piece of fabric that can be torn in two

Ahead of time, ask a volunteer to gradually dim the lights in the room when you begin the reading to create a somber and serious mood. Ask another volunteer to hold up the various props when each is mentioned in the story to help the group members visually understand the seriousness of Jesus' suffering. Here are the places where the volunteer will need to hold up each item:

- *coins:* "the chief priests picked up the coins and said . . ."
- *pitcher of water and bowl:* "[Pilate] took water and washed his hands in front of the crowd . . ."
- *whip:* "but he had Jesus flogged . . ."
- *robe:* "they stripped him and put a scarlet robe on him . . ."
- *crown of thorns:* "and then twisted together a crown of thorns and set it on his head . . ."
- *cross:* "they forced [Simon] to carry the cross . . ."
- *hammer and nails:* "when they had crucified him, they divided up his clothes by casting lots . . ."
- *piece of fabric [tear as this line is read]:* "at that moment the curtain of the temple was torn in two from top to bottom . . ."
- *rope:* "give the order for the tomb to be made secure until the third day . . ."

As you hand out copies of "Good Friday Drama," explain that the very essence of the gospel is found in this reading from Matthew 27:1-66 and that this passage can help us better understand the sacrificial love of God. Read the drama aloud, and then allow some time after the reading for the group members to think about what they have heard and to pray quietly.

no greater love

Greater love has no one than this,
that he lay down his life for his friends.

John 15:13

It was a rainy evening. A young mother and her six-year-old son were driving home from a movie when the car began to sputter. The mother pulled the car off the road and stepped out to see if she could flag down another car.

With no cars in sight, the mother decided that she and her young son would have to walk to the nearest gas station, so she bundled up her son in his jacket, and off they went. It was not too long before the mother saw headlights in the distance. She told her son to stand away from the road, and she started waving both arms frantically, trying to catch the attention of the approaching driver.

Too late, the mother realized the car was not slowing down and that it was also swerving erratically. As she watched in horror, the car suddenly swerved off the road, hitting her young son and smashing into a tree.

The mom ran to her son, only to find him lying limp, covered with blood, barely breathing. Enraged, she ran to the car, where she found a bloodied middle-aged man behind the wheel. He was barely coherent, but he managed to utter a brief phrase in a drunken drawl before he passed out: "Stupid kid, what was he doing in the street?"

A passerby came upon the scene to find the mother crying while she sat on the ground cradling her wounded child. The passerby called an ambulance, and soon the boy, his mother and the drunk were taken to the hospital.

The boy had lost a lot of blood and needed a transfusion. The hospital did not have the little boy's rare blood type but, thankfully, his mother did. Shortly after the transfusion began, the mother noticed the doctors and nurses frantically working over her son, and then one of the doctors turned to her and uttered the words no parent wants to hear: "I am so sorry. There is nothing else we can do."

Desperately, the mother ripped the needle out of her arm and grabbed her child, hoping that her love and perseverance could bring him back, but to no avail. The nurses escorted her out of the room to a nearby waiting room, where she put her head in her hands and sobbed.

A short while later, a doctor approached the woman and asked if she was the one with the rare blood type. "Yes," she answered. "Why do you ask?"

"There is another patient who needs a transfusion," the doctor said, "and you are the only possible matching donor." He hesitated for a moment, and then said, "I need to tell you, though, that the person who needs your blood is the man responsible for your son's death."

Shock came over the mother. Her first inclination was to chastise the doctor for even thinking she would save the man who killed her son. *He doesn't deserve it! How could he even consider this?* But then, her heart began to soften. *What greater love could I show for my son than to save a life in the midst of my pain?* She thought. *It will be a legacy to his life. This man will live, even though he does not deserve it, because I want the legacy of the love I have for my son to live on.*

So the mother consented, and the transfusion began.

good friday drama
matthew 27

Early in the morning, all the chief priests and the elders of the people came to the decision to put Jesus to death. They bound him, led him away and handed him over to Pilate, the governor.

When Judas, who had betrayed him, saw that Jesus was condemned, he was seized with remorse and returned the thirty silver coins to the chief priests and the elders. "I have sinned," he said, "for I have betrayed innocent blood."

"What is that to us?" they replied. "That's your responsibility."

So Judas threw the money into the temple and left. Then he went away and hanged himself.

The chief priests picked up the coins and said, "It is against the law to put this into the treasury, since it is blood money." So they decided to use the money to buy the potter's field as a burial place for foreigners. That is why it has been called the Field of Blood to this day. Then what was spoken by Jeremiah the prophet was fulfilled: "They took the thirty silver coins, the price set on him by the people of Israel, and they used them to buy the potter's field, as the Lord commanded me."

Meanwhile Jesus stood before the governor, and the governor asked him, "Are you the king of the Jews?"

"Yes, it is as you say," Jesus replied.

When he was accused by the chief priests and the elders, he gave no answer. Pilate asked him, "Don't you hear the testimony they are bringing against you?" But Jesus made no reply, not even to a single charge—to the great amazement of the governor.

Now it was the governor's custom at the Feast to release a prisoner chosen by the crowd. At that time they had a notorious prisoner, called Barabbas. So when the crowd had gathered, Pilate asked them, "Which one do you want me to release to you: Barabbas, or Jesus who is called Christ?" For he knew it was out of envy that they had handed Jesus over to him.

While Pilate was sitting on the judge's seat, his wife sent him this message: "Don't have anything to do with that innocent man, for I have suffered a great deal today in a dream because of him."

But the chief priests and the elders persuaded the crowd to ask for Barabbas and to have Jesus executed.

"Which of the two do you want me to release to you?" asked the governor.

"Barabbas," they answered.

"What shall I do, then, with Jesus who is called Christ?" Pilate asked.

They all answered, "Crucify him!"

"Why? What crime has he committed?" asked Pilate.

But they shouted all the louder, "Crucify him!"

When Pilate saw that he was getting nowhere, but that instead an uproar was starting, he took water and washed his hands in front of the crowd. "I am innocent of this man's blood," he said. "It is your responsibility!"

All the people answered, "Let his blood be on us and on our children!"

Then he released Barabbas to them. But he had Jesus flogged, and handed him over to be crucified.

Then the governor's soldiers took Jesus into the Praetorium and gathered the whole company of soldiers around him. They stripped him and put a scarlet robe on him, and then twisted together a crown of thorns and set it on his head. They put a staff in his right hand and knelt in front of him and mocked him. "Hail, king of the Jews!" they said. They spit on him, and took the staff and struck him on the head again and again. After they had mocked him, they took off the robe and put his own clothes on him. Then they led him away to crucify him.

As they were going out, they met a man from Cyrene, named Simon, and they forced him to carry the cross. They came to a place called Golgotha (which means The Place of the Skull). There they offered Jesus wine to drink, mixed with gall; but after tasting it, he refused to drink it. When they had crucified him, they divided up his clothes by casting lots. And sitting down, they kept watch over him there. Above his head they placed the written charge against him: THIS IS JESUS, THE KING OF THE JEWS. Two robbers were crucified with him, one on his right and one on his left. Those who passed by hurled insults at him, shaking their heads and saying, "You who are going to destroy the temple and build it in three days, save yourself! Come down from the cross, if you are the Son of God!"

In the same way the chief priests, the teachers of the law and the elders mocked him. "He saved others," they said, "but he can't save himself! He's the King of Israel! Let him come down now from the cross, and we will believe in him. He trusts in God. Let God rescue him now if he wants him, for he said, 'I am the Son of God.'" In the same way the robbers who were crucified with him also heaped insults on him.

From the sixth hour until the ninth hour darkness came over all the land. About the ninth hour Jesus cried out in a loud voice, *"Eloi, Eloi, lama sabachthani?"*—which means, "My God, my God, why have you forsaken me?"

When some of those standing there heard this, they said, "He's calling Elijah."

Immediately one of them ran and got a sponge. He filled it with wine vinegar, put it on a stick, and offered it to Jesus to drink. The rest said, "Now leave him alone. Let's see if Elijah comes to save him."

And when Jesus had cried out again in a loud voice, he gave up his spirit.

At that moment the curtain of the temple was torn in two from top to bottom. The earth shook and the rocks split. The tombs broke open and the bodies of many holy people who had died were raised to life. They came out of the tombs, and after Jesus' resurrection they went into the holy city and appeared to many people.

When the centurion and those with him who were guarding Jesus saw the earthquake and all that had happened, they were terrified, and exclaimed, "Surely he was the Son of God!"

Many women were there, watching from a distance. They had followed Jesus from Galilee to care for his needs. Among them were Mary Magdalene, Mary the mother of James and Joses, and the mother of Zebedee's sons.

As evening approached, there came a rich man from Arimathea, named Joseph, who had himself become a disciple of Jesus. Going to Pilate, he asked for Jesus' body, and Pilate ordered that it be given to him. Joseph took the body, wrapped it in a clean linen cloth, and placed it in his own new tomb that he had cut out of the rock. He rolled a big stone in front of the entrance to the tomb and went away. Mary Magdalene and the other Mary were sitting there opposite the tomb.

The next day, the one after Preparation Day, the chief priests and the Pharisees went to Pilate. "Sir," they said, "we remember that while he was still alive that deceiver said, 'After three days I will rise again.' So give the order for the tomb to be made secure until the third day. Otherwise, his disciples may come and steal the body and tell the people that he has been raised from the dead. This last deception will be worse than the first."

"Take a guard," Pilate answered. "Go, make the tomb as secure as you know how." So they went and made the tomb secure by putting a seal on the stone and posting the guard.

8

easter

sunday after first full moon during spring

description
Easter and Christmas are the two most important holidays for Christians everywhere. On this day, you will get a chance to celebrate Jesus' resurrection from the dead and His complete triumph over death.

key verses
"The men said to them, 'Why do you look for the living among the dead? He is not here; he has risen!'" (Luke 24:5-6).

location needed
a large meeting room

the event
The following activities will help your group members understand the significance of the Resurrection. Note that if you choose to do the play "Lucifer's Labors" (found on the CD-ROM), you will need to recruit some actors and set aside some practice time before you deliver the presentation.

easter quiz
You will need copies of "Easter Quiz" (see page 130) and prizes for correct answers. Hand out one copy of the quiz to each person and allow a few minutes for everyone to complete it. Here are the answers:

1. Who did Jesus say He was?
    - C.   The Son of God

2. What is the Sunday before Easter called?
    - B.   Palm Sunday

3. Before Jesus shared the Last Supper with His disciples, what did He do for them?
    - A.   He washed their feet.

4. During the Last Supper, Jesus broke bread and said, "Take and eat, this is my ___________, broken for you."
    - B.   body

5. What did the soldiers force Simon to carry for Jesus?
    - A.   His cross

6. Because Jesus was sacrificed for our sins, He is called the ___________ of God.
     B.   Lamb

7. Who was the first person to see Jesus alive on the first Easter morning?
     B.   Mary Magdalene

8. Which disciple would not believe Jesus was alive until he touched Jesus' wounds?
     C.   Thomas

9. After Jesus rose from the dead, He appeared to His disciples while they were doing what?
     C.   Eating

10. What do the Easter Bunny, butterflies and baby chicks represent about Jesus Christ?
     C.   New life

lucifer's labors

For this option, you will need copies of "Lucifer's Labors" (found on the CD-ROM), six actors to play the parts (Michael, Gabriel, an angel messenger, Satan, a demon named Greed and a demon messenger), any costumes you want the actors to wear, a desk and chair and a manila file folder with papers inside of it. You will also need a volunteer to dim the lights at the appropriate times in the play and someone to voice one line offstage from Jesus (this could be you or another adult leader). Ahead of time, have the actors rehearse the parts (they can also just read from the script). Set up the desk and chair in the middle of the room for scene one.

the resurrection story

This short concluding exercise will get your students into the Word to discover why the resurrection is so important for Christians. For this activity, you will need copies of "The Resurrection" (see page 131) and Bibles. Have your group members break into smaller groups and hand out one copy of the worksheet to each person and one Bible per small group. Have the groups work through each of the items on the worksheet and discuss their answers.

closing devotion

After the small groups have had the chance to work through each of the questions on the handout, gather back together. Have the small groups respond to the following questions:

- How does the resurrection of Jesus separate Christianity from other religions?
- Why do you think people deny Christianity, even after hearing of the resurrection?
- If the resurrection were a hoax, how would that affect your faith?

End with prayer, thanking God for providing us with His Word so we can be sure that the resurrection of Christ did occur. Thank God for sending His Son into the world to pay the price for our sins, and pray that we will never diminish or forget the impact of Christ's sacrifice in our daily lives.

easter quiz

1. Who did Jesus say He was?
    A. God   B. An angel   C. The Son of God

2. What is the Sunday before Easter called?
    A. Ash Sunday   B. Palm Sunday   C. Lent

3. Before Jesus shared the Last Supper with His disciples, what did He do for them?
    A.   He washed their feet.
    B.   He washed their hands.
    C.   He washed their faces.

4. During the Last Supper, Jesus broke bread and said, "Take and eat, this is my
    _____________, broken for you."
    A. heart   B. body   C. palm

5. What did the soldiers force Simon to carry for Jesus?
    A. His cross   B. His clothes   C. The crown of thorns

6. Because Jesus was sacrificed for our sins, He is called the ___________ of God.
    A. King   B. Lamb   C. Servant

7. Who was the first person to see Jesus alive on the first Easter morning?
    A. An angel   B. Mary Magdalene   C. Peter and John

8. Which disciple would not believe Jesus was alive until he touched Jesus' wounds?
    A. Peter   B. John   C. Thomas

9. After Jesus rose from the dead, He appeared to His disciples while they were do-
    ing what?
    A. Sleeping   B. Praying   C. Eating

10. What do the Easter Bunny, butterflies and baby chicks represent about Jesus
    Christ?
    A. Spring   B. Blood   C. New life

the resurrection

The most important event in history is the resurrection of Jesus Christ. This single miracle has transformed the history of the world. The Christian faith rests on the fact that Jesus Christ actually rose from the dead. Based on this knowledge, we can be assured of the following:

- All Jesus claimed about Himself must be true.
- All Jesus said about life must be true.
- Our sins are forgiven. There is new life in the resurrection of Christ.
- We have eternal life and will be resurrected from the dead, just as Christ was.

You don't have to commit "intellectual suicide" to believe in the resurrection of Jesus. There are actually a number of facts that are unexplainable if Jesus did not actually rise from the dead. Read Matthew 16:21 and 17:22-23. Why were the disciples distressed by Jesus' words?

____

____

____

If Jesus did not rise from the dead on the third day, could these verses still be true? What would that imply about the rest of the Bible?

____

____

____

eyewitness accounts

The testimony of eyewitnesses and the transformation of the disciples can only be logically explained by the resurrected appearance of Jesus. Read 1 Corinthians 15:3-8. To whom did Jesus appear after He rose from the dead?

____

____

____

At the crucifixion, the followers of Jesus were in despair. Their hopes for a Messiah had been crushed. However, when Jesus appeared to them after His resurrection, their lives were forever transformed. Read Matthew 26:69-75. What did Peter do immediately before the Resurrection?

____

____

____

Read Acts 2:14-37. What did Peter proclaim about the Resurrection?

____

____

____

the only explanation for the empty tomb

Throughout history, people have tried to disprove the resurrection of Christ. It is true that if the resurrection of Jesus can be disproved, then the cornerstone of the Christian faith would

be destroyed. Read Mark 15:46 and Matthew 27:62-66. What were the precautions taken to ensure that Jesus' body would not be stolen?

____

____

____

The following are some common theories used by skeptics to refute the resurrection of Christ:

- The disciples stole and hid the body.
- The Roman or Jewish authorities took the body.
- Jesus never died; He walked out of the tomb.
- The women and the disciples went to the wrong tomb.
- The disciples simply hallucinated that they saw the resurrected Jesus.

Based on the Scripture passages you have studied, what is the fallacy of these theories?

____

____

____

the only reason for growth of the church

Within a short time period, the Christian faith spread all over the Roman Empire and beyond. Jesus' disciples always spoke of the resurrection and the living Christ. Review Acts 2:14-37. What was the main theme of Peter's sermon?

____

____

____

Read Acts 2:40-41. What was the result of Peter's preaching to the crowd?

____

____

____

the reason we believe

Read 1 Corinthians 15:17-19. What does Paul say about the resurrection in this passage?

____

____

____

In John 11:25, Jesus said, "I am the resurrection and the life. He who believes in me will live, even though he dies." What impact does this statement have on your life?

____

____

____

How will you live differently this week because of the impact Jesus' resurrection has on your life?

____

____

____

earth day

april 22

description

Earth Day is a relatively new holiday enacted in 1970 to inspire awareness and appreciation for the earth's natural environment. The timing of the holiday coincides with Arbor Day, which allows your group to merge the two into one event.

key verses

"The land must not be sold permanently, because the land is mine and you are but aliens and my tenants. Throughout the country that you hold as a possession, you must provide for the redemption of the land" (Leviticus 25:23-24).

location needed

a large field or other outdoor area (you will also need a parking lot with cars if you choose to do the "Dirty Sock Contest")

the event

Ahead of time, decide which events you want to do with your group. Each activity requires different materials and setup, so see the specific directions that follow.

dirty sock contest

This is a great contest that doubles in a lesson for how auto emissions affect air quality. Generally, this activity works best with older group members who drive their own cars, but you can also use any of the adult leaders' cars in your group. It's also best if you ask the group members ahead of time to bring some spare, clean white socks to the event.

For the contest, each participant will place the white sock over his or her car's exhaust (or the designated adult leaders' exhaust) and run the engine for 30 seconds. The contestant with the dirtiest sock should win some sort of prize (such as a coupon to get a tune-up or one of those pine tree air fresheners). The contestant with the cleanest sock should also win a prize to reward him or her for having the most environmentally friendly car.[1]

earth day haiku

A *haiku* is a short form of Japanese poetry that consists of three lines with five, seven and five syllables, respectively. Most *haiku* also consist of a contrast between two images or ideas. Here is an example:

> After summer's rain
> God's promise is remembered
> Glorious rainbow.[2]

133

Have your group members write similar poems about the earth. Award prizes to the most creative poem, the best use of imagery, the wackiest, and so on.

guess the item

Place several items from nature (rocks, pinecones, sea shells) into a bag. Blindfold one person at a time and have him or her try to guess what the item is. Give the person a few seconds to do this. If the person is unsuccessful, he or she is out of the game. Each player who guesses correctly gets another turn. Give a prize to the last person who is able to guess each item correctly.

earth day quiz

For this activity, you will need a copy of "Earth Day Quiz" (see page 138). Read each of the questions and the multiple-choice answers to your group. Call on the person who raises his or her hand first, and award that person a point for a correct answer. If the person is wrong, call on the next person who raises his or her hand. Have another adult leader keep track of the score and award a prize to the person with the most points. Here are the answers:

1. In what year was the first Earth Day held?
   C.   1970

2. Approximately how long does it take for a banana to break down in the environment?
   B.   3 to 4 weeks

3. How long does it take for a tin can to break down in the environment?
   C.   80 to 100 years

4. How long does it take for an aluminum can to break down in the environment?
   C.   200 to 500 years

5. How long does is take for plastic to break down in the environment?
   D.   1,000 years

6. How much of the earth's surface is covered by oceans?
   D.   70 percent

7. On average, how deep are the earth's oceans?
   B.   2 miles

8. Why is earth called the "blue planet"?
   D.   Because from space the oceans and the atmosphere make it look blue.

9. In terms of size, what rank does the earth hold in our solar system?
   C.   It is the fifth largest planet.

10. Approximately how much does the earth weigh?
    C.   6.6 sextillion tons

11. What is the area of the earth in square miles?
    A.   200 million miles

12. About how fast are we hurtling through space?
    B.   66,000 miles per hour

13. How long does it take the earth to rotate on its axis?
    C.   24 hours (that's one day!)

14. How long does it take the earth to orbit around the sun?
    B.   365½ days

15. What percent of the earth's surface is used to grow food?
    B.   25 percent

letter writing and petitions

Letter writing is an excellent way to let those in your local government know what types of issues matter to you the most. At your Earth Day celebration, provide a list of your local members of government at the federal, state, county or community level. Make copies of the "Sample Earth Day Letter" (see page 140) and hand it out to your group members to give them an idea of how to structure the letter. When they have finished, provide them with addresses and stamps to mail the letters (or let them take the letters home to do this).

Another idea is to set up a petition in your community. For this option, you would draft a petition ahead of time on an Earth Day issue that is important to your group and post the document on a pole with a picture illustrating the topic. You can place the petitions on clipboards and affix a pen to the clipboard so people can sign it quickly.[3] Here are some helpful tips to consider when creating your petition:

- *Write clearly and concisely.* State your goal concisely at the beginning of the petition. Potential signers don't have a lot of time.

- *Be polite and reasonable.* State your point, but do so politely. Potential signers won't be motivated to sign petitions they deem rude, even if they agree with your position.

- *Be practical.* You want to be ambitious but realistic. Make sure the changes you are proposing are concrete and doable.

- *Think big.* Remember that you and your group have a voice. "With man this is impossible, but with God all things are possible" (Matthew 19:26).[4]

Online petitions are also quite effective. There are several sites on the Internet that provide sample templates for creating these (a good one can be found at change.org).[5]

plant a tree

Johnny Appleseed (1774–1845) made a name for himself by introducing apple trees to portions of Ohio, Indiana and Illinois. (Contrary to popular belief, he didn't plant seeds randomly everywhere he went but planted nurseries with fences around them.) Your group can do the same on a smaller scale. Ahead of time, hold a fundraiser or

other event to raise money to buy a tree to plant as a special memorial for your group. Plant the tree at your Earth Day event on the church grounds or other location where the group members will see it. This will serve as a reminder to them whenever they see the tree. (Note: Of course, be sure to get permission to plant the tree before you dig!)

recycled sculpture

For this activity, you and your group members will build some unique pieces of art using only recycled materials (newspapers, plastic jugs, aluminum cans, and the like). The group members can use duct tape to stick all of the items together, but this should be the only non-recycled material used in the sculpture. Award prizes for the most creative piece, the most aesthetically pleasing (nice-looking), the wackiest, and so on. When the event is over, make sure the group members place the recycled sculptures in the recycling bins![6]

take a hike

This is an activity in which you lead your group members through a local park or other area with wildlife. Do some research ahead of time and point out the names of trees and plants that the group members will see along the hike, and list some interesting facts about them. You can even ask the group members to look for certain trees or types of animal along the hike and award a prize to the person who spots the most.

trash pick-up

For this option, your group will need gloves and some garbage bags. Organize a crew from your group members and go to a nearby park or other location to pick up trash. Also visit lakes, beaches, rivers and trails and clear them of debris and garbage, or clean graffiti from walls in local communities. If the weather is good, you can even have a picnic at the park after the cleanup is done.

closing devotion

Begin the devotion time by explaining that in Psalm 24:1, we read that "the earth is the LORD's, and everything in it." One thing that is great about Earth Day is that it provides us with a moment to think about our world and how we are treating everything that God has provided in it. We often think that we own the earth and we have the right to do whatever we want to it, but as this passage tells us, we have a responsibility to be good stewards (or caretakers) of what God has given to us.

God gave Adam and Eve this task back in the Garden of Eden. In Genesis 1:26, He said, "Let us make man in our image, in our likeness, and let them *rule over* the fish of the sea and the birds of the air, over the livestock, over all the earth, and over all the creatures that move along the ground" (emphasis added). After He created the first humans, He said to them, "Be fruitful and increase in number; fill the earth and subdue it" (verse 28). Later, He told the Israelites, "The land is mine and you are but *aliens* and *my tenants*. Throughout the country that you hold as a possession, you must provide for the redemption of the land" (Leviticus 25:23-24, emphasis added).

Like the Israelites, we are tenants of the land the Lord has given us to occupy. God has given us this incredible world and we should thank Him for it, just as David praised God for the beauty of creation he saw all around him. We should also consider how we are doing as tenants of God's land. Are we treating His creation in the way that He would want us to treat it?

earth day

Close your time together in prayer, asking God to help the group members to better appreciate the wonders of creation that He has provided to them, and asking Him to help each person to be a better steward of this earth.

Notes

1. Adapted from "Hold a Dirty Sock Contest," *Earth Day Organizer's Guide: Earth Day Event Ideas*, Envirolink. http://earthday.envirolink.org/guide6.html.
2. Haiku by Udiah, "The Rainbow," on PoemHunter.com. http://www.poemhunter.com/poems/haiku/.
3. Adapted from "Petitions/Letters/Politicians," *Earth Day Organizer's Guide: Earth Day Event Ideas*, Envirolink. http://earthday.envirolink.org/guide6.html.
4. List adapted from "How to Write a Successful Petition," ipetitions.com. http://www.ipetitions.com/guide?campaign=1&kw=how%20to%20set%20up%20a%20petition&gclid=CKCOvtfesq8CFc4a6wodfns2hg.
5. See http://www.change.org/start-a-petition?utm_source=google&utm_medium=cpc&utm_campaign=GST_USER_GEOT2_SCHT1_PERT1.
6. Adapted from "Build a Life-sized Sculpture," *Earth Day Organizer's Guide: Earth Day Event Ideas*, Envirolink. http://earthday.envirolink.org/guide6.html.

earth day quiz

1. In what year was the first Earth Day held?
    - A.   1900
    - B.   1960
    - C.   1970
    - D.   1980

2. Approximately how long does it take for a banana to break down in the environment?
    - A.   1 to 2 weeks
    - B.   3 to 4 weeks
    - C.   1 year
    - D.   5 years

3. How long does it take for a tin can to break down in the environment?
    - A.   20 to 40 years
    - B.   50 to 70 years
    - C.   80 to 100 years
    - D.   More than 100 years

4. How long does it take for an aluminum can to break down in the environment?
    - A.   50 to 100 years
    - B.   100 to 200 years
    - C.   200 to 500 years
    - D.   500 to 1,000 years

5. How long does is take for plastic to break down in the environment?
    - A.   100 years
    - B.   300 years
    - C.   600 years
    - D.   1,000 years

6. How much of the earth's surface is covered by oceans?
    - A.   30 percent
    - B.   40 percent
    - C.   55 percent
    - D.   70 percent

7. On average, how deep are the earth's oceans?
    - A.   1 mile
    - B.   2 miles
    - C.   5 miles
    - D.   10 miles

8. Why is earth called the "blue planet"?
   - A.   It comes from a Latin word.
   - B.   Because it is colder than the planets nearer the sun.
   - C.   Because the ancients viewed it as a melancholy place.
   - D.   Because from space the oceans and the atmosphere make it look blue.

9. In terms of size, what rank does the earth hold in our solar system?
   - A.   It is the largest planet.
   - B.   It is the third largest planet.
   - C.   It is the fifth largest planet.
   - D.   It is the seventh largest planet.

10. Approximately how much does the earth weigh?
    - A.   9.2 billion tons
    - B.   12.7 trillion tons
    - C.   6.6 sextillion tons
    - D.   8.4 nonillion tons

11. What is the area of the earth in square miles?
    - A.   200 million miles
    - B.   300 million miles
    - C.   400 million miles
    - D.   500 million miles

12. About how fast are we hurtling through space?
    - A.   30,000 miles per hour
    - B.   66,000 miles per hour
    - C.   75,000 miles per hour
    - D.   100,000 miles per hour

13. How long does it take the earth to rotate on its axis?
    - A.   12 hours
    - B.   16 hours
    - C.   24 hours
    - D.   30 hours

14. How long does it take the earth to orbit around the sun?
    - A.   364 days
    - B.   365½ days
    - C.   366 days
    - D.   None of the above

15. What percent of the earth's surface is used to grow food?
    - A.   11 percent
    - B.   25 percent
    - C.   34 percent
    - D.   40 percent

sample earth day letter

Your name
Your address

Date, year
Congresswoman/Congressman [*add his or her name*]
Local District office address

Dear Congresswoman/Congressman [*add his or her name*],

Opening: This letter is to urge you to . . .
       or I am writing to request that you . . .
       or The reason I am writing this letter is to encourage you to . . .
             [*write a short statement as to what you would like your congresswoman/congressman to do*]

Facts: It is my understanding that . . .
       or I have discovered that . . .
       or It is expected that . . .
             [*write a short statement about the facts of the issue, including any policies that you know are currently in place*]

Call to Action: I am concerned that . . .
       or I strongly feel that . . .
       or I believe that we should . . .
             [*explain your idea and what you would like to see enacted*]

Closing: I genuinely appreciate the role you play in shaping our country.
       or Thank you for all you do as our representative in Washington.
       or Thank you for all your efforts in this matter.

Respectfully,
       or Warm regards,
       or Sincerely,

[*your signature*]
[*your printed name*]

Letter adapted from Americans for Department of Peace. http://www.afdop.org/.

cinco de mayo
may 5

description
Cinco de Mayo ("fifth of May") commemorates the victory on May 5, 1862, of a small Mexican army over the French occupation forces at the town of Puebla in Mexico. It is celebrated nationwide in the United States and regionally in Mexico.

key verse
"Everything is possible for him who believes" (Mark 9:23).

location needed
A large outdoor area or open indoor area with access to electrical outlets

the event
Ahead of time, choose which activities or games you want to offer to your group. Each requires different materials and setup, so see the specific directions that follow. You will need at least one person in charge of each activity, so appoint these individuals ahead of time. You will also need some simple prizes or tickets to award to those who participate in the activities (tickets can be redeemed for prizes at a separate booth). You may want to offer some activities at specific times in which the whole group can participate—such as the Mexican hat dance or the piñata.

If you are providing an outreach opportunity to families or kids in your community, have student leaders ready to greet visitors, answer questions and participate with visitors in the activities. Have a meeting beforehand to give your group members any instructions about serving in these areas. If you are sharing information about your church's involvement in missions work, have a display ready describing the people and places you support and any opportunities for your students to serve. Invite a missionary, your missions pastor, or a student who has participated in a missions or service project to give a brief devotion or share a personal story during the event.

decorations
Decorations are key in creating a festive atmosphere. If you are holding this event at night, hang strings of lights all around and consider using sombreros, chili pepper-themed party supplies, streamers and balloons in the national colors of Mexico (red, black, orange and green). You can also purchase piñatas at party stores or make them inexpensively using papier-mâché and hang them around the area.[1] As an option, have theme-oriented bandanas or strings of beads to give to group members as they arrive to serve as their admission tickets.

music
Play music in the background while the group members are enjoying the different activities. You might want to hold a large group karaoke contest (in Spanish, of course),

invite a mariachi band to perform, or have volunteers dress up as a mariachi band and lip-sync. Pepper in several worship songs recorded in Spanish to mix it up a bit.

food

It is impossible to celebrate Cinco de Mayo without food, so consider having a build-your-own-taco bar. Traditional tacos include chopped chicken/beef, black beans, Mexican rice, soft and/or hard taco shells, shredded lettuce, grated cheese, diced tomatoes, sour cream and guacamole. Include tortilla chips and several kinds of salsa, taco sauce and peppers (for the more daring participants), and have plenty of drinks on hand (milk is good with spicy food). Theme-related paper plates and napkins will brighten the area. Don't forget to recycle if you provide canned drinks or water bottles.

games and activities

The following are some of the options you can provide to your group members to get them involved in this fun and festive holiday.

piñata busting

Any authentic Cinco de Mayo celebration includes the traditional busting of the piñata. You will need at least one piñata filled with candy and prizes, some rope, a plastic baseball bat, a blindfold and a whistle. Use a length of the rope to hang the piñata about 5 to 6 feet off the ground in an open area. (For added challenge, attach the rope to a pulley so the piñata can be raised and lowered while the group members swing at it.) Arrange a 15-foot diameter rope circle on the ground centered under the piñata.

Before you begin the activity, explain the following rules to the group:

- The group members must stay behind the rope, outside the circle, until they hear the whistle—no exceptions!

- At the leader's signal (*vaya!*) each blindfolded participant will get three swings at the piñata. (Leader, don't be a casualty—stand back!)

- When the piñata breaks, the group members must wait until they hear the whistle blow before rushing in to pick up the prizes. The person who hit the piñata should drop his or her bat at this point and take off his or her blindfold.

- No candy or other piñata contents can be taken from another person.

Choose the first participant to wear the blindfold and have him or her stand within striking distance of the piñata. Turn the person around several times and stand back. Give the signal to begin and count the three swings the person takes (a miss counts). If you elected to set up a pulley, have another leader raise or lower the piñata as the person strikes at it. Give each group member a turn until someone breaks the piñata. At this point, blow the whistle and allow the group members to scramble to pick up the contents on the ground. Make sure the person who hit the piñata drops the bat, and take the blindfold off this person so he or she can grab some prizes as well.

It is a good idea to have an extra bag of candy or prizes ready to throw to the group members on the edge of the crowd. This will ensure that everyone gets a prize and goes away happy. Keep safety in mind as you do this activity and encourage the participants as they swing at the piñata.

cactus ring toss

To play this game, you can either purchase an inflatable cactus ring toss game online or at a party store or make your own cactus and rings. Create the cactus using cardboard and markers or paint. For the rings, cut two 3-foot lengths and one 5-foot length of foam pipe insulation and duct tape the ends together. Use tape or rope to create a throw line about four to five feet away from the cactus. Have the group members stand at the throw line and attempt to land the rings on the cactus. Assign a point value for each successful throw and award points, tickets or prizes as desired.

face painting

This is a fun activity especially for younger group members. Ahead of time, select some of your more creative students to serve as face painters. Have a variety of colors of face paint crayons available for them to use (be sure to include colors such as green, red and white). To make things a bit easier, you might want to purchase templates for different shapes cut out of lightweight plastic (see the scrapbooking section of your local craft store). Ideas for pictures include a green cactus, red chili pepper, the Mexican flag colors (vertical strips of green, white and red in order from left to right), flowers and stars.

mexican hat dance

The Mexican hat dance is considered to be the national dance of Mexico. There are several examples of this dance (along with music) available for you to watch on YouTube. The dance tells a story of courtship, so it works best to have a guy and a girl student leader learn the steps so that they can teach it to the others—keep it simple when doing it as a group. For fun, speed up the dance on each round until you only have one or two students still standing!

sombrero challenge

For this game, arrange five sombreros in a line, with each one a bit farther from the starting line. Assign point values to each sombrero, giving the farthest one the highest number. Give the first player three pennies (or pesos, if you have them). Have the person stand at the starting line (tape or a piece of rope can define where this line is) and toss the coins into the brims of the sombreros. Award prizes or give out tickets for scores over a certain number.

missionary corner

Ahead of time, set up a booth with a display of the different missionaries your group or church supports. Include maps that show where they serve and any pictures you may have. Recruit some adult or student volunteers to attend the party dressed as someone from the area where each missionary serves. The volunteers should be familiar with the person and work they represent. Create a page listing each missionary's name and place of ministry and room to write one fact about the people that missionary serves. Make copies of the page for attendees.

As the group members visit the booth, give each person a copy of the page you created and invite him or her to find a person representing each missionary. Tell the group members to find out one fact about the missionary and his or her work to

143

write on the page. Group members can earn points, prizes or tickets for the number of people they interview. Collect the pages near the end of the event and award prizes.

closing devotion

Regardless of which activities you choose to do, end with a short devotional time. If you chose to set up a missionary corner, ask leaders or group members who participated in a missions trip to share their experiences and how they saw God work in the lives of those they served. Ask them to focus on ways that God accomplishes His will in the world despite challenges or even what seem to be insurmountable odds.

Begin the devotion time by providing some background information as to why Cinco de Mayo is celebrated today. In 1861, a well-armed French fleet stormed the city of Veracruz in modern-day Mexico. The French troops, considered the best in the world, began to march toward Mexico City, but they were met with heavy resistance at the town of Puebla. Although the French outnumbered the Mexican forces by a ratio of two to one, were better trained and had better equipment, the Mexican patriots were victorious. On May 5, 1862, they crushed the French forces and sent them packing. There were other battles for freedom in Mexico after this, but Cinco de Mayo began to bring a sense of national unity and pride to Mexicans.

Sometimes, the trials we face in our lives seem insurmountable. In Mark 9:17-27, we read the story of a man who certainly felt this way. His son had been possessed by a demon, and the evil spirit robbed his speech and threw him into fits at times. Jesus' disciples had attempted to drive out the demon, but they had been unsuccessful. It appeared that all hope was lost.

Jesus, however, was undaunted. He asked that the boy be brought to Him, and when the evil spirit saw Jesus, he threw the boy into a convulsion. Jesus asked how long the boy had been like this, to which the father replied, "From childhood . . . it has often thrown him into fire or water to kill him. But if you can do anything, take pity on us and help us" (verse 22). Jesus replied by stating, "Everything is possible for him who believes," which made the father utter a contradictory statement: "I do believe; help me overcome by unbelief!" (verses 23-24).

When we have faith in God and put our complete trust in Him, we will be amazed at what He will accomplish in our lives. We may feel outnumbered and believe that certain defeat is imminent—much as the Mexican forces at Puebla must have felt—but God can overcome anything. All He requires of us is to put our faith in Him and believe that He can do the impossible. As Jesus said, "I tell you the truth, if you have faith as small as a mustard seed, you can say to this mountain, 'Move from here to there' and it will move. Nothing will be impossible for you" (Matthew 17:20).

Close your time together with worship and prayer, thanking God that He cares for each of us and sees our needs. Ask Him to bring His power into your group members' lives and to help each person grow in their faith.

Note
1. Check out www.piñatas.com for some ideas.

mother's day
second sunday in may

description
As Emily Dickinson once said, "A mother is one to whom you hurry when you are troubled." On this day, your group members will get a chance to thank their mothers and do something nice not only for them but also for other moms in the area.

key verse
"My son, keep your father's commands and do not forsake your mother's teaching" (Proverbs 6:20).

location needed
an indoor room with access to a kitchen

the event
Ahead of time, decide which events you want to do with your group. Each of the events requires different materials and setup, so see the specific directions that follow. Note that many of these activities require extra planning, and some will take place outside of the main group time. Also, be sure to be sensitive to those in your group who might have lost their mothers or who are not currently living with them.

mother's day information quest
You can use this quest as a small-group activity or as a crowd breaker. Ahead of time, make copies of "All About Mom" (see page 148) and give one to each person in the group. Provide everyone with pens or pencils and set a time limit for them to complete the activity. Allow the groups to work in teams of two. At the end of the time, have everyone tally their points and award prizes to the team or person with the highest score. Award extra points (and extra prizes) for the following categories:

- 300 points for the student with the most outgoing mom
- 400 points for the student who can do the best imitation of his or her mom
- 500 points for the funniest mom story

Have the group members share why their mom qualifies in these categories, and determine the winners by group vote.

mother's day meal
A great way for your group members to honor their mothers is by making a meal for them to take home. Arrange to use the church kitchen (or a home with a large kitchen) and be prepared to make a dish that can be divided into family-size servings for each person. See page 149, "Spaghetti Dinner" for a complete dinner menu with

recipes. Each recipe yields 12 servings—multiply amounts as necessary to fit your group's needs.

Have the group members plan, buy, prepare and cook the food. When the meal is finished and they have cleaned up the mess, they can take the meals back to their homes to celebrate the day with their family. (Consider using disposable containers for sending meals home.) You can also have students make cards or presents for their moms.

mother's day service project
Motherhood is one of the greatest roles in life, and perhaps the most difficult. Single moms have it especially tough. To this end, find a single mom (or just a mom in need) who could use a boost, and make an appointment for the group to spend two hours with her performing one or more of the following services:

- *Clean her house.* Bring all your own supplies.
- *Make her family a meal.* Don't forget to leave a spotless kitchen!
- *Fix something in the house that is broken.* Make sure you have a handyman or two along with you.
- *Clean the yard and plant some flowers.* If she lives in an apartment, bring her a beautiful plant or start an herb garden in a window box.
- *Give her a coupon for free babysitting* (see activity below).
- *Pray with and for her and her children.*

You and your group members are sure to make an impression and bless this mother in ways she will never forget!

mother's day babysitting service
This is another great way to bless a mother with young children. Have your group members form a pool to provide babysitting services at no cost to those in need in your church or community. You can set this up as a special event for mothers in honor of Mother's Day. Be sure to provide an adequate adult-to-student-to-child ratio and access to a phone for emergencies. Many churches have someone who could give the group members the basics of childcare, first aid and advice on how to solve problems they might encounter, so tap into these resources.

Before beginning any babysitting job, make sure there is adequate parental contact information, a listing of any allergies or special needs for the child, and the name of anyone who is authorized to pick up the child (if different from the parent). An adult leader should check in each child, and each child should wear a nametag. Ask the nursery staff and/or children's ministry director at your church for any additional information or procedures your group members should follow.[1]

closing devotion
If you elected to cook a meal for the group members' mothers, take a moment to have the students reflect on the experience. What did they enjoy about cooking the meal? What was challenging for them? How do they think their moms will react? If your group elected to do the Mother's Day service project or babysitting service, take a moment to discuss how the group members think their actions will benefit those moms. What do they hope to learn from the project? What results do they expect to see?

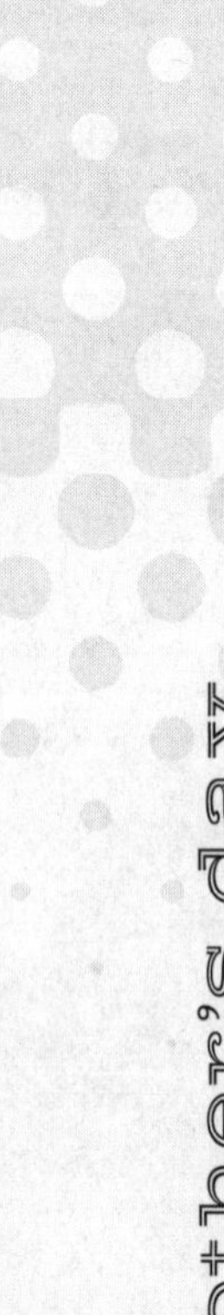

Continue by having a short devotion time. Explain that in the New Testament, we read a short note from the apostle Paul to a man named Timothy, in which Paul acknowledges the way in which Timothy's mother and grandmother raised him. Paul writes, "I have been reminded of your sincere faith, which first lived in your grandmother Lois and in your mother Eunice and, I am persuaded, now lives in you also" (2 Timothy 1:5). We know nothing else of these women, but from Paul's words, it is evident that they were instrumental in instilling faith in Timothy from a young age. In doing so, they were following the command God gave in Proverbs 22:6 to mothers and fathers everywhere: "Train a child in the way he should go, and when he is old he will not turn from it."

As you celebrate Mother's Day, think about what your own mother has taught you and what she has done to teach you about God. Even if you don't have a biological mother present in your home, you can identify someone who has performed this role in your life. Today, be sure to express your appreciation to that person, and thank her for standing by you—even if you might not always have appreciated her advice!

Note

1. Idea taken from Jim Burns, general editor, "Babysitting Service," *Uncommon Missions & Service Projects* (Ventura, CA: Gospel Light, 2011), p. 40.

all about mom

For each item listed below, write the name of a person in the room whose mom fits the category (each item is worth 250 points unless otherwise indicated).

❑ Someone whose mom was a cheerleader:

____

❑ Someone whose mom played sports in high school:

____

❑ The person whose mom has the highest college degree:

____

❑ Someone whose mom has taught a Bible study:

____

❑ Someone whose mom has lived in another country:

____

❑ The person whose mom has the most children:

____

❑ Write her children's names and earn 100 bonus points per child:

____

____

____

____

____

____

❑ The person whose mom has the best-looking kid in this group:

____

spaghetti dinner

simple homemade spaghetti
pinch of salt
2 lbs. spaghetti
4 lbs. lean ground beef
2 medium onions, minced
2 6-oz. cans tomato paste
4 large (10¾-oz.) cans condensed tomato soup
5 cups water

Preheat a large skillet over medium heat; add ground beef and onion. Cook, stirring occasionally, until meat is brown. Drain and return to pan. Add tomato paste, tomato soup and water. Cook, stirring constantly, until thickened and heated through (approximately 5 to 15 minutes). Bring a large pot of lightly salted water to a boil. Add spaghetti and cook for 8 to 10 minutes, or until *al dente,* and then drain and set aside. (Ready in 25 minutes.)

tossed greek salad
1 head Romaine lettuce, torn into bite-sized pieces
1 head red-leaf lettuce, torn into bite-sized pieces
1 8-oz. package crumbled Feta cheese
1 4-oz. can sliced black olives
1 cup halved cherry tomatoes
1 red onion, halved and thinly sliced
6 medium mushrooms, sliced
1 8-oz. bottle Italian salad dressing

In a large salad bowl, combine lettuce with Feta cheese, olives, tomatoes, onion and mushrooms. Toss with Italian dressing just prior to serving. (Ready in 15 minutes.)

toasted garlic bread
3 1-lb. loaves Italian bread
¾ cup plus 3 tbsp. butter, softened
2 tbsp. virgin olive oil
9 garlic gloves, crushed
1 tbsp. oregano
3 cups shredded mozzarella cheese
salt and pepper

While broiler is preheating, slice bread loaves in 1-inch to 2-inch thick pieces. In a small bowl, mix butter, olive oil, garlic, oregano, salt and pepper. Spread the mixture evenly on one side of each bread slice. Arrange bread slices evenly on a baking sheet; broil 5 minutes or until slightly brown. Check frequently to prevent overcooking. When done, remove from broiler; top with cheese and return to broiler for 2 to 3 minutes, or until cheese is melted and slightly browned. Serve immediately. (Ready in 15 minutes.)

apple-berry punch

1 32-oz. bottle apple juice, chilled
1 12-oz. can frozen cranberry juice concentrate
1 cup orange juice
1½ liters ginger ale
1 apple

In a large punch bowl, combine apple juice, cranberry juice concentrate and orange juice. Stir until dissolved, and then slowly pour in the ginger ale. Thinly slice the apple vertically, forming whole apple slices. Float apple slices on top of punch. (Ready in 10 minutes.)

creamy chocolate pudding

1 cup plus 2 tbsp. granulated sugar
¾ cup baking cocoa
¾ cup cornstarch
¼ tsp. salt
3 12-oz. cans evaporated fat-free milk
1½ cups water
3 tbsp. butter or margarine
1½ tsp. vanilla extract

Combine sugar, cocoa, cornstarch and salt in medium saucepan. Add evaporated milk and water; whisk to blend. Cook over medium heat, stirring constantly, for 7 minutes or until pudding thickens (do not boil). Remove from heat; stir in butter and vanilla extract. Serve warm or cold. (Ready in 15 minutes.)

memorial day
last sunday in may

description

Memorial Day, first officially observed on May 30, 1868, is an American holiday dedicated to honoring those who have died serving our country. This event will allow you to honor the memory of fallen service men and women in your congregation and in your community.

key verses

"In the future, when your children ask you, 'What do these stones mean?' tell them that the flow of the Jordan was cut off before the ark of the covenant of the LORD. When it crossed the Jordan, the waters of the Jordan were cut off. These stones are to be a memorial to the people of Israel forever" (Joshua 4:6-7).

location needed

large room or yard with a place to hang the American Flag

the event

At its core, Memorial Day is a somber holiday. Given this, you may want to begin your time with some fun activities that get your group members thinking about the meaning of Memorial Day and end with a more serious, somber time of remembrance. If you choose to do the care packages option, notify your group in advance and ask them to bring specific ingredients for the packages.

food and decorations

It is appropriate to keep decorations patriotic at Memorial Day events—and properly display the flag—but you might want to try a twist along with traditional American hamburgers and hot dogs.[1] Based on the different countries where your community has members serving in the military, provide foods typical of those countries (Japan, Korea, Italy, Germany, Cuba, the Middle East, Spain, Greece, among others).[2] Emphasize that America is a symbol of freedom and democracy around the world.

games and events

The following games and activities will get your group members focused on the significance of the Memorial Day holiday—and have fun at the same time.

american flag quiz

How much do your group members really know about the American flag? Make copies of the "American Flag True-False Quiz" (see page 155) and hand out one copy to each person. Read each of the questions and allow the group members to check

"true" if they believe the statement is accurate and the box for "false" if they believe it is not. Once you have finished, go over the following answers as a group:

1. The American flag has 13 stripes and 50 stars.

    True.

2. The stars represent the original 13 colonies and the stripes represent the 50 states in the union.

    False. The stars represent the states and the stripes represent the colonies.

3. The American flag inspired Samuel Adams to write "The Star Spangled Banner" during the War of 1812.

    False. "The Star Spangled Banner" was written by Francis Scott Key.

4. The current American flag was adopted in 1950.

    False. It was adopted in 1960.

5. A high school student created the current design for the American flag as part of a school project.

    True. A 17-year-old student named Robert G. Heft created it in 1958. He initially received a B- on the project.

6. According to the United States Flag Code, if a flag is flown at night, it must be illuminated.

    True.

7. When a flag is so tattered it can no longer serve as a symbol of the United States, it should be buried.

    False. It should be destroyed "in a dignified manner."

8. The Flag Code prohibits using the flag for advertising and printing it on cushions, napkins or boxes.

    True. This rule is generally ignored.

9. It is never acceptable to wear the flag on clothing.

    False. It can appear on uniforms and other items of clothing.

10. The first time the American flag was used on postage stamps was during World War II.

    False. It first appeared on stamps in 1926.

11. The U.S. flag has appeared on every manned spacecraft built by NASA.

    True.

12. When the Chinese first saw the American flag in 1785, they thought it resembled a duck.

    False. They thought it looked like a flower.

As a group, go over the questions and see who had the most correct answers. This is a great educational eye-opener for everyone.

care packages

Ahead of time, compile a list of servicemen and servicewomen who are associated with families in your church or community. Consider ways to support and encourage the families either by sharing with them financially, offering special events for any children, and offering practical acts of service such as yard work, babysitting or help with groceries. As a group, you can adopt several of these families.

Note that there are a variety of organizations online that can help you show love and support for our troops.[3] Many of these organizations will facilitate the delivery of care packages to deployed soldiers, and they usually offer helpful ideas of what to send. Your group can use this event as a time to bring donations and assemble the packages.

After you have put a plan in place, give your group members specific instructions for bringing items to put in the care packages. As they arrive at the Memorial Day celebration, have them sort and pack boxes, following any instructions you have obtained. Provide paper for them to write personal notes, and try to include pictures of your group or a link to a video online that the serviceperson can access.

national moment of remembrance

In 2000, Congress established 3:00 PM local time on Memorial Day to be a national moment of remembrance. During this time, Americans are asked to pause and remember the sacrifice our heroes in uniform have made for our country. You may want to plan your event to include this moment as part of a memorial service. You can also include a flag raising to half-mast (check online for procedures on how to do this—it is a good idea to practice ahead of time). An accomplished rendition of "Taps" is a great way to formally close your moment of remembrance. If you can't provide a live flag raising to half-mast or a performance of "Taps," there are several videos online that can help you create a meaningful moment.

memorial stones

In the Old Testament, God directed the Israelites to build a memorial out of stones (see Joshua 4). On Memorial Day, you can create a similar memorial out of bricks or stones. On clean, dry stones or bricks, use permanent paint to write the names of members from your church or community who have given their lives in service to their country. Invite family members of those listed on the stones to participate in a reading of the names, and work together to build a memorial out of them. You might want to incorporate a moment of remembrance at this time (see above). If you have a bricklayer or cement contractor in your congregation, you might consider asking him or her to assist you in making an appropriate and permanent arrangement. This memorial can be used and added to as needed from year to year.

closing devotion

If you have a member of the military or a veteran who would be comfortable sharing, ask him or her to tell about an experience where he or she felt God's presence during a difficult time of service. You can do this in an interview format, preparing questions ahead of time for your guest so that he or she can prayerfully consider how to answer them. Focus on how remembering God's faithfulness can make a difficult time a growing experience for yourself and others, and then share the following about the importance of remembering God's faithful love and care.

In the Old Testament, God led the Israelites out of Egypt and through the desert. The Israelites had a tough time trusting that God would care for them and always be with them, but in spite of their doubts, fears and disobedience, He faithfully led them through the desert. As they wandered, homeless, in the desert for 40 years, they had to completely depend on God. When the time was finally right, God gave Joshua, the leader of the Israelites, specific instructions for how He wanted the people to enter their new homeland. Under Joshua's leadership, they obeyed every command. When they stepped into the Jordan River to enter their new home, God miraculously stopped it up so the whole nation could cross on dry land.

God wanted this day to stand out in the Israelites' memories, and He wanted them to share this memory with future generations "so that all the peoples of the earth might know that the hand of the LORD is powerful and so that you might always fear the LORD your God" (Joshua 4:24). He had the people create a physical memorial, a pile of stones, to help them remember what He had done. He told Joshua that "these stones are to be a memorial to the people of Israel forever" (verse 7).

A special day, a physical reminder, or a strong memory can help us remember God's love and faithfulness—even when the memory may be difficult. Joshua found comfort in God's promise that "no one will be able to stand up against you all the days of your life. As I was with Moses, so I will be with you; I will never leave you nor forsake you" (Joshua 1:5). In the same way, we can be certain that God will always be with us, and we need to take time to remember His faithfulness to us.

Close in prayer and move into a time of worship, thanking God for His continual presence in each of our lives.

Notes

1. See www.usa-flag-site.org/etiquette.shtml for specific tips on proper flag etiquette.
2. See www.militarybases.com for current listings.
3. Some organizations include www.anysoldier.com; www.soldiersangels.org; www.us woundedsoldiers.com; and www.give2thetroops.org.

american flag true-false quiz

		T	F
1.	The American flag has 13 stripes and 50 stars.	☐	☐
2.	The stars represent the original 13 colonies and the stripes represent the 50 states in the union.	☐	☐
3.	The American flag inspired Samuel Adams to write "The Star Spangled Banner" during the War of 1812.	☐	☐
4.	The current American flag was adopted in 1950.	☐	☐
5.	A high school student created the current design for the American flag as part of a school project.	☐	☐
6.	According to the United States Flag Code, if a flag is flown at night, it must be illuminated.	☐	☐
7.	When a flag is so tattered it can no longer serve as a symbol of the United States, it should be buried.	☐	☐
8.	The Flag Code prohibits using the flag for advertising and printing it on cushions, napkins or boxes.	☐	☐
9.	It is never acceptable to wear the flag on clothing.	☐	☐
10.	The first time the American flag was used on postage stamps was during World War II.	☐	☐
11.	The U.S. flag has appeared on every manned spacecraft built by NASA.	☐	☐
12.	When the Chinese first saw the American flag in 1785, they thought it resembled a duck.	☐	☐

Score: __________

Source: "Flag of the United States," Wikipedia.org. http://en.wikipedia.org/wiki/Flag_of_the_United _States#The_49-_and_50-star_unions.

father's day
third sunday in june

description
It was Charles Wadsworth, a classical pianist, who said, "By the time a man realizes that maybe his father was right, he usually has a son who thinks he's wrong." On this day, your group members will get the chance to thank the father figures in their lives and do something nice for others in the process.

key verse
"Listen to your father, who gave you life, and do not despise your mother when she is old" (Proverbs 23:22).

location needed
an indoor room with access to a kitchen

the event
Each of the events requires different materials and setup, so see the following specific directions. Note that many of these activities require extra planning, and some will take place outside of the main group time. Also, be sure to be sensitive to those in your group who might have lost their fathers, never known their fathers, or who are not currently living with them.

father's day information quest
We did this activity for moms on Mother's Day, and now it's time to give fathers a turn. You can use this quest as a small-group activity or as a crowd breaker. Ahead of time, make copies of "All About Dad" (see page 159) and give one to each person in the group. Provide everyone with pens or pencils and set a time limit for them to complete the activity. Allow the groups to work in teams of two. At the end of the time, have everyone tally their points and award prizes to the team or person with the highest score. Award extra points (and extra prizes) for the following categories:

- 300 points for the student whose dad is the biggest nerd
- 400 points for the student whose dad eats the strangest foods
- 500 points for the student whose dad has done the weirdest or most daring things

Have the group members share why their dad qualifies in these categories, and determine the winners by group vote.

father's day skit
This is a great skit that your group members can put on for their fathers or just for the other students in the group. You will need copies of "Noah and Sons" (found

on the CD-ROM), a narrator, four actors to play the parts (Noah, Ham, Shem and Japheth), any costumes you want the actors to wear, and the following props:

- a table
- roll of two or three large sheets of paper
- three lawn chairs
- a tape measure
- two lengths of wood (about four inches different in length)
- pencils
- hand tools, such as a hammer and saw (optional)

Ahead of time, have the actors rehearse the parts (they can also just read from the script).

father's day service project
There are probably some single dads in your church (or just dads in need of help) who could use a boost. In addition to the ideas listed previously for moms on Mother's Day, the following are some ideas to give that special dad a memorable gift of service:

- *Make two family meals:* one to eat that night and one to freeze for another night. Don't forget to leave a spotless kitchen!

- *Create a family photo collection to display in a picture frame.* You can purchase frames with precut areas for pictures or you can make your own using card stock and a standard picture frame.

- *Pray with and for him and his children.*

You and your group members are sure to make an impression and bless this father in ways he will never forget!

closing devotion

If your group elected to do the Father's Day service project, take a moment to discuss how the group members think their actions will benefit those dads. What do they hope to learn from the project? What results do they expect to see?

Continue by having a short devotion time. Explain that in the Old Testament, we find a book of wisdom known as Proverbs. This book is basically a collection of teachings from a father to a son. As we read in Proverbs 1:8, the author states, "Listen, my son, to your father's instruction and do not forsake your mother's teaching." Why did the author (who is believed to be King Solomon) feel the need to write this information down?

One reason is because God commanded fathers (and mothers) to pass on instruction to their children. In Deuteronomy 6:6-7-2, Moses told the Israelites, "These commandments that I give you today are to be upon your hearts. Impress them on your children. Talk about them when you sit at home and when you walk along the road, when you lie down and when you get up." Parents have a biblical command to teach their children about faith in God.

Likewise, children have a biblical command to follow those teachings. In Ephesians 6:2-3, the apostle Paul (quoting Deuteronomy 5:16) states, "'Honor your father

and mother'—which is the first commandment with a promise—'that it may go well with you and that you may enjoy long life on the earth.' " So we see that the relationship goes both ways: fathers (and mothers) are to instruct their children, and their children are to obey what their parents say.

As you celebrate Father's Day, think about what your father has taught you and what he has done to teach you about God. Even if you don't have a biological father present in your home, you can identify someone who has performed this role in your life. Today, be sure to express your appreciation to that person and thank him for standing by you—even if you might not always have appreciated his advice!

all about dad

For each item listed below, write the name of a person in the room whose dad fits the category (each item is worth 250 points unless otherwise indicated).

❑ The person whose dad has the most chest hair:

____

Earn 100 bonus points if that dad has a lot of back hair too!

❑ The person whose dad has the least amount of hair on his head:

____

❑ Someone whose dad cries at movies:

____

❑ Someone whose dad has served in the military:

____

❑ Someone whose dad played football in high school or college:

____

If this dad has an old football injury, add 250 bonus points.

❑ The person whose dad works the farthest away from home:

____

❑ Someone whose dad has coached his or her sports team:

____

independence day
july 4

description

Ah, the Fourth of July. Summer weather, barbeques, picnics, parades, get-togethers . . . and FIREWORKS! The following will give you some ideas of fun things you can do together as a group as a lead-up to a pyrotechnic display at night.

key verses

"But thanks be to God that, though you used to be slaves to sin, you wholeheartedly obeyed the form of teaching to which you were entrusted. You have been set free from sin and have become slaves to righteousness" (Romans 6:17-18).

location needed

an outdoor field or other large venue

the event

What could be a more American way to celebrate this holiday than with typical American food—watermelon—and with an American pastime—playing Frisbee? The following are some great ideas for having fun with both. (For those of you in the north, there is also a game in here to celebrate Canada Day on July 1!) Each of these events requires different materials and setup, so check the following individual options.

melon fest

Did you know that watermelons originally came from southern Africa? Today, they are generally associated with summertime picnics and holidays like the Fourth of July. What follows is a collection of games that use this oversized piece of fruit to its fullest.[1]

bobbing for melons

This game requires a pool or some other large body of water. Fill a pool with all kinds of melons, and even a few vegetables of choice (cucumbers, squash, zucchini, and so forth). Divide into several teams, and give each team a certain amount of time to retrieve the produce. You can increase the degree of difficulty by doing this activity at night with no lights or by putting petroleum jelly all over the produce.

seed-spitting contest

Have players take a big mouthful of watermelon, collect the seeds, and then see who can launch them the farthest. Award prizes to the winners.

helmet contest

Divide the group members into two teams and have each team carve a helmet (or helmets) out of watermelons. They can go for the gladiator look or more of the Darth Vader look—their choice. The team members can wear their helmets throughout the day's melon-themed events, or you can just hold a contest and vote on the best helmet. Award prizes to the winner.

melon armor

Give each team a ball of string, a roll of duct tape, a knife and about five melons of different varieties. Have each team dress one of their team members in *full melon armor*. That's right: they must dress up this person in as much armor, made of melons, as humanly possible. (You may want to make the armored team member a guy!)

steal the melon

This is like a good ol' game of Steal the Bacon, *except* with a greased watermelon in the center. Divide the group into two teams, and have them line up facing each other. Place a watermelon covered in petroleum jelly in the center of the field. Number the team members off, and then call out a number. The players with that number have to grab the watermelon and get it back to their side.

watermelon toss

Get your strongest group members to do a take-off on the age-old egg toss. Divide the participants into teams of two and have the teammates line up facing each other. One person tosses the watermelon to the other, and then both take a step back. Have them continue backing up after each toss. The melon *can't* hit the ground. The last pair still tossing wins!

cantaloupe football

Form two teams. Much like football, the goal of this game is for each team to try to get to the opposing end zone with the "ball"—which in this case is a cantaloupe. Instead of a kickoff, just have one team start on its side of the field. Teams work their way down the field, passing the melon to each other until they score. Note the following rules:

- When players catch the cantaloupe, they can take only three steps and then they must toss it.
- There is no knocking the melon down out of the air.
- If the melon is knocked out of play, possession goes to the opposite team of the last person who touched the melon before going out of bounds.
- Defensive players must give opponents who are holding the melon at least three feet of space around them.
- If no one catches a toss and the melon drops to the ground (without being touched), possession goes to the opposite team.
- As an added twist, if one team busts the cantaloupe, the other team automatically scores. Have extra cantaloupes available.

Play to a certain number of points, and then call the winning team.

frisbee° games

The flying disc was created in 1938 when a man and his future wife were offered 25 cents for a cake pan they were tossing back and forth on the beach. From this simple design came what would be known as the "Frisbee," which was introduced to the

world in 1957. Today, you can celebrate this wonderful invention by playing a few Frisbee-themed summer games.[2]

float on
Divide participants into two teams of three, and have them stand some distance apart. One team will throw the Frisbee high above the other team. If someone catches it, that team is awarded 100 points. The person who caught it will then throw the Frisbee back and give the other team a chance to score. The winner is the first team to score 500 points.

knock it over
For this game, you will need traffic cones or other objects that can be knocked over (such as bottles). Divide the players into two teams of six people. Have them face each other in a line, and place one cone directly in front of each person. Give each team three Frisbees. The object of the game is for one team to knock over the other team's cones. Players must throw from behind their cone, and if the other team knocks over their cone, they are out of the game. Any player may retrieve a disc from the "no-man's land" between the teams, but they cannot go behind enemy lines. No goal tending is allowed, and a receiver cannot touch a Frisbee until it passes the line of cones. The first team to knock over all of the opposing team's cones is the winner.

kanjam
For this game, you will need a trashcan or other large container. Divide the group members into teams of two people, and have them stand a set distance apart from each other. Place the can in front of one of the players. The object is for one teammate to toss the Frisbee directly into the can or into the air in a way that allows the other teammate to "jam" it into the can. Award 10 points for hitting the can, 20 points for knocking the disc into the can, and 30 points for throwing the Frisbee directly into the can.

frisbee diver
This is a simple game where players try to catch a Frisbee while jumping off a diving board of a pool. Award one point per catch and various additional style points for especially dynamic catches.

canada day
♫ *"Ô Canada! Terre de nos aïeux!"* ("Oh, Canada! Our home and native land!") ♫
Canada Day is a commemoration of the act made on July 1, 1867, that united three British colonies into one country, forming the nation of Canada. To celebrate this day, try this maple-leaf sock toss. Here is what you will need:

- a large cardboard box
- red and white paint
- a paintbrush
- red and white socks
- sand
- red fabric paint

Ahead of time, decorate the cardboard box to look like the Canadian flag. Next, have the participants gather up all of the white and red socks and fill them with sand. Tie off the end of the sock. Give each player three white socks and two red ones. Players must stand five feet away from the box and attempt to land the socks in it. Award one point for each white sock and two points for each red sock that makes it into the box without tipping it over. When everyone has had a turn, have the players move back a step and try again. The first person who reaches 50 points is the winner.[3]

closing devotion

After the games are complete—and before the fireworks begin—you might want to get the group together for a short time of devotions. Begin by asking the group which of the activities they enjoyed the most. Also ask for volunteers to explain what comes to their minds when they think of the word "independence." Why is it important to celebrate the Fourth of July holiday each year?

Celebrating an event on an annual (or more frequent) basis allows us to remember what important event took place on that day that has contributed to our current way of life. In the case of the United States, July 4, 1776, is the date when the Founding Fathers signed the Declaration of Independence and stated to the world that the nation was no longer under the dominion of British rule. The firework displays serve to remind Americans what accompanied that declaration: a bloody American Revolutionary War, when gunfire and rockets lit up the night sky. The American war for independence was costly, with 25,000 lives lost on the American side alone.[4] However, for the colonists, it was a price they were willing to pay for their freedom.

In Romans, Paul tells that we were once slaves to sin, but now we "have been set free from sin and have become slaves to righteousness" (6:18). We are no longer under the dominion of Satan's rule but under the rule of God the Father. Like the American Revolution, there was a high price for this freedom—it cost God the life of Jesus, His Son, on the cross. This was a cost He was willing to pay because of His great love for us. Because of Jesus' sacrifice, we can know we are free (see John 8:36).

Close in prayer, thanking God for your nation and asking Him to guide and protect its leaders. Thank Him for His gift of salvation and for freeing each person from the bondage of sin.

Notes

1. The following ideas are adapted from Jonathan McKee, *The Top 12 Resources Youth Workers Want* (Ventura, CA: Gospel Light, 2002), pp. 118-120.
2. The following ideas are adapted from "List of Frisbee Games," Australian Flying Disc Association (AFDA). http://www.afda.com/juniors/games.htm.
3. Adapted from "Maple Leaf Toss," TLC Family. http://tlc.howstuffworks.com/family/canada-day-activities2.htm.
4. Interestingly, only about 8,000 of these deaths occurred in battle; 17,000 occurred as a result of disease.

163

labor day
first monday in september

description

Use this event to mark the end of summer and as a time to relax and enjoy a rest from work and daily commitments. This is a great time to talk about finding rest and refreshment by spending time with the Lord and His people.

key verses

"Come to me, all you who are weary and burdened, and I will give you rest. Take my yoke upon you and learn from me, for I am gentle and humble in heart, and you will find rest for your souls" (Matthew 11:28-29).

location needed

a park, beach or large backyard/lawn area

the event

Labor Day traditionally signals the end of summer and the beginning of the school year. On this day, take some time to relax together, build friendships and just have fun. This is a great opportunity to invite friends from outside your group or to welcome graduates who are "moving up" into your group.

You will want to have a large area to play the group games (see the instructions for specific setup and equipment required). A BBQ is standard for cooking up hot dogs, hamburgers and corn on the cob (throw the whole ear of corn on—husk and all—and turn every 10 minutes for 30 minutes). Summer fruit and veggies are at their best, so fruit kabobs or finger foods make a great addition. It may be hot, so have plenty of liquids on hand to drink.

You may also want to have some pop-ups available to provide shade or protection should rain show its ugly face. Keep insect repellent and citronella candles nearby to avoid becoming the main course at the party. Have the eating area well lit with tiki torches or strings of lights, and have the guests BYOC (bring your own chair) or bring blankets to lay on the ground.

flag football

Use cones to mark off the playing area and strips of cloth in two colors (or hats) for team members to wear. Include as many people as possible, keeping the rules to a minimum. The more serious players can either arrive early for a regulation game or start one after everyone has had a chance to share the fun. As always, goofy (but kind) sideline cheers are welcome from fans.

tug-of-war

Add some "labor" to your Labor Day with an old-fashioned game of tug of war. For this activity, you will need a heavy rope or length of garden hose, two teams of 6 to

8 people each, and a grassy, sandy or other open area with a soft surface. Wrap a piece of colored tape or tie a strip of cloth around the center of the rope. Stretch the rope out on the ground and mark two spots with cones 6 to 10 feet out from the center of the rope. The teams will line up on opposite ends of the rope, grab on and, at your signal, pull as hard against each other as they can. The first team to pull the center of the rope past its own cone wins.

stack those boxes

For this game, you will need two equal sets of 6 to 10 boxes (the bigger the boxes, the greater the challenge). Mark a start line 20 feet from each set of boxes. On your signal, participants (one on a team at a time) will run to the boxes, pick one up and carry it back to the start line. Repeat this until all the boxes are collected. At this point, the participants will stack all their boxes up, one on top of the other (in single layers). The first to complete the task and have their stack stand for 30 seconds wins.

water games

On a hot day, no one is too old for a little water fun. Provide water cannons or squirt guns, water balloons and a water balloon launcher (available online or at stores such as Walmart or Target), and plenty of targets. To add to the fun, place distance markers on the field for the group members to hit, and scatter large objects (such as overturned trash cans) about so they can hide behind them. Award points or prizes for the most accurate or farthest shots. A game of commandos with squirt guns can be fun as well—sunglasses are recommended for this as eye protection.

watermelon-eating contest

Cut watermelons into quarters lengthwise. Line the pieces up on a plastic-covered table and, on your signal, have volunteers (with hands behind their backs) eat a piece of watermelon as fast as possible. The winner is the first one with no fruit left. As with any eating contest, supervision is required to avoid choking hazards, food fights or other gross-outs.

storytelling under the stars

For this activity, you will need flashlights and blankets. Take a short hike at night away from city lights and find an open area where you can see the stars. Have a contest to see who can see the first shooting star, satellite or even an airplane. (If you have someone with a smartphone app like Starmap, have him or her point out some planets or constellations). Following this, have a story or two prepared to share with the group, and let the group members tell their stories as well. This is a great time of bonding for the group, and it will allow the group members to get to know each other better.

bonfire at the beach

For this option, you will need to first check out what the local laws are for having a bonfire. Have a responsible adult in charge of monitoring the fire and keeping an eye out for the pyro-types in the group. Having s'mores supplies handy to roast marshmallows is a great end to any summer evening. A bonfire or campfire is also a great place to sing together, share stories from the summer, talk about what God has done in the lives of students and dream about what He has for your group in the future. The following short devotion is provided to help you get started.

closing devotion

Begin the devotion time by sharing that summer is a great time to rest and relax. The stress of school eases up, and the weather invites us outdoors. It can be a time to learn something new, such as changing the oil in the car, playing the guitar, surfing or gardening. Or it can be an opportunity to earn some money, travel, go to camp or visit relatives.

In order to lead healthy lives, we all need time to rest, change our routine, and have some fun. In the summer, we tend to focus on physical rest or social fun, but we can also invest in a relationship with Jesus—and improve our spiritual health. Jesus invites us to come to Him to find rest for our souls. In Matthew 11:28-30, He says, "Come to me, all you who are weary and burdened, and I will give you rest. Take my yoke upon you and learn from me, for I am gentle and humble in heart, and you will find rest for your souls. For my yoke is easy and my burden is light." Taking Jesus' "yoke" upon us means following alongside Him and letting Him guide us. He gives us direction, and He is gentle and humble in showing us the best way to live. The result is peace for our souls—even if our circumstances aren't calm or relaxing.

Conclude by stating that Labor Day is a great time for the group members to look back at where they've been this year. Maybe they've graduated from school or moved here from somewhere else or are just moving on to the next grade. It is also an opportunity to look forward to what is ahead, which can be uncertain in terms of what joys and challenges they will come up against. But it can also be a time to experience the peace that comes from having Jesus walk beside them, guide their steps and point them in the right direction. The promise of peace in our soul is worth pursuing.

Close your time in prayer. Be available to talk with any interested students who want to know more about having a healthy relationship with Jesus. This is a great time to sing around the fire or continue your evening with some stargazing.

patriot day
september 11

description

Life, as we knew it, forever changed on September 11, 2001, when planes slammed into the World Trade Center and the Pentagon. The following events will help you recognize those who died and those who took part in rescue and recovery of what has become known as "9/11."

key verse

"To you, O LORD, I lift up my soul; in you I trust, O my God" (Psalm 25:1).

location needed

any indoor meeting area appropriate for the size of your group (you will need access to audio/video equipment for some activities listed below)

the event

Use this time to honor those who serve our country at home—policemen, firefighters, rescue workers—as well as those who lost their lives or loved ones on September 11, 2001. During this time, focus on the importance of putting our trust in the Lord, who is our source of hope for the future.

talk with a firefighter

Invite a firefighter and/or police officer to talk about the events of 9/11. Ask questions about how they felt, what they did at the time, and what they think it must have been like to be a part of the rescue services. Take time to pray for firefighters and police in your local area and around the world.

interview a survivor

Interview someone via phone, Skype® or in person who was in the area where the 9/11 tragedy took place. You can often find people who are willing to talk about the events of that day from websites centered on 9/11. One group talked to an uncle of a student who was in the tower at the time of the tragedy. Another group had a phone conversation with two pastors who were directly involved in ministry to people in their church and others throughout New York.

bring in an expert

Bring in a history professor or other expert and have them explain the politics and events that created the background for this terrible event. Invite someone from the military to talk about the effects of 9/11 on his or her job.

hold a DVD night

Film can get your students thinking about serious topics and open the door for discussion. There are several films about 9/11 that focus on finding hope. If appropriate

for your group, consider showing *The Cross and the Towers* (available at www.christian cinema.com). Prepare a few discussion starter questions to get your group talking about finding hope in the midst of a crisis.

create a presentation

Create an inspirational PowerPoint presentation set to music. Many of the websites committed to 9/11 have photos that you can download.

remember the victims

Take time to remember those who died. Sing hymns of memorial. Light candles to remember the many lives that were lost. Pray for those in authority over our government and the other institutions that will never be the same.

closing devotion

Begin the devotion time by stating that September 11, 2001 reminded us, as a nation, that we are vulnerable, that evil is real, and that we shouldn't take our security for granted. It was also a wake-up call for where we place our security. As David wrote in Psalm 25:1-5:

> To you, O Lord, I lift up my soul; in you I trust, O my God. Do not let me be put to shame, nor let my enemies triumph over me. No one whose hope is in you will ever be put to shame, but they will be put to shame who are treacherous without excuse. Show me your ways, O Lord, teach me your paths; guide me in your truth and teach me, for you are God my Savior, and my hope is in you all day long.

These verses tell us that those who trust in God will not be put to shame, that we can cry out to God when we feel afraid, and that God will teach us how to live with an attitude of hope because He is our Savior. We know that we have enemies and that evil exists, and it can seem overwhelming to understand how God can allow evil to accomplish the things that it does. But evil can only triumph in the lives of those who turn their hearts away from God. In the life of a follower of Christ, the difficult—even evil—circumstances that happen can be turned around to glorify God. As Paul says in Romans 8:28, "We know that in all things God works for the good of those who love him, who have been called according to his purpose."

We may wonder why God doesn't just step in and destroy evil right now. He has promised that someday He will. But He is waiting for this day for a reason: His love for us. In 2 Peter 3:9, we read, "The Lord is not slow in keeping his promise, as some understand slowness. He is patient with you, not wanting anyone to perish, but everyone to come to repentance." We all have people in our lives who don't know Jesus, and we want them to have the opportunity to trust in Him. So, in the meantime, we navigate a world that is vulnerable to evil, putting our trust in God and offering others the hope that He offers.

Close with a time of worship and prayer, focusing on God's power over evil and His love for the lost. Allow time to talk to students who might be interested in starting or strengthening a relationship with God. Also be available to answer any questions from group members who want to talk about the tragedy or discuss any fears they might have about the future.

halloween
october 31

description

Attitudes in Christian churches toward Halloween are diverse. Some churches hold harvest festivals in place of Halloween (see pages 20-24), some focus on Christian traditions associated with All Hallow's Eve, and others choose not to have any associations with the holiday at all. The following activities are for groups who would like to do something together on this day, and they involve helping others in the local community.

key verse

"See to it that no one takes you captive through hollow and deceptive philosophy, which depends on human tradition and the basic principles of this world rather than on Christ" (Colossians 2:8).

location needed

A large indoor area and a parking lot (specific activities below require other locations such as a thrift store and a hospital)

the event

The traditions associated with Halloween are about *getting—getting* costumes, *getting* candy, *getting* sick—so, for a twist, try these activities to get your group in the spirit of *giving* to the local community.

costume party

There are two ways to do this party: (1) a thrift-store option, and (2) a donated-clothing option. Each requires specific materials and preparation in advance of the party, so check the following details.

thrift-store option

Arrange with the manager of a local thrift store to have the store remain open (or reopen) for 20 minutes on the night of the party. Have the group members come to the party dressed *normal*. (Well, maybe "normal" isn't the right word—how about dressed in their usual attire?) Ask each student to bring five dollars to the party. While this may not seem like much, five dollars can be a lot to some families. (Be sure to encourage those who can't get the money to contact you or a co-leader ahead of time so you can arrange for a scholarship.) When the group members arrive, tell them they have 20 minutes to purchase a costume from the thrift store and come back to the party. Have prizes for the funniest costumes, the most beautiful, the ugliest, the most unique, and so on. (Note: You could buy prizes at the same thrift store while the group members are searching for their costumes!)

donated-clothing option

A variation of this activity is to invite church members and students to donate clothes to your group during the weeks before Halloween. Then, on that night, allow group members to rummage through the donations and come up with a costume. Make sure there are also weird hats, wigs and plenty of makeup available. Come up with various prizes for the most creative costume, the ugliest, the strangest, the best looking, and so forth. When the party is over, bring the clothing to a local thrift store.

children's hospital visit

Make arrangements with a local children's hospital to have the group members visit the children there on this night. The group members can dress in costumes (scary costumes and medical clothing are *not* allowed), give out candy (if agreed upon by the hospital), and just visit with the kids. (Note: This activity could also be done for the elderly at a local nursing home or a senior care center.)

pumpkin carving

This option works as a great fundraiser for your church or an organization that helps the needy. Ahead of time, you will need pumpkins and safety knives for carving. Instead of having the group members carve scary faces on their pumpkins, have them write words with meaning and witness, such as "Jesus," "God is love," "joy," "peace" or "love." Display the carved pumpkins or sell them as part of the fundraiser for your group.

pumpkin jigsaw game

For this game, you will need pumpkins, safety knives (for carving) and prizes. Form teams of four or five people, and give each team a pumpkin and a knife. Give the teams two minutes to cut their pumpkins into eight-piece jigsaw puzzles. After two minutes, have the teams exchange pumpkins. The first team to put its pumpkin puzzle together wins. Give prizes to everyone!

trunk or treat

For this option, you will need access to a parking lot and tons of candy or other prizes. Have students put on an alternative Halloween celebration for the children in the church and the surrounding neighborhood. The group members can decorate their or their family's cars in the church parking lot and fill the trunks of the cars with candy. Award prizes for best (or tackiest) decorations, most unique costumes, and so forth. (Note: This could be a great activity for the whole congregation and the group members' families to get involved, but allow the students to organize and run it.)

closing devotion

At the end of your event, you might want to have a brief time of devotions. Begin by stating that Halloween is *not* a Christian holiday—it is typically associated with ancient Celtic festivals—but it is believed to have been influenced by two Christian holy days: (1) All Saints' Day, and (2) All Souls' Day. These two holidays, which fall on November 1 and November 2 respectively, are practiced primarily in the Catholic and Eastern Orthodox Church. They are days to remember those in the faith who have died.

Wearing masks on Halloween is an interesting and unusual tradition that developed in Europe out of these two holidays. A commonly held superstition during medieval times was that the souls of the dead wandered the earth until these holy days arrived. It was believed that "All Hallow's Eve," the day before All Saints' Day, gave the dead one last chance to get back at their enemies before moving on. Of course, this tradition is completely unbiblical, but many believed it was true, and so they began wearing masks to disguise their identity from these supposed wandering souls.

It's easy to laugh at these individuals, but today many of us do the same thing. We put on "masks" to hide our identity from others. These are not physical masks like the ones children wear on Halloween, but rather false fronts we put up so others will not know our weaknesses. Maybe we are embarrassed about things in our past and are afraid others will make fun of us, so we put on a mask. Or we worry that showing our true selves will make us unpopular, so we put up a false identity. We might even be concerned that others won't accept us if they know we are Christians, so we try to hide this fact from others. Masks come in many shapes and sizes.

In Colossians 2:8, Paul warned believers not to be taken captive "through hollow and deceptive philosophy, which depends on human traditions and the basic principles of this world rather than on Christ." When we listen to the world, we are deceived into putting on masks that hide who we are. When we listen to Christ, however, we put aside these masks and embrace who God has made us to be. This allows us to recognize that we are "fearfully and wonderfully made" (Psalm 139:14) and praise God for it.

Close in a time of prayer, asking God to help the group members put aside any masks they have put on and to embrace their true identity in Christ. Also pray for God's protection over the group members. Ask that He will use them to push back the darkness in this world and continue to advance His kingdom on earth.

thanksgiving
fourth thursday in november

description

Thanksgiving is a time for eating turkey, watching ball games, spending time with family and—above all—giving thanks to God for all He has done. The activities listed below will serve as a good lead-in to get the group members thinking about the true meaning of this holiday.

key verse

"Give thanks to the LORD, for he is good; his love endures forever" (Psalm 107:1).

location needed

an indoor area (and outside locations for the Thanksgiving Day scavenger hunt)

the event

The following are some ideas for activities your group can do in the weeks and days leading up to the Thanksgiving holiday. Each of these requires different materials and advance preparation, so check the requirements that follow for the specific options you want to do with your group.

thanksgiving affirmation experience

For this option, you will need copies of "I Am Thankful" (found on the CD-ROM) and pens or pencils. This activity is best done in small groups, and it is better if the group members know each other (it can also be a *very* powerful family experience). Plan ahead to allow plenty of time for sharing!

Give each student one "I Am Thankful" card for every other person in the group (for instance, if you have 20 students total, you will give each student 19 cards). Have students write the names of their group members on the cards and then write three reasons why they are thankful for each person. After everyone has had time to write about the other group members, start with one name and have the students go around a circle and share why they are thankful for that person. After students have their turn, they can give their card to the person about whom they shared. When the group finishes sharing about each person, ask one person to pray for that individual.

thanksgiving scavenger hunt (with a purpose)

You don't have to wait for Thanksgiving to do this great project! Ahead of time, you will need copies of "Hunt It Down!" (see page 175) and pens or pencils. This is a scavenger hunt to gather food, clothing and toys for the needy. Distribute copies of the handout and award prizes as you would for any other scavenger hunt, but donate the collected items to charities. You might want to arrange for student participation in a service project or ministry to the people to whom the items will be given. You can also have group members help deliver the items to a rescue mission and help sort and put away the items; have them serve a meal at a soup kitchen to which they have donated food items; or have them clean and repair toys to be given to a homeless shelter.

let's talk turkey quiz

Quick! Before your group members' brains turn to football mush, give them a Thanksgiving quiz. You will need copies of "Let's Talk Turkey" (see page 176) and pens or pencils. Be sure to award prizes (plastic turkeys are great!). Here are the answers:

1. How long did it take for the Pilgrims to reach the New World?
   B. 66 days

2. What was the name of the covenant signed by the Pilgrims following their landing?
   C. The Mayflower Compact

3. In what year did the Pilgrims have the first Thanksgiving feast?
   C. 1621

4. Which of the following items was not part of the first Thanksgiving meal?
   B. Potatoes

5. What are the oldest remaining documents about the first Thanksgiving?
   B. Letters by a Pilgrim

6. In 1676, a day of thanksgiving was proclaimed. In what month was this day to take place?
   A. June

7. Which United States President established Thanksgiving as a national holiday?
   B. Abraham Lincoln

8. Which United States President moved the official date of Thanksgiving two times during his presidency?
   C. Franklin D. Roosevelt

9. Why was Thanksgiving finally moved up a week?
   C. To lengthen the Christmas shopping season

10. The Macy's Thanksgiving Day Parade was first held in what year?
    A. 1924

thanksgiving cards

For this activity, the group members will be making Thanksgiving Day cards for special people in the church and for their families. You will need the following materials:

- card stock or construction paper
- crayons, felt-tip pens or colored pencils
- scissors

173

- glue or tape
- decorative items (feathers, leaves, stickers)

The cards should be large enough for the group members to write or draw something that represents their thankfulness to the people they've chosen. Encourage them to make Thanksgiving cards for church staff members such as the custodian, church secretary, Sunday School teachers, nursery workers—the unsung heroes that every church has! The senior pastor would also be greatly blessed to receive a few cards. You might conclude the experience with a short devotion on thankfulness.

closing devotion

Close your time together with a brief Bible study on thankfulness. If you chose to do the Thanksgiving cards option, your group members could use these passages of Scripture in the text of their cards. Ask volunteers to find and read the following verses:

- "You turned my wailing into dancing; you removed my sackcloth and clothed me with joy that my heart may sing to you and not be silent. O Lord my God, I will give you thanks forever" (Psalm 30:11-12).

- "Enter [God's] gates with thanksgiving and his courts with praise; give thanks to him and praise his name" (Psalm 100:4).

- "Give thanks to the Lord, call on his name; make known among the nations what he has done" (Psalm 105:1).

- "Give thanks to the Lord, for he is good; his love endures forever" (Psalm 107:1).

- "Do not be anxious about anything, but in everything, by prayer and petition, with thanksgiving, present your requests to God" (Philippians 4:6).

- "Let the peace of Christ rule in your hearts, since as members of one body you were called to peace. And be thankful" (Colossians 3:15).

- "Give thanks in all circumstances, for this is God's will for you in Christ Jesus" (1 Thessalonians 5:18.)

Go around the room and ask each person to name at least one thing for which he or she is thankful. Close in a time of praise and worship, thanking God for the incredible blessings that He gives to us each and every day.

hunt it down!

This scavenger hunt is a little different than most. Everything you collect will be donated to families in need. Points are calculated per *item*.

25 points

- [ ] item of clothing
- [ ] potatoes
- [ ] bag of rice

50 points

- [ ] $5 bill
- [ ] toy suitable for a child
- [ ] canned food
- [ ] a pumpkin, berry or apple pie
- [ ] a bag of candy
- [ ] a family-sized dessert

75 points

- [ ] $10 bill
- [ ] a new pillow

100+ points

- [ ] a frozen turkey or a canned ham (100 points)
- [ ] a blanket (125 points)
- [ ] $20 bill (150 points)

let's talk turkey

Did you know that eating turkey can actually make you sleepy? It's true! Test your Thanksgiving knowledge with the following quiz. Circle your answers.

1. How long did it take for the Pilgrims to reach the New World?
   - A. 38 days
   - B. 66 days
   - C. 96 days

2. What was the name of the covenant signed by the Pilgrims following their landing?
   - A. The Mayflower Truce
   - B. The Mayflower Treaty
   - C. The Mayflower Compact

3. In what year did the Pilgrims have the first Thanksgiving feast?
   - A. 1608
   - B. 1615
   - C. 1621

4. Which of the following items was not part of the first Thanksgiving meal?
   - A. Fowl
   - B. Potatoes
   - C. Fish

5. What are the oldest remaining documents about the first Thanksgiving?
   - A. Travelogues by an explorer
   - B. Letters by a Pilgrim
   - C. Essays by an English official

6. In 1676, a day of thanksgiving was proclaimed. In what month did that day take place?
   - A. June
   - B. October
   - C. November

7. Which United States President established Thanksgiving as a national holiday?
   - A. Thomas Jefferson
   - B. Abraham Lincoln
   - C. Dwight D. Eisenhower

8. Which United States President moved the official date of Thanksgiving two times during his presidency?
   - A. Abraham Lincoln
   - B. Woodrow Wilson
   - C. Franklin D. Roosevelt

9. Why was Thanksgiving finally moved up a week?
   - A. To fulfill a political promise
   - B. To make the celebration closer to the first Thanksgiving's date
   - C. To lengthen the Christmas shopping season

10. The Macy's Thanksgiving Day Parade was first held in what year?
   - A. 1924
   - B. 1927
   - C. 1931

hanukkah
late november to late december

description

Hanukkah (or Chanukkah), also called the Festival of Lights, is a time of rededication. You can use this event to help your group members learn about the Jewish traditions surrounding this holiday and focus on Jesus as the Light of the world.

key verse

"I am the light of the world. Whoever follows me will never walk in darkness, but will have the light of life" (John 8:12).

location needed

A large indoor area that you can darken (you will want to have room for group members to gather for worship as well as an area for enjoying food and games)

the event

The historical events surrounding Hanukkah fall during the time between the Old and New Testaments. In 165 BC, a ruler named Antiochus IV Epiphanes desecrated the Temple in Jerusalem by sacrificing a pig on the altar. This caused an uprising of the Jews that eventually resulted in the purification and rededication of the Temple. Part of this rededication included the lighting of the Menorah—which miraculously stayed lit for eight days on one day's supply of olive oil.

The eight-day holiday of Hanukkah is celebrated in remembrance of the miracle of the oil and the rededication of the Temple. The word "Hanukkah" refers to the date of the celebration—the twenty-fifth day of the month of Kislev (on the Jewish calendar). Use the following activities to give your group members a taste of this Jewish holiday and also celebrate God's grace and mercy when we commit our lives to Him.

decorations

The traditional colors for Hanukkah are silver, blue and white. Chocolates covered in foil can also be placed in silver bowls around the room. Use battery-operated candles to add atmosphere in every corner.

food

Because of the significance of oil in the holiday, fried foods are popular. The most popular of these are potato pancakes called *latkes*. Use the following recipe to fry some up. They are often served with applesauce, sour cream and chopped green onions.

- 2 cups uncooked potatoes, peeled and grated
- 1 tbsp. onion, grated
- 3 eggs, beaten

- 2 tbsp. white flour
- 1½ tsp. salt
- ½ cup oil

Immediately after grating the potatoes, use an absorbent cloth to remove as much moisture as possible. Mix the potatoes, onion, eggs, flour and salt together. Pour the oil into a heavy skillet over medium-high heat. When hot, spoon the potato mixture into the pan to make ¼- to ½-inch thick patties. Cook until brown on one side; then turn and cook until brown on the other side. Drain on paper towels for a moment and serve while hot.[1]

games and activities

There are two activities that are popular during Hanukkah time: playing dreidel and lighting the menorah. Check the specific instructions below for materials needed.

dreidel game

A "dreidel" is a four-sided wooden top. Each side of the dreidel bears a letter of the Hebrew alphabet: נ (Nun), ג (Gimel), ה (Hei) and שׁ (Shin), which together form the acronym for נס גדול היה שם (*Nes Gadol Hayah Sham*—"a great miracle happened there"). Begin by setting up several tables for four to six participants. You will need the following materials:

- A copy of the "Dreidel Game Rules" (see page 180)
- bowls (one for each table)
- A dreidel (available online or at many educational supply stores)
- 10 to 15 foil-covered coins or wrapped candies in a resealable bag (one for each person)

Tape a copy of the rules to each table and place the bowl in the center. Ask a few student leaders to learn the rules of the game so they can help others get started. As the group members arrive, give them a bag of candy and a dreidel, and then invite them to gather in groups of four to six to play the game. This activity is a great mixer for the group, and you can add background music featuring traditional Hanukkah songs such as "Hanukkah O Hanukkah" and "The Dreidel Song" for added effect. (Many of these are available for free download on the Internet.)[2]

menorah lighting

A "menorah" is a nine-branched candle holder. You can either acquire one of these online or at a supply store or just use eight handle holders with candles all the same height. You will need an additional candle to use to light the others. (This is called a *shamash* or "helper" candle and is usually placed in the center of a menorah—thus the nine branches). Traditionally, the candles are meant to burn for at least a half hour and only at night.

Begin with a time of music and worship. In Jewish homes, Hanukkah is celebrated for eight days with a candle added and lit on each day until the menorah is full and all candles are lit. For your observance, place candles one at a time in a row from right to left until all eight are in place. Take a moment to pray, thanking God for the miracle of the oil celebrated on Hanukkah. Then thank God for bringing all of you to this celebration of rededication. Following this, from left to right, use the additional candle to light each candle. After this ceremony, you can lead into your devotion time.

closing devotion

Begin by stating that Hanukkah, the Jewish celebration of rededication, was intended to remind the people of Israel that the Temple was a house dedicated to worshiping God according to His instructions. During the time the Greeks ruled over the Jews, the Temple had become a place of pagan sacrifice. Then, according to tradition, the Jews fought back against the Greeks, were triumphant, and cleaned and purified the Temple.

To celebrate this victory, the Jews held a ceremony of rededication and lit the lamp in the Temple. In Exodus 27:20-21, God had instructed the Israelites to keep the lamp burning from evening to morning, but there was only enough olive oil to keep the lamp burning for one day. Miraculously, the oil kept the lamp going for *eight* days, which is where we get the celebration of the eight days of Hanukkah. (Note: You might want to show the "Candlelight Video" at www.maccabeats.com as a fun way to share a bit more about the history of Hanukkah.)

There are times in our lives when we need to "clean house." In 1 John 1:7, we read, "If we walk in the light, as he is in the light, we have fellowship with one another, and the blood of Jesus, his Son, purifies us from all sin." When we first put our faith in Jesus, He takes our sin away, and we receive eternal life. But the battle to live Jesus' way—to walk in the light—is a daily effort to dedicate and rededicate our lives to Him. Jesus said, "I am the light of the world. Whoever follows me will never walk in darkness, but will have the light of life" (John 8:12). When we get off the path, Jesus promises to help us find our way back. Living Jesus' way helps us see clearly, and He promises to lead us and give us the light we need for life!

Close in prayer, thanking Jesus for His life-giving power to walk daily in the light of life. Encourage your group members to take a moment to reflect on their lives, do any necessary housecleaning, and rededicate their lives to Christ. Be available after your time together to talk to students who want to put their lives in order God's way.

Notes

1. Recipe adapted from "Chanukkah," Judaism 101. http://www.jewfaq.org/holiday7.htm.
2. Ibid.

dreidel game rules

1. Begin by having each player place one piece of candy in the bowl.

2. The first player spins his or her dreidel and, based on the Hebrew letter that ends up on top when it falls, does the following:

   נ (Nun), do nothing (the next person spins)

   ג (Gimel), the person wins the contents of the bowl

   ה (Hei), the person gets half of the contents of the bowl (round up if the number is uneven)

   ש (Shin), the person puts a piece of candy in the bowl

3. If the bowl becomes empty at any time, each player must put one candy in the bowl, and play resumes until someone wins everyone else's candy.

4. At the end of the game, the winner gives each other player two pieces of candy.

christmas
december 25

description

Christmas and Easter are the two most important holidays for Christians. The following games and activities will help your group focus on the true meaning of this holiday—Jesus' birth into this world—as they prepare for the Christmas season.

key verses

"Today in the town of David a Savior has been born to you; he is Christ the Lord. This will be a sign to you: You will find a baby wrapped in cloths and lying in a manger" (Luke 2:11-12).

location needed

a large indoor area

the event

Ahead of time, decide which activities you want to do with your group. Each of the options requires different materials and setup, so see the specific directions below. The first section includes fun games and events you can do with your group as part of your Christmas celebration. The second section focuses on ways your group can give back to the community at large during this holiday season.

group games and activities

These are great activities you can use to have some fun together as a group.

through the eyes of an angel

This is a monologue that you can read to the group to show them the miracle of Christmas from the perspective of an angel. For this option, you will need one copy of "Through the Eyes of an Angel" (see page 187) and a white choir robe to wear (optional). Read through the monologue several times to familiarize yourself with it— the more comfortable you are with it, the more students will hear the angel speaking instead of just you!

the meaning of the candy cane

For this option, you will need Bibles, copies of "The Meaning of the Candy Cane" (see page 190), and candy canes for everyone in the group. Although the story is likely more fiction than fact, it is still a *sweet* way to share the gospel with the group. After reading the story, give each person a candy cane as a reminder of God's great love and provision of our Savior, Jesus Christ.

random acts of kindness advent calendar
To do this activity, you just need copies of "Advent Calendar" (found on the CD-ROM) for every person in the group. Have the students use this blank advent calendar to record one random act of kindness for each day of Advent.

christmas story quiz
Make copies of "Christmas Story Quiz" (see page 191) for each person, and hand out pens and pencils. After the group members have had a few minutes to answer the questions, discuss the answers together as a group:

1. Who told Joseph and Mary to go to Bethlehem?
    D.   Caesar Augustus.

2. How did Mary and Joseph travel to Bethlehem?
    D.   Who knows? (The Bible doesn't say.)

3. What did the innkeeper tell Mary and Joseph?
    D.   None of the above. (He isn't even mentioned.)

4. Which animals does the Bible say were present at the birth of Jesus?
    E.   None of the above. (The Bible doesn't say specifically; however, because a manger is a feeding trough for barnyard animals, it's probable that there were barnyard animals present.)

5. Who saw the star in the east?
    E.   None of the above. (It was Magi, "wise men," not kings.)

6. How many angels spoke to the shepherds?
    A.   One. (Just one angel spoke, though a multitude praised God.)

7. Where did the wise men find Jesus?
    D.   In a house. (The wise men found Jesus more than a year after His birth.)

8. When did the baby Jesus cry?
    D.   When He needed something, just like other babies. (Although Jesus was fully God, He was also fully human and communicated the way all babies do.)

9. What did the angels say in praise to God while with the shepherds?
    C.   "Glory to God in the highest."

10. Which one of the following statements is false?
    E.   All of these statements are true.

Have the group members give themselves a point for each correct answer. Determine the winner and hand out prizes.

For this option, you will need copies of "What Do You Know About Christmas?" (see page 193) and pens or pencils. Hand out one copy to each person and award points as indicated below. Here are the answers to this fun little bunch of queries:

1. Name all nine of Santa's reindeer. (The first letter has been provided.)

   Dasher, Dancer, Prancer, Vixen, Comet, Cupid, Donner, Blitzen, Rudolph. **(One point for each correct answer.)**

2. What is a crèche?

   It's a representation of the Nativity scene. **(20 points.)**

3. Name the 12 gifts given in the song "The Twelve Days of Christmas."

   (1) A partridge in a pear tree, (2) turtle doves, (3) French hens, (4) calling birds, (5) golden rings, (6) geese-a-laying, (7) swans-a-swimming, (8) maids-a-milking, (9) ladies dancing, (10) lords-a-leaping, (11) pipers piping, and (12) drummers drumming. **(Five points for each correct answer.)**

4. Who were the three spirits that visited Mr. Scrooge in *A Christmas Carol*?

   (1) the Ghost of Christmas Past, (2) the Ghost of Christmas Present, and (3) the Ghost of Christmas Yet-to-Come. **(Two points for each correct answer.)**

5. Who said "God bless us everyone" in *A Christmas Carol*?

   "Tiny Tim" Cratchett. **(Five points.)**

6. Finish this line from a famous Bing Crosby song: "I'm dreaming of a . . ."

   White Christmas. **(Five points.)**

7. What was the original opening line to "Have Yourself a Merry Little Christmas"?
   C.   "Have yourself a merry little Christmas, it might be your last." **(20 points.)**

8. Name the three gifts the wise men brought to the baby Jesus.

   (1) Gold, (2) frankincense, and (3) myrrh. **(Five points for each correct answer.)**

9. According to legend, what were the three wise men's names?

   (1) Balthazar, (2) Melchior, and (3) Caspar **(Ten points for each correct answer.)**

10. What does Santa leave for bad boys and girls?

    Lumps of coal. **(Five points.)**

11. What is the flower most commonly used at Christmas?

    Poinsettia. **(Five points.)**

12. What are you supposed to kiss under?

    Mistletoe. **(Five points.)**

13. What does *Feliz Navidad* mean?

    It means "Merry Christmas" in Spanish. **(10 points.)**

14. Where is a stocking traditionally hung on Christmas Eve?

    Wherever your family puts them, although traditionally they go on the fireplace mantle. **(Five points.)**

15. Who helps Santa make the toys?

    Elves. **(Five points.)**

christmas movie trivia

For this option, you will need copies of "Christmas Movie Madness" (see page 195) and pens or pencils. This little trivia sheet is great for small groups or anytime you just want to see how much you—uh, your students—know about Christmas movies. Here are the answers:

1. What is the occupation of Bill Murray's character in the movie *Scrooged*?
    B.   A coldhearted TV executive

2. According to Buddy in the movie *Elf*, what are the four food groups?
    B.   Candy, candy canes, candy corns, syrup

3. What is the name of George Bailey's guardian angel in *It's a Wonderful Life*?
    C.   Clarence

4. In *It's a Wonderful Life*, what does George Bailey injure as a young boy?
    D.   His ear

5. Who wrote the screenplay for *The Nightmare Before Christmas*?
    A.   Tim Burton

6. Which state was the setting for *White Christmas*?
    D.   Vermont

7. Who plays the army buddy of Bing Crosby's character in *White Christmas*?
    C.   Danny Kaye

8. Which actress played the little girl who is skeptical about Santa Claus in *Miracle on 34th Street*?
    A.   Natalie Wood

9. The setting for *Miracle on 34th Street* revolves around which department store?
    B.   Macy's

10. Who played the Grinch in *How the Grinch Stole Christmas*?
    C.   Jim Carrey

11. What happens to the character played by Tim Allen in *The Santa Clause*?
    D.   All of the above

According to the National Institute of Health, psychiatrists and psychologists report a high rate of depression among their clients at Christmastime. One North American survey even reported that 45 percent of people dread the holiday season.[1] For this reason, Christmas is an excellent time for your group to get focused on helping those in the church and in the community. The following are some practical ways that you can do this.

toy collection

For this activity, you and your group will collect toys for underprivileged children. There are probably many organizations in your area that would be glad to distribute the gifts your group collects, but it can be powerful to have students distribute the gifts themselves. Many churches throw a party for needy children, either at the church itself or where the underprivileged children live. There are several national organizations that can also help you with gifts for children, including Angel Tree Ministries (www.angeltree.org) and Operation Christmas Child at Samaritan's Purse (www.samaritanspurse.org). When you give to these organizations, you know the gifts are given along with the love of the gospel to truly needy children.

present wrapping

Christmas wrapping can be big business and raise a great deal for missions, or it can just bless someone who needs help getting his or her gifts wrapped! Arrange for a specific day or days for group members to be available to wrap gifts, and be sure to advertise the event ahead of time. Make flyers, use word-of-mouth advertising, and ask the pastor to announce it during several consecutive Sundays. Once the day arrives, people can bring their presents to be wrapped. You can either charge per item, ask people to donate to your group's mission fund, or do it for free. Encourage some of your more artistic students to create homemade Christmas wrapping paper. The group members will love the opportunity to be creative, and the people will often give more to the cause!

christmas tree pickup or delivery

Grab a couple of trucks, some energetic group members and some adult volunteers to drive. Once word spreads that you'll pick up or deliver trees, you'll have more than enough work! You can charge a flat fee, ask for donations to your group's mission fund, or just use the opportunity to bless others. Note that there may also be others in your area who would love to have some help decorating their trees. Group members can offer to help with the tree, lights, wrapping, cleaning, cooking—whatever needs doing. This not only provides ministry opportunities for your students but also brings great joy to folks during what can be a lonely time of the year.

christmas holiday babysitting service

This idea is a wonderful service to stressed-out parents. Open up the church on several afternoons and evenings for parents to drop off their children for a fun, safe time at the church while the parents go shopping (or out to dinner or indulge in an uninterrupted nap!). Make sure you have plenty of adult supervision and lots of standby help in case all the parents in your church take you up on the offer at the same time. Once word gets out, you might need to have parents reserve the time they want to use the services of the group.

closing devotion

Regardless of which activities you choose to do, consider ending your time with a short devotion. Hand out Bibles to the group and have the students read the Christmas story from Matthew 1:18–2:12 and Luke 1:26-65; 2:1-20. Following the reading, invite volunteers to pretend they are one of the Christmas story participants and tell the story from that person's point of view. The characters are as follows:

- Mary
- Joseph
- Angel
- Shepherd
- King Herod
- Elizabeth
- The innkeeper
- God the Father

Continue by discussing what the two Gospel accounts have in common and what are some of the differences. Close in prayer, thanking God for sending His Son, Jesus, into the world to be our Savior. Also ask that He would help those in the group to continue to keep the focus on Christ and share their time with those who are lonely or depressed during the holiday season.

Note

1. Ray B. Williams, "Why People Get Depressed at Christmas," *Psychology Today*, November 28, 2010. http://www.psychologytoday.com/blog/wired-success/201011/why-people-get-depressed-christmas.

through the eyes of an angel

a monologue

I know what you're wondering: *Who are* you *supposed to be?* Well, I'm an angel, and my name is Gabriel.

Now you're thinking, *You're crazy! First, angels do not look like you. Where are your wings? Where is your harp? And an angel definitely would not look like [your name]—I thought they were supposed to be beautiful. Besides, [your name] isn't even dead yet.*

Well, to answer your question, an angel can take any form God chooses. Some of you have visited with some of my fellow angels before and didn't even know it. The Bible tells you, "Do not forget to entertain strangers, for by so doing some people have entertained angels without knowing it" (Hebrews 13:2).

Another misconception you humans have about angels is that we are the spirits of people who have died and then have earned our angel wings. I think you've been watching too much TV. Once again, if you read the Bible, it clearly states that we were created long before man and that our job is as "ministering spirits sent to serve those who will inherit salvation" (Hebrews 1:14).

Enough of this, though. I was not sent to give you a lesson on angels. I was sent to give you a new perspective on Christmas: an angel's perspective.

First, let me give you a little glimpse into what it is like to be an angel. Can you imagine being in constant fellowship with the Creator of all things? I was there when God created the heavens and the earth. Talk about creative! You've probably heard about the Big Bang Theory in school. Well, let me tell you, I was there and I saw it— God said it, and *bang!* It was done. It was fun to watch Him come up with the different plants and animals. Talk about variety!

When He was finished creating your world, He created humans. At first, all of us angels were jealous. We were all wondering, *Aren't we good enough?* Why did God have to create these inferior beings? Then we realized that God wanted to have fellowship with a being who would serve and love Him without having to see Him. I still don't know how you humans do that.

I was there and witnessed the fall of one of our own, a beautiful angel named Lucifer. His name meant "son of the morning," "shining one" and "anointed cherub who covers," and he was God's number one angel. That is, until he saw that God created you. When he saw that you worshiped God, he wanted to be worshiped too.

Well, you all know there is only one God, so obviously Lucifer was overstepping his place. He wound up getting kicked out of heaven. You call him Satan now. His new name means "adversary" or "enemy"—and, be assured, that name definitely fits now. He is one bad apple. The really sad thing is that he took many of my fellow angels with him. You call them demons. We call them angels with an attitude.

I was there to witness the fall of man. I wondered, *Why? Why would you give up everything for a piece of fruit when you could have anything else you wanted?* I never will understand that. Over these many, many years, I have watched you grow and fall over and over again—and the patience and love God has had for you have totally amazed me. In fact, watching humankind throughout history has puzzled me. At times I've

wondered why God doesn't just wipe out all humans and start again. But then I realize that I can't even begin to fathom His love for you.

Anyway, we angels knew that God had a plan to redeem mankind, but we had no idea what His plan was. About 2,000 years ago, rumors began to circulate around heaven that God was about to act. I still remember getting together with other angels and trying to figure out how God was going to save you from yourselves. Some of us thought He was just going to touch down and tell the people, "Serve Me, or else." Others, like myself, had some inside information that God was going to become a human being, so we figured He would come as a great king and wipe out His enemies and set up Eden all over again. You know, to give you a second chance and all that.

Then one day, God came to me and said, "Gabriel, I want you to go to Nazareth in Galilee. I want you to find a young woman named Mary." In Luke 1:30-33, you can read what God wanted me to tell her: "Do not be afraid, Mary, you have found favor with God. You will be with child and give birth to a son, and you are to give him the name Jesus. He will be great and will be called the Son of the Most High. The Lord God will give him the throne of his father David, and he will reign over the house of Jacob forever; his kingdom will never end."

Well, talk about a surprise! God was coming to earth as a baby. I didn't understand why a deliverer would start out as a baby. After all, God never did it this way before—well, there was Moses, but he was a human. So we angels began wondering all kinds of things. Would He be a superbaby? Would He have to eat that nasty earth food? Would His earthly mom and dad tell Him what to do? How could all of God fit into such a tiny package? I decided that God would come as a baby, grow up in a palace and be crowned king of the world. This Mary must be some sort of princess, I thought. After all, I knew she was a descendant of David, so this made sense, right?

After God gave me some more instructions, I left to find this Mary. When I arrived in Nazareth, I was surprised to find that it was a dirty little town—no palace, no kings, no princes . . . nothing but peasants. I thought I had the wrong place, but I knew God didn't make mistakes, so I knew Mary had to be there somewhere. I found her in a humble dwelling. She was a plain young woman and very poor. She wasn't a princess—and to top it off, she was not even married! Was God going to be born to an *unwed* mother? You humans have a derogatory term for that, and I was sure that God did not want His Son to be called that name.

What is God thinking? I thought. Then I remembered that God always knows what He's doing, so even though I didn't understand the whole thing, I decided to just shut up and do my job.

Even though Mary wasn't a princess, there was something about her. She had an inner beauty that drew me to her. She was humble and willing to do whatever God wanted, even at the risk of her own life. I didn't know there were still humans like that in your world. I wanted to stay and talk with her, but I had other assignments.

After seeing Mary, God told me to go and convince her future husband, Joseph, that she was pregnant with God's Son. Knowing how skeptical humans can be, I figured it would be an interesting task. I was successful, but what a challenge!

Next came the fun part. God sent me to tell the people of the area that He was coming. I thought my next destination would be the palace—or at least the homes of the kings and noblemen—where I would announce there was a new king on the block. However, when I got to the place God had told me about, there was no palace, no king, no queen—nothing! And I mean nothing! It was a pasture, right smack dab in the middle of nowhere. All I could see were some shepherds and their mangy sheep.

Hey, this could be fun, I thought. I mean, think about it: shepherds huddled around a fire with nothing around them as far as they could see. They were a bit skittish already, worrying about attacks from wild animals. I could just pop in and scare the living daylights out of 'em!

Well, my conscience got the best of me (angels have a conscience too), and I decided I should probably continue on with my mission the way I was told to do it. When I first appeared, the shepherds were scared, but once they realized who I was, they were really happy. I got all excited too, and pretty soon I called on some of my angel buds to sing a song written by the Heavenly Host Rockers. You can read some of the lyrics in Luke 2:14: "Glory to God in the highest, and on earth peace to men on whom his favor rests." Anyway, it was awesome! *No wonder God sent me to these guys,* I thought. Those kingly types would never have accepted this news with such joy.

Then it was time to go to see the God-child's birth, so I was off to a place called Bethlehem. I knew there were no palaces there, but I thought there must be a nice house for Him to be born in. Wrong again! When I got to the place where the baby was born, I was angry. This is God's Son, people! Do you have any idea what you are doing? A stinky, cold, dirty stable? Suddenly, it occurred to me: God came to be a man so He could relate to man. He came to the common man because He doesn't care about earthly titles or earthly status. He was born to a humble couple in a humble setting to show that He was willing to do anything to show how much He loves you humans. He gave you the greatest gift—Himself—so you would see that giving is more important to Him than receiving.

Sometimes I think that maybe humans will understand how far God has gone to show you that He loves you. That maybe you will get the message and share God's love with others. Maybe this gift-giving thing will even become a tradition. You never know, right?

Note: This monologue was written by Pete Aubin.

the meaning of the candy cane

Many years ago as the Christmas season approached, a humble candy maker living in a small town in the state of Indiana wanted to create something with his hands that would be symbolic of the true meaning of Christmas.

As a believer, the candy maker began with pure, hard, *white* candy—white to symbolize the virgin birth and the sinless nature of Jesus, and hard to represent Christ as the solid rock, the foundation of the Church, and the firmness of the promises of God.

The candy maker then shaped the candy into the form of a *J*. This represented both the precious name of Jesus and also His staff as the Good Shepherd, who reaches down into the ditches of the world to lift out His fallen lambs and bring them into eternal salvation.

The candy maker stained the candy with *red stripes* to represent the scourging Jesus received and the blood He shed on the cross as redemption for all who believe in Him and accept Him as Lord.

The candy maker's final touch was to make his creation and all that it stood for available to everyone. So he hung the candy canes abundantly on the Christmas tree in his candy shop, around the shop window and door frame. He offered it free to anyone who would simply ask, just as salvation is offered free to those who ask Jesus Christ to come into their heart.

Source: Adapted from Jim Burns and Mike DeVries, *Intense Illustrations* (Ventura, CA: Gospel Light, 2002), pp. 118-119.

christmas story quiz

1. Who told Joseph and Mary to go to Bethlehem?

    A.   An angelic messenger
    B.   Mary's shamed relatives
    C.   King Herod
    D.   Caesar Augustus
    E.   No one told them

2. How did Mary and Joseph travel to Bethlehem?

    A.   Camel
    B.   Donkey
    C.   Joseph walked, and Mary rode a donkey
    D.   Who knows?

3. What did the innkeeper tell Mary and Joseph?

    A.   "There's no room in the inn."
    B.   "I have a stable you can use."
    C.   Both A and B
    D.   None of the above

4. Which animals does the Bible say were present at the birth of Jesus?

    A.   Cows, sheep, goats
    B.   Sheep and goats only
    C.   Lions, tigers and bears (oh, my!)
    D.   Miscellaneous barnyard creatures
    E.   None of the above

5. Who saw the star in the east?

    A.   Shepherds
    B.   Three kings
    C.   Mary and Joseph
    D.   Both A and B
    E.   None of the above

6. How many angels spoke to the shepherds?

    A.   One
    B.   Three
    C.   A multitude
    D.   None of the above

7. Where did the wise men find Jesus?

    A.   In a manger
    B.   In a stable
    C.   In a field
    D.   In a house
    E.   None of the above

8. When did the baby Jesus cry?
    A.   When the doctor slapped him on his bottom
    B.   When the little drummer boy kept on playing
    C.   Not once, just as the Bible says
    D.   When He needed something, just like other babies

9. What did the angels say in praise to God while with the shepherds?
    A.   "Joy to the world, the Lord is come"
    B.   "Alleluia!"
    C.   "Glory to God in the highest"
    D.   "My sweet Lord"
    E.   None of the above

10. Which one of the following statements is false?
    A.   Mary was a virgin when she delivered Jesus.
    B.   Mary was pledged to be married to Joseph when she became pregnant.
    C.   Mary left town when she found out she was with child.
    D.   Joseph was a dreamer.
    E.   All of these statements are true.

what do you know about christmas?

1. Name all nine of Santa's reindeer. (The first letter has been provided.)

   D _______________________   D _______________________
   P _______________________   V _______________________
   C _______________________   C _______________________
   D _______________________   B _______________________
   R _______________________

2. What is a crèche? ____
   ____
   ____

3. Name the 12 gifts given in the song "The Twelve Days of Christmas."

   1. __________________   7. __________________
   2. __________________   8. __________________
   3. __________________   9. __________________
   4. __________________   10. _________________
   5. __________________   11. _________________
   6. __________________   12. _________________

4. Who were the three spirits that visited Mr. Scrooge in *A Christmas Carol*?

   1. ____
   2. ____
   3. ____

5. Who said "God bless us everyone" in *A Christmas Carol*? _______________

6. Finish this line from a famous Bing Crosby song: "I'm dreaming of a . . ."
   ____

7. What was the original opening line to "Have Yourself a Merry Little Christmas"?

   A. "Have yourself a merry little Christmas, let your heart be light"
   B. "Have yourself a merry little Christmas, let your day be bright"
   C. "Have yourself a merry little Christmas, it might be your last"
   D. "Have yourself a merry little Christmas, it has come at last"

8. Name the three gifts the wise men brought to the baby Jesus.

   1. ____
   2. ____
   3. ____

9. According to legend, what were the three wise men's names?

   1. ____

   2. ____

   3. ____

10. What does Santa leave for bad boys and girls? _______________________________________

11. What is the flower most commonly used at Christmas?

    ____

12. What are you supposed to kiss under? _______________________________________

13. What does *Feliz Navidad* mean? _______________________________________

14. Where is a stocking traditionally hung on Christmas Eve?

    ____

15. Who helps Santa make the toys? _______________________________________

christmas movie madness

1. What is the occupation of Bill Murray's character in the movie *Scrooged*?

    A.   A coldhearted banker
    B.   A coldhearted TV executive
    C.   A coldhearted police officer
    D.   A coldhearted politician

2. According to Buddy in the movie *Elf*, what are the four food groups?

    A.   candy, spaghetti, soda pop, sugar
    B.   candy, candy canes, candy corns, syrup
    C.   candy, soda pop, sugar, jelly beans
    D.   candy canes, candy corn, jelly beans, soda pop

3. What is the name of George Bailey's guardian angel in *It's a Wonderful Life*?

    A.   Ariel
    B.   Henry
    C.   Clarence
    D.   Frank

4. In *It's a Wonderful Life*, what does George Bailey injure as a young boy?

    A.   His foot
    B.   His arm
    C.   His eyes
    D.   His ear

5. Who wrote the screenplay for *The Nightmare Before Christmas*?

    A.   Tim Burton
    B.   Steven Spielberg
    C.   Jimmy Stewart
    D.   Ozzy Osbourne

6. Which state was the setting for *White Christmas*?

    A.   Colorado
    B.   Montana
    C.   New Hampshire
    D.   Vermont

7. Who plays the army buddy of Bing Crosby's character in *White Christmas*?

    A.   Jimmy Stewart
    B.   Dean Martin
    C.   Danny Kaye
    D.   Bob Hope

8. Which actress played the little girl who is skeptical about Santa Claus in *Miracle on 34th Street*?

    A.   Natalie Wood
    B.   Audrey Hepburn
    C.   Anne Bancroft
    D.   Shirley Temple

9. The setting for *Miracle on 34th Street* revolves around which department store?

    A.   Bloomingdale's
    B.   Macy's
    C.   Sax Fifth Avenue
    D.   Neiman Marcus

10. Who played the Grinch in *How the Grinch Stole Christmas*?

    A.   Will Farrell
    B.   Tim Allen
    C.   Jim Carrey
    D.   Eddie Murphy

11. What happens to the character played by Tim Allen in *The Santa Clause*?

    A.   He gains weight.
    B.   He grows a beard.
    C.   He gets fired.
    D.   All of the above

SPECIAL EVENTS

event: \i-vent\ **1a:** something that happens: occurrence **b:** a note-worthy happening **c:** a social occasion or activity; **2:** any of the con-tests in a program of sports **3:** a subset of the possible outcomes of an experiment

birthday ideas

description ♪

♪ Happy birthday to you, happy birthday to you . . . ♪

the event

The following are some creative ways to celebrate your group members' birthdays and make them feel special on this important day.

birthday drop-off

Prepare a bag of goodies for the birthday guy or gal. Include affirming notes, fun food and even a devotional book. Drive by the honoree's home before school (or before he or she wakes up on a weekend or school break) and leave the goodie bag on the front doorstep. As an option, consider developing a birthday committee for making the drop-offs happen and handling the logistics. This is an excellent way to involve students who are not outgoing or don't like to be up front—it can be very affirming to let them handle the details of honoring the birthday people. Don't forget to honor the committee members when *their* birthdays roll around too!

breakfast bash

With the approval of the honoree's parents, sneak into the birthday person's home and decorate the house with posters and balloons. Provide birthday cake and ice cream. After the decorations are up (and after Mom or Dad has checked to make sure there's no dirty underwear on the floor!), walk into the honoree's bedroom and wake him or her up. Then have a fun time together—and don't forget to clean up whatever mess your group made.

breakfast kidnap

This is an oldie but goody. Drop by the birthday person's house early in the morning and take him or her to a fast-food restaurant for breakfast. Make sure to check with the parents of the birthday person *first* to avoid any unforeseen surprises.

kidnap the guests

Here's a twist for a surprise birthday party: kidnap the guests! Ahead of time, arrange with your group members' parents the exact time and plan for the event. Then go to each guest's house and kidnap him or her for the party. You can ask parents to pack a bag with a swimsuit for a pool, lake or beach day—or whatever you're planning to do.

birthday recognition

Some groups choose to recognize birthdays at their meetings on a weekly or monthly basis. This is a great way to get to know each other better. The usual way to celebrate is by singing "Happy Birthday" to the birthday honoree(s). You might also want to create an information piece about each birthday person. To do so, you will need to gather information about each honoree ahead of time and obtain a photo of him or her. Paste the photo to a sheet of poster board and make a huge birthday card with some fun facts about the birthday honoree. Here are some ideas for what to include:

- full name
- nickname
- date of birth
- place of birth
- favorite food
- favorite musical artist(s)
- favorite Scripture verse(s)
- favorite vacation spot
- favorite color
- little-known fact (remember not to embarrass the honoree *too* much!)
- a hope and a prayer for the coming year

As an option, you can also shoot a short video with a digital camera and show it to the person at the event. Have the group members make a short statement about what they like about the person or appreciate the most about him or her, or have them share some fun memory they shared together.

199

graduation banquet

description

Graduation is an important time of transition for your group members. This event will allow you to celebrate the occasion with a special banquet in their honor.

the event

Make this a time of affirmation and blessing for the graduates of your youth group, whether they are graduating from elementary school, middle school or high school. Serve a fun meal and create a festive, celebratory atmosphere. Here are a few ideas:

- Create a smorgasbord of food. Ask for volunteers in the church who would be willing to provide one dish—main course, salad or dessert—for the banquet.

- Make placemats for each graduate. Decorate large sheets of construction paper with photos, congratulatory comments, blessings, verses and remembrances. Use clear Con-Tact paper to preserve the placemat.

- Invite parents or other family members to attend the celebration and share an encouraging word or blessing for the graduate. (Keep comments to one minute or so, as this can get very long.)

- Create a short video or PowerPoint presentation depicting the person(s) being honored. This could include pictures from fun outings together as a youth group.

- Offer a different "Most Likely to . . ." award to each graduate. Make sure all awards are affirming—moving on to a different level in life is tough enough!

End the night by bringing the graduates up front and praying for each one while others in the group lay hands of blessing on them. At this point, you might present each graduate with a gift—perhaps a Bible, a Bible study or a short devotional book.

3

car ride games

description

These activities are similar to those "I Spy" car games you might have played as a kid and are great for those long drives with your youth group.

the event

Let's face it: long car rides can be borrrrring. Here are some fun games for your group members to play when you are looking to fill your driving day. For this game, your students will need digital cameras (which they most likely have on their phones). The idea is for your group members to take pictures out the window based on each of the following themes. At the end of the drive, you can award points to the person who captured photos from each theme, or who took the most original/creative photo, or who captured the most different shots in each theme, or whatever else you decide. Note that photos should be of items *outside* the car.

cross theme

Have the group members take pictures of various crosses. For example, the Red Cross symbol, a cross on a church, a cross made by the wood in a window, a cross found in nature, a cross from electrical wires, and so forth.

cow theme

Only photos of cows or pictures of cows allowed.

potato theme

In this option the group will be looking for creative potato photos. This could include billboards or advertisements of potato chips.

red theme

In every photo, the color red must be the dominant color. (You could also have a green theme if your drive is taking place near St. Patrick's Day.)

international theme

Every photo the group members take must be a picture of something international or have the word "international." (IHOPs count.)

sports theme

Search for creative sports shots or advertisements of sports-related products.

joy theme

Each photo must describe the word "joy" in some way. For example, the group members could take a picture of an advertisement featuring happy people, or take a shot

201

of a serene meadow or still lake, or a kid jumping up and down, or anything else that captures the feeling of joy.

God theme
Like the joy theme, the group members will take pictures of items that depict where they see God or things that make them think of God.

scavenger hunts

description
Can't get enough of scavenger hunts? Here are some more options to try!

the event
As with the other scavenger hunt activities listed in this book, you will need check-lists, prizes and other specific items for your group members to do the hunt. Check each of the specific requirements given below.

couch potato hunt
This is a fun twist on the typical scavenger hunt. For this option, you will need:

- copies of "Couch Potato Hunt" (see page 205)
- pens or pencils
- an old couch
- a truck
- digital cameras (could be cell phone cameras) for each team
- responsible adult drivers
- prizes

Load up a couch onto each truck and give each team a copy of "Couch Potato Hunt." Teams will drive around town taking photos as directed on the handout. Most of the fun will be in telling the stories and showing the photos when everyone returns. (You can also post these photos online to Facebook or another website after the event is over.) Set a time limit, but be sure to allow enough time for the group members to complete most of the tasks. The team with the most pictures from the list wins!

edible scavenger hunt
This activity works best with at least four members per team (unless you've got some *really* big eaters!). To do this hunt, you will need the following:

- copies of "Incredible Edibles Hunt" (see page 206)
- pens or pencils
- prizes (probably not a good idea to award cabbage, sardines, popcorn, soda, cookies, pickles, pasta, milk or candy)

This scavenger hunt involves edible items *not* purchased at a store. When everyone has returned, calculate the point totals and explain that this does *not* represent the final point tally. Next, conduct an eating relay as follows:

- *popcorn*: each team who can eat the entire bag of popcorn wins 200 points (there can be no popcorn left on the floor)

203

- *cabbage*: the person who can eat an entire head of cabbage wins 300 points for his or her team
- *sardines:* the person who can eat an entire can of sardines wins 500 points for his or her team
- *soda*: the first team to have each member drink an entire can of soda and then burp out loud wins 500 points
- *cookies and pickles:* the first team to have each member eat a cookie and a pickle and sing "Yankee Doodle Dandy" wins 500 points
- *candy:* the first team to have each member eat his or her candy wins 1,000 points
- *leftover dinner:* the person who can eat everything on the plate and drink the milk wins 500 points for his or her team

As with all food-eating games, safety is paramount. Make sure that the group members do not eat so fast that they choke on the food (popcorn can be especially tricky). Set up parameters, and if you see someone choking or eating too fast, call a halt to the game.

bigger and better

This is an old standard that never fails to be fun. Ahead of time, arrange for adult volunteers to drive the teams (or set a boundary around the local neighborhood). You will need the following materials:

- small objects (marbles, eggs, pencils, pennies—anything small and unimpressive)
- prizes

Begin by having the group members form teams of 4 to 6 people. Hand each team a small object and tell them to trade it with a person in the neighborhood they don't know for something bigger and better. Make sure they inform the person that he or she will *not* be getting the item back, as the group members will be trading it up at the next stop. Explain the following rules:

- teams must trade each item they receive for the next item
- nothing can be offered in addition to the one item
- teams must stay together

After 45 minutes, the teams must bring back whatever treasure they have collected. Award prizes to the team who collected the "biggest and best" object. (Note: Don't be surprised if you need a truck to bring back the last bigger and better item. We're *not* kidding!)

couch potato hunt

Take a photo with the entire team sitting on—or at least touching—the couch at each of the following locations. Points are calculated *per item*.

250 points

- ❏ On an athletic field (250 extra points if there is a game in progress)
- ❏ In the pastor's office
- ❏ In front of a sign at a high school or middle school (250 extra points for each administrator, teacher and/or janitor sitting on the couch as well)
- ❏ Inside a grocery or department store in your area (250 extra points if you can get the manager to sit on the couch)

300 points

- ❏ Inside the garage of someone's home whom you do not know (Note: Get their permission *first!*)
- ❏ In front of a statue or a fountain

400 points

- ❏ Inside a fast-food restaurant
- ❏ In front of a store that sells ice cream—with everyone on your team eating ice cream
- ❏ At a movie theater

500 points

- ❏ In front of a police officer's car (500 extra points if an officer is sitting on the couch)

bonus points

You can earn 1,000 points for the most unique photo!

incredible edibles hunt

Collect each of the items listed below. Note that these items *cannot* be purchased at a store. Points are calculated *per item*.

100 points

☐ a bag of microwave popcorn, already popped

200 points

☐ a head of cabbage

☐ a can of sardines

☐ a can of soda for each team member

☐ a cookie *and* a pickle for each team member

☐ a piece of chocolate candy for each team member

300 points

☐ An entire leftover meal consisting of meat (or pasta), salad, dessert and a glass of milk (100 extra points for buttermilk!)

5

snow days

description

For those of us in warmer climates, a snow day (or night) is created purely in our minds. Here are some tried-and-true ideas for turning your meeting room into a winter wonderland.

the event

Don't let the lack of snowy weather get you down. Here are some ideas to simulate the experience of a cold and frosty day (you can also use these ideas to cool down on a hot summer day):

- Use newspaper to create snowballs. Marshmallows are another idea, but they get sticky or hard after a while.

- Wrap students in toilet paper to make snow people.

- Use shaving cream to mold snowmen.

- Have snow cones for dessert.

- Make a big winter treasure chest out of a refrigerator box by filling it with white shipping peanuts and small trinkets.

- Create ice sculptures from blocks of ice. Do this fast before they melt.

- Use paper and scissors to make snowflakes. Have a snowflake contest and decorate the room with the results.

- Go cardboard sledding on a grassy hill, or (with permission) on the gym floor. You could also use blocks of ice on a grassy hill, but once again, get permission from the property owner!

- For that oh-so-lovely frostbite sensation, have contestants, using only their bare feet, search for pool diving sticks or rings (or marbles!) in buckets filled with ice water.

- Sprinkle white confetti all over the floor and build a six-foot-tall snowman with chicken wire and papier-mâché.

Let it snow!

super bowl sunday

description

Super Bowl Sunday, or just "Super Sunday," is the most-watched annual television program in the United States. Why not turn it into a youth group party?

the event

Ahead of time, decorate the room where you will be watching the game with team colors, balloons and other memorabilia. If you live in a place where it is snowing or cold, you might want to choose a tropical theme using party favors with palm trees and hula dancers. You will need the following:

- copies of "My Super Bowl Predictions" (see page 209)
- pens or pencils
- prizes for winners of the football pool (candy always works!)
- food—lots of it!

Before the game starts, give everyone a copy of "My Super Bowl Predictions" and have them fill out what they think will happen. After the game, award prizes for correct guesses. If you're gathering at the church and you have room, play a game of indoor or outdoor co-ed flag football during halftime, or have the group members rank their favorite commercials. You can also ask students to pay admission with one nonperishable food item, and then give the food collected to a local food pantry.

my super bowl predictions

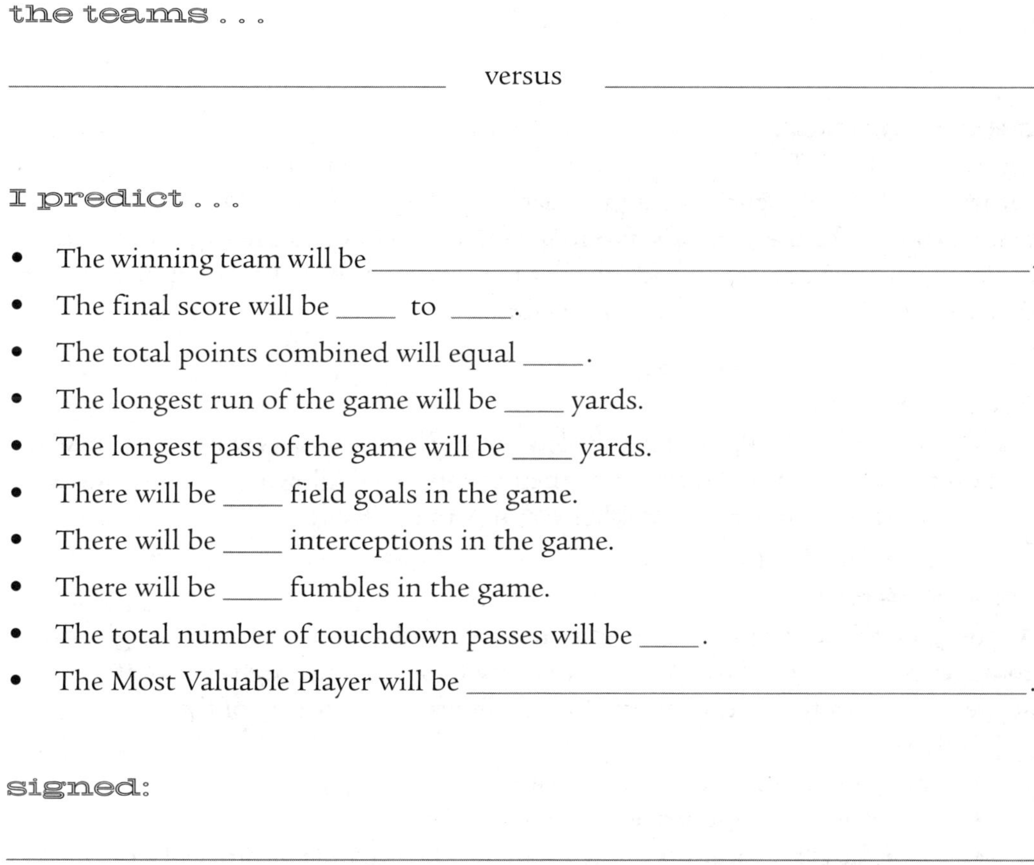

the teams . . .

_____________________________ versus _____________________________

I predict . . .

- The winning team will be _____________________________________.
- The final score will be ____ to ____.
- The total points combined will equal ____.
- The longest run of the game will be ____ yards.
- The longest pass of the game will be ____ yards.
- There will be ____ field goals in the game.
- There will be ____ interceptions in the game.
- There will be ____ fumbles in the game.
- The total number of touchdown passes will be ____.
- The Most Valuable Player will be ________________________________.

signed:

____

see you
at the pole event

description

See You at the Pole™ (www.syatp.com) is a global movement of young people who gather around their school's flagpole each year on the fourth Wednesday in September to pray for their friends, families, teachers, school and nation. It is student-initiated, student-organized and student-led. This is a special and important event that you and your group won't want to miss.

the event

Because See You at the Pole is student-led, your group members will need to take the lead on planning and organizing it at their school. The following are some ideas for how to help them prepare for, publicize and plan the event.

preparation

As the group leader, you should pray for the students, asking God to give them courage to make a stand for Him and to bring Him glory through the event. See You at the Pole also advises students to do the following in advance of the event:

- inform their school administration
- plan the exact time and let everyone know
- plan the exact location of the event—at the flagpole or other place
- determine an alternate meeting place in the event of bad weather
- encourage other students to promote the event to their friends

It is important for student leaders to know that adults from their churches, communities and schools support them. You may also want to invite other local youth ministries to be involved. Encourage them to pray regularly that God would direct the prayer movement in their area and raise up obedient student leaders. Local youth ministers may want to work together to organize pre-pole rallies or follow-up rallies in their area. Refer to the "See You at the Pole Checklist" (see page 212) for additional preparation.

publicity

Have the students get the word out to their friends! They can create posters, flyers, T-shirts, Facebook pages, Tweets, YouTube clips and other methods to publicize the event. Free publicity and clip art for creating materials are available on the See You at the Pole website, in addition to promotional resources (videos, brochures, posters, banners, wristbands) available for purchase. The website also has a promotional clip that you can show at Bible studies, church services and other gatherings.

planning

A pre-pole rally is a great way to get everyone together to talk about what they will do during the event. Sing worship songs, pray, read Scripture and ask former participants to give testimonies during this time. Some groups have found that the Sunday night prior to the actual event is a convenient and effective time for the rally. Student groups, individual churches or a group of local churches can host the rally, and it can include testimonies from previous See You at the Pole events, the showing of the "See You at the Pole" promo video, special speakers, a worship band—whatever you think will get students fired up for the event. Include a time of commissioning, during which students stand or come to the front and church leaders say a prayer of dedication, spiritual protection and intercession over them.

youth group prayer time

One evening (or on a Saturday) prior to the See You at the Pole event, take students by van or bus to their schools. Gather around the flagpole to pray for that school and for the students who attend it. Share testimonies, have worship music and try to make it a celebration of what God is going to do on their campuses in the new school year. You may want to consider asking students to fast for the evening meal. For inspirational stories about students and leaders who have participated in this event, refer to "A Testimony from See You at the Pole" by Jim Burns (see page 213).

211

see you at the pole
checklist

❑ Have you informed the principal of the school about this event? (Note: Although there is no requirement to ask the school board or administration for permission to hold the event, it is wise and courteous to inform the administration about it.)

❑ What time will you begin the event on your campus? Will it be held before school, during lunch or after school?

❑ Where exactly on the campus will the gathering take place?

❑ Do you have an alternative meeting place off the school property?

❑ Do you have an alternative meeting place in case of rain?

❑ Do you have more than one flagpole on campus to choose from?

❑ Should students wear T-shirts promoting the event?

❑ How will you handle traffic noise, onlookers and other distractions?

❑ How will you begin the event? Who will lead it off?

❑ Will there be elements other than prayer (such as singing)?

❑ Will you hold hands, kneel down, break into small groups, or remain in a large group?

❑ What will you pray for or about during the event?

❑ Will you have audible prayer or silent prayer?

❑ How will you end the event? How will people know when it is over?

❑ Have you informed the adult representative(s) of the Fellowship of Christian Athletes (FCA) and/or other Christian organizations at the school?

❑ How will you answer questions regarding your participation in this event?

❑ How can participants help to promote the event beforehand?

❑ Will you have a post-See You at the Pole rally?

❑ Will you be at the flagpole, even if no one else will?

Source: Adapted from Scott Bennefield, "Questions to Conisder," See You at the Pole.™ See www.syatp.com for additional information.

a testimony from see you at the pole

Bernice Ayer Middle School in San Clemente, California. One kid—a small, wiry seventh grader wearing a surf T-shirt and shorts with his arms outstretched almost hugging the flagpole—is praying. School didn't start for another hour and 40 minutes. It was just him, the flagpole and God.

What was he praying about? What motivated this young man with no peers around him to stand alone at the pole and pray?

Some years ago, Suzanne, a 17-year-old homeschool student from Orange County, California, asked if I would be willing to stand at the flagpole at the department of education building with some of her homeschool group to pray with them and give a brief talk. "If you talk for more than 10 minutes, the group members will get bored," she informed me. I smiled. Suzanne was in charge, and she had it programmed to the hilt.

On the day of the event, most of the students had a Scripture passage to read. It was just them and me—though a few supportive moms and several nervous employees of the department of education were watching from a distance. They weren't sure what this was all about. Some kind of protest against no more prayer at football games?

We started with a scratchy recording of a patriotic song, and then one of the group members read the powerful words from 2 Chronicles 7:14: "If my people, who are called by my name, will humble themselves and pray and seek my face and turn from their wicked ways, then will I hear from heaven and will forgive their sin and will heal their land."

Suzanne began our time of prayer. Most of the students prayed. Some were long-winded; some prayed specifically for a need in their life. The dominant themes were prayers of thanksgiving for the country and freedom to pray at the flagpole. The flagpole brought out their patriotic side. In light of the increase in violence on school campuses, they all petitioned God for safety in schools. Most prayed for a family member or a friend who needed God.

By the end of the time of prayer, all the mothers (and even a few Christian employees of the department of education) had come much closer around the pole, inspired by the spiritual fervor. The group members were encouraged to take a stand for God. I spoke to a receptive little audience, but they really didn't need my part of the program. The students had done it on their own.

When we finished our final prayer, the group members stood around in groups, talking about their classes and what they were going to do on Friday night. We adults— who had been much less comfortable around the flagpole—spoke in hushed tones. Somehow, observing those group members praying inspired us to believe just for a moment that the flagpole had become holy ground.

The millions of group members who stood around flagpoles in most of the 56,000 junior and senior high schools in America praying that morning came for a variety of reasons. Some, like Tanya, age 16, came in defiant protest because the courts have "disallowed prayer at football games, but they can't stop us at the flagpole." Eric Wakeling, the junior-high youth pastor at my own church, announced

that he would be there with donuts (mostly chocolate). His presence and his donuts brought an enthusiastic applause at the See You at the Pole pre-rally. The event was student-run, but Eric and thousands of youth workers in America like him were there to cheer the group members on and bring the donuts.

My daughter came to See You at the Pole because it was an event and her Christian friends were there. Her beloved youth worker was an encouragement to all the group members who showed up early to pray. There is negative peer pressure on campus, but this event just might be about positive peer influence. Yes, some of the adolescents stood by the pole and giggled through the prayers while others fervently got on their knees, recited Scriptures and prayed for renewal and revival. See You at the Pole is part of the new and positive movement of young people leaning toward a deeper, stronger faith—a radical faith.

When it comes to spirituality, there are two types of students in America on parallel tracks. One group was not at See You at the Pole, and they probably won't even know it happened at their school. These students haven't visited any kind of church in their life except for an occasional wedding or funeral. They don't know the meaning of Easter or Christmas and have barely even heard of the Ten Commandments. Their parents probably left the church in the 1970s, and these group members are products of a previous generation's lack of interest in spiritual things.

The other group—the ones at See You at the Pole—are those who are seeking a deeper spirituality than the previous generation. These are the students who don't want to just play at church anymore. They seek a radical commitment. Worship is of primary importance to them. Serving through hands-on mission experience is on the upward swing, and these same group members tell us they will stand for God at the flagpole, in the classroom, at home and on the streets. These are the same ones who are leaving the flagpoles to join campus Bible studies and serve at soup kitchens. They are bringing passion back to faith, they are disturbing our comfort level, and they may just be the best thing that has happened to the Church since a few fishermen, a prostitute and a handful of others followed the Lord to the cross more than a thousand years ago.

see you at the pole event

service projects
year-round

description

Any time of the year is a good time for your group members to do service projects that will help those in need in your church and community.

the event

The following themed service project ideas will take your group through the calendar year and allow them to bless others with their acts of kindness.[1]

january: new year's eve party for seniors

Take your group to a local retirement center or nursing home and include the senior citizens in your party. Sing old hymns and even "Auld Lang Syne"—the seniors will probably know the words, but students may need to practice ahead of time. This event could be done in the early evening. Here are some ideas to add to the fun:

- Make a clock and have your own countdown to the new year.
- Bring hot cider and cookies for treats.
- Bring confetti, streamers and noisemakers (check with the facility manager or director first to make sure this is okay).
- Bring a digital camera and record students interviewing seniors about their lives and the New Year's celebrations they have experienced.

february: valentine's day love notes

Love notes are not only great to receive but are also fun to send. Explain to the group members about sharing Christ's love with others and encourage them to write notes to one or more of the following:

- missionaries
- church staff
- grandparents, parents and siblings
- special people in their lives
- teachers and coaches
- military personnel
- hospital personnel or patients
- police officers and firefighters

march: easter egg hunt

Organize an Easter Egg Hunt for a local children's home or an inner-city community. Use plastic eggs filled with goodies and give out candy and refreshments. An appearance by the lovable rabbit is always a special treat. You can incorporate drama,

video presentations or readings to share the Easter message. Have students brainstorm additional ideas.

april: showers of food

Thanksgiving and Christmas are popular times for food drives. Just to be different, why not have one in the middle of April? After all, there are people every day in every month of every year that could use some help. Your food drive can take place over a period of weeks or it can be a one-day event. Here are some ideas to make your food drive fun (and hopefully get more food):

- Have students compete in teams to see who can bring in the most cans.

- Have a scavenger hunt for cans of food with different types of food having different point values.

- Have students take empty shopping bags door to door and deliver them with a note that explains the purpose of the food drive. They should also include in the note that someone will come back the next day to pick up their donated food cans.

may: flowers for mothers

There's an old saying: "April showers bring May flowers." So how about giving flowers to some well-deserving moms? In fact, how about recognizing some moms who might not be getting flowers from their own children? For example, there are moms in nursing homes whose children have moved away or who are otherwise unable to visit. And what about the wonderful women who have no children of their own but are moms to everyone they know? Here are some additional ideas for showing these special women that they are loved:

- Buy fresh flowers from a local wholesale florist and have students arrange them into bouquets, tying them together with ribbon.

- Have students make tissue-paper flowers and write affirming notes to attach to the bouquet.

- Bake cupcakes or cookies and decorate them with flower-shaped candies or icing swirled in the shape of flowers.

Note: If your group members know any single-parent dads, it is completely okay to honor these men with this activity as well!

june: fishing with dad (or mom)

Involve your group members in organizing a fishing trip for themselves and their dads (or moms). If fishing isn't practical in your area, they can try a golf day, a movie night or something else that fits your community. The point is to encourage them to take the time to make some special memories with their parents.

july: water for the masses

Give away bottled water to thirsty spectators at your local community's fireworks show. Buy or get donated bottles of water and ice them down. Large, clean trash cans or the lined bed of a pickup truck may be used as a temporary cooler.

august: water day

This is a great event to have at a local children's home. If there is not one in your area, make arrangements to hold a water day at a local park or even on your church grounds. Advertise the event, and remember to apply for any necessary permits if you are hosting it at a community park. Students will have fun dreaming up water games, but here are a few ideas to get you going:

- Have water-sliding relays using a large tarp as a Slip 'n Slide.
- Use wet sponges for a sponge toss.
- Use water bottles with squirt tops for target games, having tag-team water fights, or filling up buckets.
- Contact the local fire department and see if they will bring out a fire truck to spray water upward and create a fun waterfall to play under, in and through.

september: remember community servants

Take the month of September to do something nice for the police and fire personnel in your community. Here are just a few ideas:

- Arrange a car wash for police and fire personnel, where off-duty police officers and firefighters can take their cars to your church parking lot for a free wash.

- Take group members to a specific precinct or firehouse and wash the cars for those on duty.

- Bake cookies and have the group members write thank-you notes to the men and women who serve us every day. Deliver the cookies and notes to precincts or firehouses in your community.

october: act-of-kindness rally

Instead of the traditional scavenger hunt, have the group members perform little acts of kindness. Set a time limit and have them try to do as many acts of kindness as they can in the given time. Make sure there are cameras on hand to document the kind acts. Remind the group members not to accept tips or gifts for doing their acts. Make a list of ideas and assign a point value to each act. Here are some suggestions to get you started:

- give a flower to a teacher (100 points)
- give a shoulder rub to a firefighter (100 points)
- sing a song to a cashier (200 points)
- buy a stranger a meal (150 points)
- take a card to someone who is sick (250 points)
- pump someone's gasoline and clean the windows of his or her car (175 points)

november: community outreach

During the Thanksgiving and Christmas holiday season, there are more community service events than usual. Plugging into these events can help your group members get involved in service and clearly see the difference their involvement can make. It

will also help them make connections with others in their community. Here are a few projects to look for in your area:

- Feed the homeless on Thanksgiving Day or during the Thanksgiving weekend.
- Deliver food to shut-ins over the long Thanksgiving weekend, as many who volunteer year-round may be taking time off during the holiday.
- Participate in the Angel Tree program (see page 185).
- Collect food and deliver it to a local food bank.
- Collect toys for the Toys for Tots program.

december: cookies, caroling and children

Great Christmases always involve cookies, caroling and children, and this is a great activity for helping students to discover the love in Christmas while brightening the season for unfortunate or sick children. Here are just a couple of ideas:

- Have students bake cookies and arrange with a children's home or hospital for a time when your group can deliver the cookies and sing Christmas carols with the children.

- Have students each adopt a child in your church and as a group take the children caroling at a local senior center or nursing home. Then come back to the church for cookies and hot chocolate.

Jesus said, "Whatever you did for one of the least of these brothers of mine, you did for me" (Matthew 25:40). Let your group members be the "hands and feet" of Jesus all year round!

Note

1. For additional project ideas, see Jim Burns, *Uncommon Missions & Service Projects* (Ventura, CA: Gospel Light, 2011).

compassion project

description

According to UNICEF, some 21,000 children die each day due to poverty.[1] This project will help your group members team up with organizations that address this problem and support children and mothers in need.

the event

According to Compassion International, if group members understand the following four ideas, they can keep learning about poverty and what to do about it for a lifetime:

1. *If poverty were simple, we would have solved it by now (but it's not rocket science either).* Poverty is created by several factors, any one of which can make life difficult if it's out of balance. But those factors are not so complicated that no one can understand them.

2. *When life gets out of balance, children are the first to suffer.* Coal miners used to take small songbirds into the shafts with them as an early warning system. If the bird died, the miners knew they had just a few minutes to get out before the gas would kill them as well. Children are like that. Suffering children are the first warning sign that there is serious trouble in a society.

3. *Children don't create poverty; they just have to live with it.* Children don't smuggle drugs, originate pornography or start wars. Those are adult jobs. They don't create poverty, either—but when adults do things that cause poverty, children suffer for it.

4. *Doing the right things for the right reasons makes a big difference.* Your group members can't do everything, but they certainly can do *something* significant.[2]

With these items in mind, consider partnering with hunger-relief organizations such as World Vision (www.worldvision.org) and Compassion International (www.compassion.com) to support a specific child in a third-world country. By sponsoring a child, your group can assure that he or she is given food, water, shelter, basic medical care and an education. The organization usually sends the sponsor a picture of the child, brief information about the child and his or her country, and an address to send letters to the child.

Once you have decided on an organization, plan an event to promote awareness among your group members. Most of the organizations have free promotional films available to aid in your presentation. The purpose of the event is to educate students

219

on the needs of others around the world and encourage them to sponsor a child for at least one year. Sponsorship of a child usually costs about two dollars a day. You may want to have the entire group adopt one child or have individual students or small groups of students adopt a child. The trick is to stretch students without over-committing them. Display the sponsored child's picture on a bulletin board and include prayer for the child and letter writing as a regular part of your meeting times.[3]

compassion project

Notes

1. Anup Shah, "Today, Around 21,000 Children Died Around the World," Global Issues, September 24, 2011. http://www.globalissues.org/article/715/today-21000-children-died-around-the-world.
2. "Four Big Ideas" in "About Compassion and The Compassion Project," The Compassion Project, March 2003.
3. Adapted from Jim Burns, *Uncommon Missions & Service Projects* (Ventura, CA: Gospel Light, 2011), p. 91.

true love
waits event

description

Created in 1993, True Love Waits is an international grassroots movement that challenges teenagers and college students to go against the grain of today's culture and make the commitment to remain sexually abstinent until marriage.

the event

According to a study conducted by the Heritage Foundation in Washington, DC, programs such as True Love Waits dramatically reduce the rate of out-of-wedlock births. The study showed that women who took a pledge to remain sexually pure were 40 percent more likely to be virgins when they marry, as compared to young women who did not make such a pledge. A similar study conducted by the *American Journal of Sociology* found that teenagers who pledge to remain sexually abstinent until marriage are 34 percent less likely to have sex than those who do not pledge.

Given these statistics, why not have a True Love Waits event with your youth group? A sample order of the service is available at www.truelovewaits.com along with videos, study plans and other downloads to help you structure the event. Here is the suggested order of events:

- Opening comments, in which you explain the purpose and goals of the event
- A hymn sung together—either a traditional one such as "Take My Life, Lead Me, Lord," or a contemporary song such as "We Are an Offering"
- A Scripture reading by a group member (Luke 11:11-13)
- A prayer by the youth minister or other adult leader
- A hymn focusing on God's faithfulness—either a traditional one such as "Great Is Thy Faithfulness" or a contemporary song such as "Prepare Me to Be a Sanctuary"
- A student testimony (prepared in advance of the event)
- An "open letter," in which a parent writes a note to his or her teen
- A sermon (notes are available for download)
- A responsive reading, "We Commit to God and Each Other"
- A special ring ceremony, in which parents purchase a ring or some other gift for their teens (these serve as a symbol of their mutual commitment to a lifetime of purity)
- Closing invitation and reception[1]

You will find a reproducible copy of "Purity Pledge" on page 222 (and also on the CD-ROM) for your group members to complete. Simply copy the page on card stock

and cut out individual purity pledge cards to give to group members who are ready to make a commitment to purity.[2]

PURITY PLEDGE

Believing that God's best for my life and others is to keep my life sexually pure and refrain from sexual intercourse until the day I enter marriage, I commit my body to God, my future mate and my family.

___________________________________   _______________

Signature   Date

Notes

1. Adapted from "True Love Waits Commitment Service." http://www.lifeway.com/Article/true-love-waits.
2. For a weekend retreat focusing on sexual purity, see "Love, Sex and Dating: How to Handle the Heat!" in Jim Burns, *Uncommon Camps and Retreats* (Ventura, CA: Gospel Light, 2011), pp. 137-154.

EVENT PLANNING FORMS

plan: \ plan\ **1a:** a method for achieving an end **b:** an often customary method of doing something; procedure **c:** a detailed formulation of a program of action **d:** goal; aim **2:** an orderly arrangement of parts of an overall design or objective **3:** a detailed program

This section contains several sample information sheets for planning youth parties and ministry events. You can use the sheets as a complete event outline in a one-committee planning session or assign specific planning committees and give each one its related planning sheet. All forms are available on the enclosed CD-ROM. Adapt these forms for your individual ministry needs.

event planning and purpose

Event: ____

Date(s): ______________________________ Time: ________________

Location: ____

Main Contact: _____________________ Phone Number: ______________

Emergency Contact During Event: _______________________________

What is the purpose of the event?

____

____

____

What is the goal, or anticipated outcome, of the event?

____

____

____

Who is the target audience?

____

____

____

What is the anticipated or desired environment?

____

____

____

What is the plan for following up with event attendees?

____

____

____

logistical information

Event: ____

Date(s): _________________________ Time: _________________________

Event contact person(s): _________________________ Phone: _____________

Facilities contact person(s): _________________________ Phone: _____________

element timing

How much time is expected for each element of the event?

Load in: ____

Set up: ____

Program: ____

Cleanup: ____

Load out: ____

securing the location

Are reservations needed to secure the desired location? ❑ Yes ❑ No

If yes, have necessary contacts been made? ❑ Yes ❑ No

Has confirmation been received? ❑ Yes ❑ No

facilities requirements

Is electricity needed? ❑ Yes ❑ No

Are there sound and/or video needs? ❑ Yes ❑ No

Has audio/visual been requested? ❑ Yes ❑ No

Are there rest rooms for attendees? ❑ Yes ❑ No

personnel

Event: ____

Date(s): _________________________________ Time: _______________________

adult leadership and volunteers

How many event leaders are needed? _________

How many volunteers are needed? _________

What is the plan for recruiting them? _______________________________
____
____

Is special training needed for participation in the event?
____
____
____

Is there a plan for staffing of on-site medical personnel, if needed? ❑ Yes ❑ No

If yes, what is the plan? ____
____
____

If not, how will your staff handle medical emergencies that might arise?
____
____
____

individual assignments

(Note: Give those individuals responsible for a particular element a copy of the "Schedule for Individual Assignments" on page 238.)

Assignment   Person Responsible

________________________   ________________________

________________________   ________________________

________________________   ________________________

________________________   ________________________

hospitality

Will thank-you notes be sent to volunteers after the event? ❑ Yes ❑ No

If yes, who is responsible for sending them?
____

budget and financial concerns

Event: ____

Date(s): _________________________________ Time: _______________________________

approved budget

What is the approved ministry budget? $_____________________________

Is funding coming from a line item?   ❑ Yes   ❑ No

anticipated cost

What is the anticipated total cost of the event? $_____________________________

How will this be covered?

____

____

____

Is a cash advance needed?   ❑ Yes   ❑ No

secretary/treasurer

Who is responsible for handling receipts and filing necessary financial statements after the event? _______________________________

promotion and registration

Event: ____

Date(s): ___________________________ Time: ______________________

promotion

What is the timeline for promoting the event? ______________________

What methods will be used for promotion (verbal or video announcements, bulletins, flyers, posters, telephone contacts, emails, social networking/websites)?

____

____

____

registration and medical release forms

Who is the main contact for attendee registration? ______________________

What is the deadline for registration? ______________________

What will attendees need to bring (e.g., sunscreen, towels, sleeping bags)?

____

____

____

Who is responsible for obtaining medical release forms? ______________________

Where will these release forms be kept during the event?

____

____

____

medical and liability release

Event: ____

Date(s): _______________________________ Time: _______________________________

I/We, the undersigned, am/are the parent(s) of _______________________ (child's name) a minor child, _________ years of age, or the person having legal custody pursuant to authority of _____________________ or the legal guardian of the (designate authority, if applicable) minor child pursuant to an order of ___________________ ___________________ (designate authority, if applicable) and now have, and am/are entitled to the full and complete custody of said minor child.

medical care

I/We hereby authorize ____ (church or ministry name and address), its agents, servants, employees, officers and directors, or other adult sponsor bearing this written authorization, in whose care the above mentioned minor child has been entrusted by me/us, to obtain proper medical care from a licensed medical or dental doctor or facility. The medical/dental care may include, but is not limited to, any X-ray examination, anesthetic, medical or surgical diagnosis or treatment and hospital care to be rendered to said minor under the general or special supervision and upon the advice of a licensed medical doctor or dentist.

It is understood that this authorization is given in advance of any specific diagnosis, treatment or hospital care being required, but is given to provide authority and power on the part of __________________ (church or ministry) and said adult person, to give specific consent to any and all such diagnosis, treatment or hospital care which a treating physician and/or dentist in the exercise of his/her best judgment may deem advisable in the event of injury to or illness of the minor. This authorization shall include transportation to receive the medical or dental care.

guidelines

It is understood that while participating in activities sponsored by ____________ _______________________________ (church or ministry), my child/ward is to follow the guidelines set by the adults in charge. Should my child/ward not cooperate with these guidelines, I agree to pick up him/her from the activity.

risk

I am aware that these activities may involve some hazards. I have considered these risks, and I still wish my child/ward to participate. Furthermore, I agree not to bring legal action against __________________ (church or ministry), staff or sponsors as a result of any injuries suffered in the course of his/her participation.

financial responsibility

In the event of injury to my child/ward, I agree that I/we and my health care insurer shall be financially responsible for any medical treatment required by my child/ward as a result of any injury or illness suffered during his/her participation in any activities during the term of this agreement.

dispute

In the event a dispute arises between me and _________________________ (church or ministry) concerning injuries to my child/ward, then I agree that a Christian arbitrator acceptable to both sides shall resolve the dispute. The cost of the arbitrator is to be shared equally by the parties. All applicable statutes of limitation shall apply and arbitration must be requested within the appropriate period in order to preserve a right to recovery.

term of agreement

This authorization shall remain in effect through _________________ (date), unless sooner (last day of scheduled activity) revoked by the undersigned in writing delivered to _____________________ (church or ministry), its agents, servants, employees, officers and directors.

signatures

_______	______________________________		___________	___________
(Date)	(Mother's Signature)		(Home Phone)	(Work Phone)
_______	______________________________		___________	___________
(Date)	(Father's Signature)		(Home Phone)	(Work Phone)
_______	______________________________		___________	___________
(Date)	(Custodian/Guardian's Signature)		(Home Phone)	(Work Phone)

additional medical information

Other emergency contact: _______________________________ Phone: ___________
Family doctor: _______________________________ Phone: ___________
Ophthalmologist: _______________________________ Phone: ___________
Insurance company: _______________________________ Phone: ___________
Policy/Group #: _______________________________ Phone: ___________

Date of last tetanus immunization: _______________________________________
Medications/allergies: ____
Will you allow blood transfusions if physician prescribes? ________________
Other special health instructions: ______________________________________
____
____
____

transportation

Event: ____

Date(s): _________________________________ Time: _______________________

type needed

What types of vehicles are needed? ____________________________________

How many drivers are needed? __________

If buses or vans are needed, who is responsible for securing the reservations?

____

____

____

directions and cost

Do drivers need maps?   ❑ Yes   ❑ No

Who will produce or obtain maps? ______________________________________

Have drivers been informed of the process for reimbursement of gas and expenses?

                                                         ❑ Yes   ❑ No

volunteer driver form

Event: ____

Date(s): _________________________ Time: _________________________

Name: _________________________ Driver's License #: _____________

Phone: (H) ___________ (C) ___________ Expiration Date: ___________

Address: ____

Email: ____

Car Model/Year #1: _______________ Car Model/Year #2: _______________

Number of working seat belts in Car #1: __________ Car #2: __________

License plate number for Car #1: ______________ Car #2: ______________

liability insurance

Minimum required amount of liability insurance: (1) $100,000 liability per person for bodily injury, (2) $300,000 liability per incident for bodily injury for all vehicle occupants, and (3) $50,000–$100,000 liability for property damage. Amount on this (these) car(s):

car #1

Insurance Company: _______________________________ Policy #: __________

(1) $______________ (2) $______________ (3) $______________

Uninsured/underinsured motorist coverage?   ❑ Yes   ❑ No

car #2

Insurance Company: _______________________________ Policy #: __________

(1) $______________ (2) $______________ (3) $______________

Uninsured/underinsured motorist coverage?   ❑ Yes   ❑ No

driving history

Are you licensed to drive a commercial vehicle?   ❑ Yes   ❑ No

Have you been in an accident in the last three years?   ❑ Yes   ❑ No

If you answered yes, describe the accident and its cause:

____

____

____

____

Have you been ticketed for moving violations within the last three years?
     ❑ Yes   ❑ No

If you answered yes, describe the infractions:

____

____

____

____

Have you been convicted for WDWI/DUI, or had your license suspended for moving violations, hit and run, eluding an officer, reckless or negligent operation of a vehicle, or driving while under suspension or revocation within the last five years? (**Note:** We will not be able to use volunteers with a "yes" answer.)　　❑ Yes　　❑ No

❑　I possess a valid driver's license. Please attach a photocopy of your driver's license and first page of your car insurance policy(ies).

declaration and signature

Students riding in my vehicle(s) seated in both the front and back seats will be secured with individual working seatbelts. (No double belting of children is permitted.) To my knowledge, my vehicle is in safe operating condition (brakes, tires, and so forth). I affirm that I will carefully transport students under my care, including obeying all traffic laws. I also declare that by signing this driver form I will not have ingested alcohol, a controlled substance or any other medication that impairs my driving abilities, during or within six (6) hours before the trip.

Signed: ____ Date: ____________________

food and supplies

Event: ____

Date(s): _______________________________ Time: _______________________

menu

Will food be provided?   ❑ Yes ❑ No

If yes, what is the planned menu?

____

____

____

____

Are there any diet restrictions that should be addressed?   ❑ Yes ❑ No

If yes, what restrictions?

____

____

____

____

____

When should the food be purchased? _______________________________

Who is responsible for this? _____________________________________

preparation of food

Who is responsible for food preparation? _________________________

What supplies are needed for preparation?

____

____

____

____

serving of food

Who is responsible for supervising the food service? _____________

How will food be served?

____

____

____

____

event planning forms

235

What is needed for serving?

____
____
____
____

What is needed for eating?

____
____
____
____

cleanup

Who is responsible for cleanup? ____

What supplies are needed (trash bags, storage containers for leftover foods)?

____
____
____
____

additional equipment and miscellaneous needs

Event: ____

Date(s): ___________________________ Time: ___________________

additional equipment

What, if any, additional equipment is needed?

____

____

____

Who is responsible for securing and returning the equipment? _______________

Who is responsible for setting up and taking down additional equipment?

____

miscellaneous

Is housing needed?   ❑ Yes   ❑ No

Who will arrange for housing? ____

Are there special concerns for this particular event, such as wheelchair access or any special seating requirements?   ❑ Yes   ❑ No

Who is responsible for accommodating special needs?

____

____

____

237

schedule for individual assignments

Event: ____

Date(s): _________________________________ Time: ______________________

Participant: ____

Event Assignment: ____

Dear _______________________________,

Thank you for the contribution of your time for this event! Your participation makes a difference. This is an outline of your assignment. If you have any questions or concerns, please contact ____ at

____.

Thanks again, and may God bless you for your participation!

Your portion of the event will begin at _______ AM/PM and will end at ________ AM/PM. Please plan to arrive no later than ______ AM/PM. Should a personal emergency arise that will prevent you from attending this event, please contact ___________________ at _______________________________ as soon as possible before you are scheduled to attend.

Additional instructions:

____

____

____

____

____

____

uncommon
leader's resources

uncommon
games & icebreakers

Jim Burns, General Editor
Manual w/ CD-ROM
ISBN 978.08307.46354

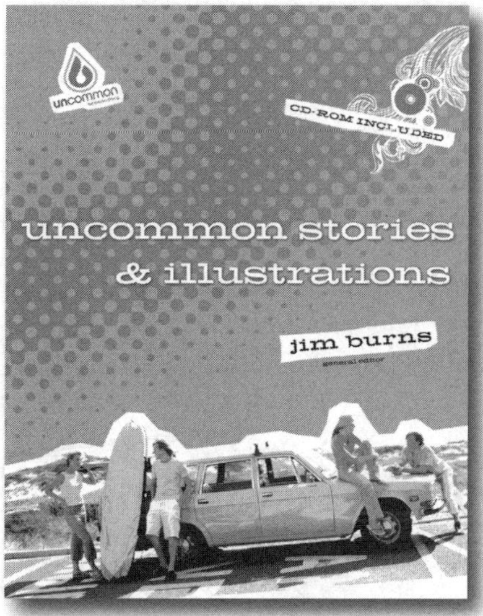

uncommon
stories & illustrations

Jim Burns, General Editor
Manual w/ CD-ROM
ISBN 978.08307.47252

uncommon
worship experiences

Jim Burns, General Editor
Manual w/ CD-ROM
ISBN 978.08307.54830

uncommon
object lessons &
discussion starters

Jim Burns, General Editor
Manual w/ CD-ROM
ISBN 978.08307.50986

uncommon
dramas, skits &
sketches

Jim Burns, General Editor
Manual w/ CD-ROM
ISBN 978.08307.57917

uncommon
camps &
retreats

Jim Burns, General Editor
Manual w/ CD-ROM
ISBN 978.08307.56476

Available at Bookstores Everywhere!

Uncommon is a decidedly different program for junior high and high school ministries. Now you can equip ministry leaders to hit the ground running with a complete package of proven and effective materials.